Glasgow Works

Glasgow Works

*An account of
the economy of the city*

Michael Boulton-Jones

Published by Dolman Scott

Copyright © Michael Boulton-Jones 2009
The right of Michael Boulton-Jones to be identified as author of this work has
been asserted by him in accordance with the Copyright, Design and
Patents Act 1988

ISBN: 978-1-905553-35-8

Printed in the United Kingdom
Dolman Scott Limited
www.dolmanscott.com

Front cover image: *QE2 nearing completion in Clydebank in 1967. The two screws represent the power of the Clyde and the QE2 represents its end.*

CONTENTS

Acknowledgements

It took me four years to research and write this book. I undertook the project in order to educate myself about the city which had become my home. This is the perspective that you should have when reading since I am neither an historian nor an economist. I am deeply grateful to several people who have given me help. Robin Stott patiently educated me about global warming and I have made use of that in the last chapter. Ronnie Sharp lent me Jack Webster's book on the history of the car industry in the West of Scotland. Ruth Tillyard, Crawford Gordon, Martin Smith, Maura High and Hilary Murdoch were kind enough to read the script and make suggestions for improvements. Neil Guthrie allowed me to use some of his photographs to illustrate the book and Ken Davidson supplied the photograph of the Royal Infirmary (below). My wife would like to express her gratitude to the book for keeping me busy and out of her way for so many years after my retirement – a time of great stress for women, she tells me.

Milngavie, 2008.

INTRODUCTION

The first time I saw Glasgow was in the summer of 1967 when I was driving through on my way for a belated honeymoon on the Isle of Skye. I cannot remember much of the city and especially, try though I do, I cannot remember the splendours of the Great Western Road. I certainly drove along it but can only remember rather mean housing and grime. The grime of Northern cities like Glasgow and Leeds was quite a shock to people brought up in the South and it may have been an effective camouflage. Furthermore, at that time, Victorian art and architecture were considered heavy and ugly and the fashion was for Scandinavian design with its elegance and light. Therefore, the first time that I really saw Glasgow was in winter 1974 when I came to look at a job in the Royal Infirmary. I arrived in Central station, whose elegance I also failed to recognise, and out into the sturdy grandeur of Gordon Street. It wasn't beautiful but it was a firm statement that Glasgow should be taken seriously. The Royal Infirmary was the same. It seemed monolithic, important and slightly forbidding. It also took itself seriously enough to dominate its neighbour, the Cathedral. It took me years to forgive the shabby, grimy rather forlorn exterior of the cathedral and come to admire its inner charms.

The Royal Infirmary was a revelation. I had worked in two teaching hospitals in London, one was the hospital where I trained and the other was Hammersmith Hospital which as the Royal Post Graduate Medical School represented the best that British medicine had to offer at that time. In my teaching hospital, famous in its day, the generalist reigned supreme and private practice often meant that consultants were missing in action a bit too often. This was compensated for by the high standard of the junior staff but clinical standards were maybe a little lower than patient satisfaction. On the other hand, Hammersmith Hospital was organised into specialty units with research and presentation being a requirement of all staff. Patients were interesting or not according to whether they happened to contribute to the stories that the doctors were trying to tell. And some of the stories were very interesting indeed and the whole world listened. However, from the patients' point of view, the care may have seemed a little distant. Glasgow Royal Infirmary seemed to me to be an amalgam of what was best in those two hospitals. It was generously staffed and organised into specialties many of which had acquired a national or international reputation. A little booklet on the activities of each of the specialties was produced every two years and this recorded that quite a lot was going on. What is more, the consultants did receiving and post-receiving ward rounds which, at that time, were considered an unnecessary expenditure of time for London hospital consultants.

As I was waiting for the train to go back to London, I was given a quick account of the pros and cons of living in Glasgow. First, I was told, it was easy to get out of and beautiful country lay just to the north and, second, it was really quite a nice place to live as long as you were middle class. I watched a steady drizzle falling outside the window and was struck by the number of people who stopped and talked apparently oblivious to the rain; many did not even wear coats and this was in December. Despite this greyness, I decided to apply and was short-listed. This was a very brave decision, as a civil servant might tell his minister, and my wife told me, for two reasons. One was that Glasgow did not appoint outsiders, which comforted my wife, and the other was that Southerners never moved North unless they were banished for some misdemeanour. However, rather surprisingly I was offered the post and accepted.

1

I then had to set up house and start work. What was Glasgow like and why was its reputation so bad in the rest of Britain? Every Tuesday and Thursday the *Glasgow Herald* produced an edition that contained houses for sale. With no local relatives or friends and no prejudices, the whole city was available to me. Not so, explained my new colleagues. Some 80% of the houses in the city were owned by the Council so that there was no private housing in vast swathes of the city. The middle class ghettoes were confined to the fringes of the city or the west end and it would be rank foolishness to stray outside those areas. I toured a seemingly endless stream of houses on both sides of the river and learned how to navigate around the city. In the end, because of schooling the search was narrowed to Milngavie or Bearsden. We have lived in Milngavie since.

First impressions of living in Glasgow were somewhat daunting. As Alasdair Gray wrote in *Lanark*, it seems as though the sky is going to fall down and smother the city. The buildings were dark, Victorian and heavy, particularly when wet. Equally obvious were the number of gaps between buildings. It looked like a bombed city and often the only building standing in an area of compacted red rubble was a single-storey pub. Alcohol problems were a major factor in the patients I saw, far more than in London. But what impressed me most in those early days in the late 1970s was the stoicism of the women who had to deal not only with their husbands' alcohol problems and the consequent shortage of money but also with damp inadequate houses. Not many men seemed to have jobs and that did not change much in all the years I worked in the Royal Infirmary. I also became conscious that patients regarded visits to the doctor as a possible source of income and I quickly learned to give them what they wanted. Indeed, Mrs Thatcher encouraged us to do so as she tried to reduce the unemployment rate by converting as many as possible on to the disability living allowance. I learned that there was another side to the East End. At that time, it was not uncommon for a general practitioner to ask a consultant to visit patients in their homes to assess them medically and to make a plan for their care. This was a necessary education for me. My impression was of poorly cared for estates with litter lying everywhere. The closes were covered in graffiti and were dingy and often smelly but once inside the flat everything was neat and sparkling. More often than not, there would be a picture of a child or grandchild graduating at Glasgow University on the dresser. Everyone was courteous and considerate. Other consultants warned me that my car would be vandalised and I should consider paying the nearest teenager to guard it. I never did and it survived unscathed.

The years rolled by. I was aware of the massive programme of cleaning all buildings that occurred in the 1980s, of the formation of GEAR (Glasgow Eastern Area Renewal) and the appearance of new low density housing in various parts of the town such as the Maryhill corridor; of the campaign to improve the image of Glasgow with its ambiguous slogan 'Glasgow's Miles Better' strung across the gasworks beside the motorway approaching the city centre; of the Garden Festival in 1988; and when, in 1990, Glasgow was the European City of Culture. I marvelled at the way various buildings in the city centre were demolished leaving just the façade standing between some completely inadequate-looking scaffolding and then rebuilt. I heard the junior doctors saying what a buzz there was in Glasgow, confirmed by English and German doctors. On walks around the city centre, I saw that old buildings which had housed banks and other businesses had been turned into bars and restaurants. How could these places survive in a city whose sources of wealth had all but disappeared? Then I heard that Glasgow was the best rated shopping centre after the West End of London. Who had the money to buy the goods to justify all this investment by national retailers? I remember going to a play about the old shipyards and one character asking what does Glasgow actually make nowadays. The answer was nothing. This intrigued me and, when I retired, I resolved to find out how Glasgow made a living and could afford to keep all those restaurants and shops going. The following account starts with a brief look at the economic history of the city and then goes on to more recent events.

PART ONE
HISTORY

Aerial view of the Clyde with some of the old docks with the Science Centre and SECC with the Armadillo on the North Bank with the Squinty Bridge in operation 2006 (Scotland's images)

CHAPTER 1

HISTORY UP TO 1800

It was Glasgow's good fortune that it became a bishop's burgh in 1175, rather than a royal burgh like Rutherglen or Dumbarton, because the church in the early Middle Ages was the most important source of jobs in the service industries. Sure enough, Glasgow got not only a cathedral, with jobs in construction over a prolonged period from 1197 to 1250, but a university in 1451. These two factors were probably enough for Glasgow to become the dominant town in the west of Scotland. A third cause was that it was built at a convenient crossing point of the Clyde linking the west Highlands with the Lowlands and far enough from the sea to discourage Viking raiders. However, it faced Ireland and an undiscovered America rather than the North Sea and Europe, so it was at a trading disadvantage compared with the ports on the east coast of Scotland which grew more quickly. During the Wars of Independence, the Bishop of Glasgow, Robert Wishart, was a key figure in the Scottish resistance to Edward I, and it was he who absolved Robert the Bruce of the murder of the Red Comyn, which triggered Bruce's rebellion, and continued to support him through thick and thin as the rightful claimant to the Scottish throne.

Glasgow was important enough to be upgraded to an Archbishopric in 1492 and the see extended from the Antonine Wall to the Solway Firth. The Cathedral had 32 canons in the middle of the 15th century, more than any other in Scotland. Despite the importance of the bishopric, the population of Glasgow was probably only 2,000 when the University was founded and only 12,000 when the Act of Union was signed in 1707 but then grew rapidly reaching about 77,000 in 1800.

During this era, Glasgow was the principal market town of the West of Scotland. Fat cows, herring and salmon, wool, ox hides, butter and cheese were exported to the countries in the East and all kinds of corn to the peoples in the West. The only early industry which was more than a cottage undertaking was the production of pottery near Calton set up in 1585 using local clay deposits. Increasing prosperity led to the building of substantial stone houses including the Tolbooth in 1626 and a Town Hall next to it ten years later. The University was rebuilt in about 1650 below the Cathedral off High Street but was pulled down after the move to Gilmorehill in the 19th century to make way for a railway marshalling yard. Indeed, only the Tolbooth steeple at Glasgow Cross, the cathedral itself and Provand's Lordship (built 1471) remain of the buildings of that time.

From its foundation Glasgow was run by its Bishop until 1560, when James Beaton, the last Roman Catholic bishop, fled to Paris before the ferocious gale brewed by John Knox. The estates of the church were appropriated by local powerful families, among whom Walter Stewart of Minto got the most. Glasgow did not have another bishop until the Union of the Crowns. The attempt by Charles I to impose his choice on the people was one of the causes of the Bishops' War which evolved into the Civil War. Once again, from 1638 until the restoration in 1660 there was no incumbent bishop. Instead of a bishop, the City Council was run by prominent citizens.

One of Cromwell's initiatives was to organise a complete inventory of the British Isles. The agent sent to Glasgow was the happily named Thomas Tucker. He reported on Glasgow's trade with Ireland, France and Norway and the attempts to trade with the West Indies which had been abandoned because of losses. Most of the inhabitants of the city were traders, dealers or students. The goods it exported included plaid, coal and herring. Tucker noted that Glasgow had twelve ships, the same as Kirkcaldy and Montrose and fewer than Leith.

In 1652, the Great Fire of Glasgow burned down a third of the houses in the town, affecting a thousand families. As a result, a fire engine was constructed for future emergencies. Rebuilding must have been rapid and of good quality because only four years later Robert Baillie, a Glasgow Presbyterian minister, noted that "our people have much more trade in comparison than any other: their buildings increase strangely both for number and for fairness; it has more than doubled in our time." A second fire in 1677 led to planned developments and the new city impressed all visitors. Clearly, the civil wars had been successfully negotiated. However, Glaswegians did not all escape unscathed. The new king, Charles II restored in 1660, insisted on making episcopacy compulsory and those dissenting ministers who refused to take the oath because of their Presbyterian principles, drawn up in the Covenant which had started the Civil Wars, started to preach in the open. James Graham of Claverhouse was ordered to hunt them down and harass their congregations. Some Glaswegians supported the Covenanters but were defeated at Bothwell Bridge in 1679. Several city dignitaries were sent to Edinburgh for trial and many were condemned.

There was a quickening in pace as new industries were developed, encouraged by the Scottish Parliament in order to reduce imports. Soap production was successfully established in 1667 but an attempt to build a whaling fleet to supply the raw material failed. A joint stock company was set up for sugar production in the same year and expanded to seven factories over the following years. Rum was distilled from the products in at least two of them. A few years later, a Frenchman introduced the art of papermaking and set up production in Cathcart. In 1681, another joint stock company was set up for the manufacture of woollen products.

After the Glorious Revolution of 1688 which made William and Mary joint rulers of the separate realms of England and Scotland, the Presbyterian Church was re-established in Scotland and Glasgow was given a Royal Charter to elect its provosts, baillies and magistrates. The injuries felt by many of the Scottish gentry as a result of William's policies did not affect the city too severely. These injuries included dragging Scotland into war with France and press-ganging Scottish seamen into the English Navy which then did little to protect Scottish coastal trade from French privateers. In 1708, the population of Glasgow was 12,766 and was the second biggest burgh in Scotland, contributing about 12% of taxes imposed on burghs compared to Edinburgh's 33%. At this time, Glasgow was a largely self-contained marketing town trading successfully, but on a small scale. It was indistinguishable from dozens of other similar towns around Europe apart from its peripheral position. Even if it was beginning to prosper, the people in the surrounding areas were poor, and sometimes near to starving. A series of poor harvests in the 1690s may have led to a temporary decline in Glasgow's population. Another blow at that time was the huge loss of wealth to the whole country caused by the failure of the Darien Adventure of 1698–99: it is estimated that Scots invested about half the available national capital (about half a million pounds) in the scheme and lost the lot. Furthermore, the 1690s were a time of protectionism so that many countries slapped tariffs on Scottish exports and, in particular, the English raised taxes on linen from Scotland in 1698, leading to a halving of the value of the trade in the next few years. These problems, argued the proponents, could be solved by union with England. Those against the idea, and most Scots probably were, cited the loss of national identity for which their forefathers had fought and the higher taxes levied on the English for their wars with France. They worried that their money would simply disappear southwards.

In the event, the Act of Union in 1707 may have been the starting gun which led to the transformation of Glasgow and the surrounding counties. At a stroke, Scots had free access to one of the wealthiest European markets and its colonies and their ships were permitted to trade with the same rights as their English rivals. It is worth emphasising the low base from which Scotland started. At the time of Union, Scotland had 20% of the UK population (about 1.25m) but contributed only 3% of taxable income. There are no accurate figures about average incomes in the two countries but the average Englishman probably had about seven times the income of the average Scot. This was why so many impoverished Scottish nobles married wives from south of the border and this helped seal the Union. Since the difference in wealth was dramatic, it is not surprising that it took a few years for the Scottish economy to benefit. For example, one crushing deficiency was the availability of funds for investment which was not helped much by the Bank of Scotland, founded in 1695, because it adopted a very conservative approach, perhaps aware of the poor record of investment in Scottish enterprises in the late 17th century. Matters eased after the Royal Bank of Scotland was set up in 1727 and introduced the overdraft a year later. Much of its initial capital of £111,347 came from the compensation given to the Company of Scotland, which had financed the Darien Adventure, as a condition of the Act of Union. Thus the Darien Adventure may have served Scotland better than its reputation allows. Another problem was the quality of goods produced in Scotland which was not good enough to penetrate the English market successfully. Only the trade in black cattle did well and even then the Scots thought that the English middlemen made most of the profit.

The Glasgow merchants were to exploit their opportunities brilliantly by improving linen manufacturing and establishing the tobacco trade. Even before these developments had really begun, James McUre published *A View of the City of Glasgow* in 1736 in which he described a glassworks, opened in 1730, for containers in which to export locally produced beer. There were rope works, tanneries, tobacco spinning factories and printers. Wool was used to manufacture carpets and coarse woollens. Clothes, hats and gloves were produced mainly for local use. The number of ships on the Clyde increased from 15 in 1707 to 195 five years later. The first local paper, the *Glasgow Courant*, started appearing in 1715. McUre also described a large stone building for making all sorts of metal objects from locks to anchors which were exported in increasing amounts.

Glasgow was clearly prospering but it was transformed by the rise (and fall) of two new developments: linen production and the tobacco trade.

Linen

Linen had been a minor industry before the Act of Union. Its evolution into a major industry was probably sparked by the Malt Tax Riots in Glasgow in 1725. One of the major differences between Scotland and England before the Act of Union was that Scotland was lightly taxed compared to England and fear of tax increases was one of the main reasons for objecting to the treaty. It was not too surprising that a tax on beer would lead to protests and Glasgow's riot was the biggest and the best. The Government responded by setting up a Board of Trustees for Improving Fisheries and Manufacture in Scotland in 1727. It had £6,000 to spend each year. Of all its investments the only success was in linen production. It systematically set about raising the standards of the existing manufacture.

First, the Board attempted to improve the quality of flax grown in Scotland with only partial success so the trade remained dependent on imports from Ireland and continental Europe. The preparation of the flax was mechanised with machines designed in Holland. Foreign workers, mainly from Holland and France, taught local men how to weave and women how to spin. At first this was done by part time workers in their own homes but, as mechanisation improved, clusters were formed around rivers with water-powered machinery and operated by full time workers. Bleaching of the cloth was a prolonged process involving washing in alkali (derived from wood ash or kelp) followed by weak acid (sour milk). The washed cloth was then laid out in fields to expose it to sunlight. Bleaching fields were subsidised and covered large areas to the south of Loch Lomond and green spaces in and around Glasgow itself, the first at Pollokshaws. The cloth went through several cycles which took months. The Board asked Professor Black of Glasgow, Professor Home of Edinburgh and others to investigate how sulphuric acid, which had been adopted in Holland, might be used more efficiently. Their solution cut the time necessary for the bleaching process from months to days and dramatically increased productivity as well as reducing the capital tied up in the process. Vitriol production was started and expanded rapidly so that early in the 19th century there were half a dozen factories for its production in Glasgow around Port Dundas. In 1742, calico printing was introduced, again by setting up invited workers from England and Holland in works established near the bleaching processes. The Board next set about improving the marketing of the finished product. Only cloth approved and stamped by the Board could be sold. The increasing mechanisation of the process required capital for investment, something that was scarce in the West. The Board itself had few funds but the British Linen Company was set up in 1746 in Edinburgh to finance production with capital of £100,000. Expansion was dramatic. The value of the trade in the West of Scotland increased from £21,264 in 1728 to £248,299 in 1768 and its share of Scottish production went up from 20.6% to 41.4% over the same time. Only Dundee enjoyed a similar growth. Some two million yards of linen was produced in 1770, and Glasgow was Britain's leading centre of linen production and much of it was of high quality.

Some pertinent conclusions may be drawn. First, a Government committee, equivalent to Scottish Enterprise today, masterminded the development of this industry. Second, the role of skilled immigrants was vital. They were invited in and must have been supported initially. They taught their skills which were widely adopted by local manufacturers. Third, the University was asked to use its expertise to solve a major problem causing a huge bottleneck in production. Fourth, capital was mobilised on the necessary scale to finance developments. Lastly, about two-thirds of Scottish linen production went to England and its colonies. This market was protected from European competition by tariffs which no longer applied to Scottish exports. Although none of the key steps in the production process was due to Scottish innovation, the organisation of the industry was unique and its products competitive. The Board of Trustees deserved considerable credit.

Tobacco

The other great development of the 18th century was the tobacco trade which more or less coincided with the growth of linen manufacture. It owed everything to the Act of Union because the Navigation Laws had excluded Scottish ships from the trade with the English American possessions but, after 1707, the Scots were included and, in turn, protected from Continental rivals. With almost incredible speed, Glaswegians came to dominate this trade. Initially, tobacco was smuggled on a huge scale. This was not too surprising as excise duties were heavy because they were the government's main source of revenue. Everyone smuggled but the Scots were perhaps more enthusiastic than most because they thought the new British government was unnecessarily expensive. In the early years of the trade, they may have paid no more than half the duty due on their imports of tobacco. This gave them an initial cost advantage and caused an English outcry which led to reform of the Customs Service in 1723, after which smuggling declined.

The other reasons why Glasgow came to dominate the trade are not totally clear. After all, Liverpool and Bristol had a few years' start. It helped that the voyage from the American tobacco-growing states to Glasgow was shorter (and safer whenever Britain was at war with France, which was not infrequently) but the real trump card played by the Glasgow merchants was that they were more efficient. They paid cash to the tobacco farmers for the crops as they bought them, not as they sold them which the English merchants tended to do (the Cunninghame family was owed £135,000 at the time of the American Revolution which they had to write off). They also stored the tobacco at depots near the farms to be ready for the arrival of a ship thus reducing turn-round times. Tobacco was imported into Glasgow and re-exported all over Europe, particularly to France and Holland. The scale of the trade and the rate at which it increased were staggering. In 1715, Glasgow merchants processed about 2.5 million pounds of tobacco; in 1752 it was 21 million lbs and in 1775 it was 44.8 million lbs which was valued at about £2.25m or about ten times the value of linen production. Glasgow's share of the American tobacco trade was about half the total. Tobacco accounted for 38% of all Scottish imports and 44% of exports. Ships did not return to Virginia and Maryland empty but filled with goods, some of Glaswegian origin such as woollen and linen products, whisky, glassware and pottery. Factories were set up to supply the goods: the largest boot manufacturer employed 700 people and used locally produced leather: a pottery, the Deltfield Company, was founded in 1748 by some Dutchmen and eventually employed thousands. The tobacco trade made these new investments possible by providing finance and a market.

The tobacco trade was controlled by a handful of merchant families of whom Cunninghame, Ritchie, Spiers and Glassford were the most successful. They were of relatively humble origins but succeeded because of their innovative business methods. They rewarded themselves by building grand town houses (the Cunninghame town mansion became the Royal Exchange, Stirling library and then the Glasgow Gallery of Modern Art) and country estates, and marrying into the gentry. Since it took so long for the ships to cross the Atlantic, these rich merchants had the money and leisure to patronise the arts, donate money to the University and found discussion clubs such as one that met in the Tontine Hotel. They also subsidised a working class man, Robert Foulis, who became a high quality publisher and opened a bookshop. He went on to found the School of the Art of Design. This was taken under the wing of the university and his publishing house became the official University Press. Others followed and, although Foulis and his brother failed financially, the number of books published in Glasgow multiplied several times in the middle of the 18th century. The associated artisan skills also increased.

> By the 1770s the city could boast fourteen booksellers as well as three engravers, four architects, two marble cutters, an import carpet warehouse, two coach builders, fourteen saddlers, three fine jewellers, and twenty-three different cabinet makers…Service industries and consumer goods, or what the more old fashioned called luxuries, were now a fixed part of the Glasgow scene. 'Whenever capital predominates' Adam Smith noted 'industry prevails, which increases the real wealth and revenue of all its inhabitants.' This 'trickle down' economics turned overseas tobacco money into local jobs.
>
> Arthur Herman *The Scottish Enlightenment* 2003

Some of the Tobacco barons' money was invested in other local developments such as the wine and sugar trades, cotton production and even iron foundries. These activities were barely interrupted by the Jacobite rebellions. In 1745, Glasgow declared loyalty to the Hanoverian regime and was left undisturbed until Bonnie Prince Charlie marched into town on his way back from Derby and demanded supplies which the city authorities were in no position to refuse but, like all good businessmen, asked for government compensation after the Prince was defeated (and got £50,000 some years later to help fund the Forth and Clyde canal).

The end of the tobacco trade was even more abrupt than its beginning. American independence removed the need for middlemen and the Americans duly took the trade into their own hands. The volume imported to Glasgow dropped from 44.8 million lbs in 1775 to 0.3 million lbs three years later. It might have been catastrophic for Glasgow and Scotland. That it was not depended on two new developments. First, the merchants switched their attentions from tobacco from North America to sugar, rum and molasses from the West Indies. Two local army men, Colonel McDowall and Major Milliken, married rich young women while on duty in the West Indies. Their wives owned sugar plantations and they used the wealth of their wives to found James Milliken and Company in Glasgow which also brought much trade through the city. They prospered and in 1733, Milliken bought an estate near the river Cart where he built a mansion which was burned down in 1801 but was replaced by his son. The sugar trade continued well into the 19th century and was an important source of wealth to a few families.

The second development was the birth of a new industry, cotton, which lasted much longer than the tobacco trade and created a huge need for workers and was responsible for a colossal increase in population.

Cotton

Lancashire pioneered the cotton industry with three crucial inventions. Hargreave's Spinning Jenny, developed from 1764, increased the amount of cotton thread that could be spun. It was small enough and cheap enough to be accommodated in cottages. Arkwright's Water-Frame (patented in 1769) was capable of spinning a cotton yarn strong enough to use in production of cloth. Crompton's Mule introduced in 1779 produced a finer yarn. The latter two were suitable for use in a factory. Since cotton was easier to spin by machine than flax, the linen manufacturers in the West of Scotland must have been tempted to switch from linen to cotton but were inhibited by the fact that the Lancastrians had a 20-year lead, during which time they had developed the necessary skills

Cotton Mill at New Lanark early 19th century (Glasgow University Archives)

and markets. Glasgow was doing well from the linen trade but production was no longer increasing and revenue had started to fall from £248,299 in 1768 to £242,937 ten years later. The switch to cotton in the West of Scotland began when James Montieth, a linen weaver, discovered how to weave an Indian muslin using cotton alone. His secret was quickly out and other linen manufacturers followed hoping to increase their profits because, if successful, cotton offered a different scale of return. The Scots had three advantages: they could learn from the Lancastrian experiences; the linen business had developed an organisation and skilled workforce which could be adapted relatively easily; and they had links with America which provided both cotton and a large market. Since the Lancastrians had specialised in relatively cheap cloths, the Scots, learning from their experience with linen, concentrated on finer products.

The first mill was opened on the Isle of Bute in 1779 and within 14 years there were 39 mills. The rivers of Lanarkshire, Ayrshire and Renfrewshire powered 15,000 looms operated by an average of nine people: men, women and children or 135,000 souls. The most famous was that founded by David Dale at New Lanark in 1786. It was equipped with the help of Arkwright himself and later managed by Dale's son-in-law, Robert Owen. Workers, usually destitute, were sucked in from the Highlands and Ireland in huge numbers. New Lanark alone employed 1,300. Unlike the linen workers, most of these worked outside the city's boundaries but within a radius of 20 miles. The earliest steam powered spinning mill was built in 1792 in the east end of Glasgow. Watt's patent on his steam engine ran out in 1800 and, since all convenient riverside sites had been exploited, steam became more common thereafter. Once the 'Slubbing Billy', capable of producing a wide range of yarns, had been introduced, the yarn produced by the domestic Spinning Jenny became redundant. The last part of the process of mechanisation of spinning was an invention by Neil Snodrass of Glasgow in 1797 which cleaned and prepared the cotton wool for spinning. Thereafter the whole process could be undertaken in factories. The application of power, whether water or steam, meant that anyone, even children, could operate the mules. Arkwright rued the help he had given and told his Lancastrian colleagues that he had put a razor in the hands of a Scotsman who would shave them all.

Weaving, as opposed to spinning, was a skilled occupation learned in the linen trade and practised by about 20,000 in the west of Scotland in 1790. The provision of large quantities of yarn led to a doubling in this number over the next 40 years with 20,000 in Glasgow alone. Initially it was carried out at home in all the small towns of the region, much to the advantage of the owners and detriment of the workers who were laid off when trade was slack. Cartwright invented the powered loom in 1784 but it took years of modifications before it was a worthwhile investment. The first in the West of Scotland was installed in 1801 by John Monteith in his spinning factory in Pollokshaws. It was constructed locally and heralded anguish for the weavers, who were skilled, disciplined and relatively well paid at the turn of the century.

By 1800, the industries of cotton spinning and weaving were the major employers in the region. The products were not directly competitive with those of Lancashire and markets were being established.

The 18th century beginnings of the industries of the 19th century

Coal was traditionally mined by serfs, essentially slaves, who had no choice in their occupation. Not surprisingly, it was difficult to attract freemen to an occupation so stigmatised. The abolition of the state of serfdom in 1799 freed the industry to recruit more widely just at a time when the cotton industry faced major troubles. But coalmining was beset by other technical problems such as ventilating mines of any depth, pumping out water to keep the seams dry and hauling coal up to the surface. Then there was the problem of transporting the coal to markets across poor roads.

These problems made mining any but superficial seams close to towns impractical. Drainage was improved by the use of steam engines from 1769. However, it was some time before they were powerful enough to pump water from deep mines. Even so, by the end of the century, coal production in the West had grown by a factor of six, from 100,000 tons to 600,000 tons, much of it exported to Ireland. It was used locally for small scale glass production and smelting iron.

The chemical industry served the linen and cotton industries. Dyes were important in the production of cloth and mordants were required to fix the dyes. Two dyes were produced in or near Glasgow by the end of the century. Turkey Red was a French discovery but Glaswegians had a practical monopoly of its use. In 1785 George Macintosh, with the backing of David Dale, opened a factory in Barrowfields in the East End for its production and sold it to Henry Monteith in 1805. It continued in production for several years. Macintosh also manufactured Prussian Blue and cudbear, derived from lichens, which could be used for dyeing wool or silk. He set up a factory to the east of Glasgow for its production. A Liverpool company manufactured coppera at Hurlet, just to the south of Glasgow, from 1753. These, together with sulphuric acid, were the beginnings of a chemical industry that flourished in or around the city in the 19th century

Whisky was transported to America in locally manufactured glass bottles. The industry was relatively small in scale as whisky was not much drunk by Glaswegians at that time. The industrial production of whisky was a 19th-century phenomenon; there were only eight legal distilleries in the whole of Scotland at the end of the 18th century but 400 illegal ones, mostly in the Highlands, for local consumption.

The iron industry started in Scotland because of its abundant supply of charcoal. English iron ore was shipped north, smelted in Invergarry (1727), Taynuilt (1753) and Furnace (1755) where a sufficient supply of the necessary timber was available, and then the product was re-exported to England where it was worked. However, early in the century, it became clear that coke derived from coal could replace charcoal. This was first demonstrated by Abraham Darby in Shropshire in 1709. Thus the Highland smelting towns had a short history. The Carron Iron Works was founded in 1759 just north of Glasgow to take advantage of Darby's discovery. This famous factory was established by Roebuck and Garbett, who worked together in the Prestonpans vitriol works, and William Cadell, a merchant. It used locally-mined coal to smelt and forge iron. The site proved susceptible to flooding and the owners asked James Watt to build an engine to pump out the water. Roebuck was a major backer of Watt until he went bankrupt in 1773 as a result of an economic depression; Watt then moved on to Birmingham. Perhaps the most famous product of the Carron Iron Works was the guns, small and manoeuvrable, which were popular with merchant ships to beat off privateers. By the end of the 18th century, there were ten iron works in and around Glasgow but the quality of the iron produced was brittle and therefore only of use for local cheap products, such as nails, ploughs, pots and pans.

Shipbuilding started on the Clyde when Scott's was founded in 1711 but the area contributed less than 5% of the British total, launching about 4,000 tons per year by the end of the century.

Development of the region's infrastructure

The result of the industrial growth in and around Glasgow during the 18th century led to profound changes. The most notable was that the population increased by a factor of six to 77,000 by 1801. Wealth also changed the city's architecture with the building of new churches, civic structures and private houses. The area around Glasgow Cross was made up of colonnaded buildings called piazzas. It was more like a Dutch or Italian town than a British one. St Andrew's church was completed in 1756. The centre of the city, with its near-by University, was thought to be very attractive according to Defoe, Smollett and Dorothy Wordsworth. As far back as 1605, the

Carron Iron Works in the 19th Century (Scotland's Images)

city had enough skilled workmen to form the Trades' House of Glasgow, which included bakers, weavers, tailors, wrights and coopers. This organisation became an important pressure group in regulation of trade and business and even in the governance of the city. In 1792, Robert Adam designed and built the Trades' Hall for the organisation that is still in use.

The City Council undertook two major projects which made feasible the transport of goods in bulk. In 1667, the Town Council bought land down the Clyde on which to build docks for Glasgow's trade: prosaically it became Port Glasgow and handled much of the tobacco trade. The long term goal, to move the docks into Glasgow itself, was frustrated by the shallowness of the Clyde. As early as 1768, John Golborne was asked to advise on ways of deepening the Clyde in Glasgow. He suggested building jetties below Glasgow, serving as a partial dam thus quickening the flow of the river which, together with raking the bottom, washed away some of the river-bed to deepen the river in Glasgow itself. By 1781, the river was 14 feet deep and ships of 100 tons could sail into the centre of the city where an ever-increasing number of docks were built. The process of dredging and blasting the bed of the Clyde continued so that bigger and bigger boats could dock in the city. By 1836, the river gave access to the city harbour for ships of 300–400 tons. It was an expensive operation costing about £1.5 million over 60 years but proved a shrewd investment. In 1799, there were 382 linear yards of quays providing a water area of four acres. By 1898, this had increased to 14,568 linear yards and 206 acres respectively. The revenue from the docks increased from £3,319 to £430,327 over the same period.

The second major project was the building of canals. The Forth and Clyde canal was completed in 1790 and the Monklands canal two years later to exploit the coal seams of the West of Scotland. The Union canal was completed by 1822. Thus coal could be shipped around the Central Belt and exported from either coast. The coalmine owners made sure that supplies to Glasgow were restricted in order to maintain the price they got for their coal. The Monklands canal made significant profits until the arrival of railways about 40 years later yet, because its construction was grossly over budget, no dividend was paid for many years.

The road system was also much improved and extended so that food and other materials could be brought into the city. An important Agricultural Revolution had been initiated in 1723 when a Society of Improvers of Knowledge of Agriculture was formed at the instigation of Cockburn. Turnips and potatoes were introduced and experts were invited to advise landowners on ways of increasing output. Farming methods were revolutionised and, as a result, famine was no longer a regular threat. Improved agricultural output and its efficient distribution were vital steps needed to feed the people sucked in by the new industries.

Glasgow was dramatically richer by the end of the 18th century and dependent on no single trade. This was recognised by the founding of the Royal Chamber of Commerce and Manufacturing in 1783 (the first of its type in the United Kingdom) to ensure the merchants' and manufacturers' interests were properly represented. The population increased from 12,766 in 1708 to 83,769 by 1801. Many large villages had been built around the city to house weavers and their looms (Calton and Bridgeton) and to work seams of coal (Parkhead and Shettleston). There were funds, albeit limited, available for reinvestment. In the 1750s and 1760s, three local banks were established for this purpose but banking did not prove a strong suit for Glasgow. Unlike elsewhere in Britain, the Glasgow banks were set up to supply funds for the development of commerce and industry and their duty to shareholders appeared to be secondary. They tended to offer higher rates of interest but had lower reserves. If one of their major debtors ran into financial difficulties, they were unusually vulnerable and crashes occurred in the 19th century. Even so, the older Edinburgh banks, the Bank of Scotland and the Royal Bank of Scotland, were the biggest investors in the West of Scotland up to the 1830s. Many industrial plants were set up with private capital obtained by personal associations sometimes achieved in the time-honoured way of marrying judiciously. Profits were frequently reinvested.

Why had Glasgow risen to such prominence so quickly? Why did it thrive after the Act of Union rather than succumb as Ireland did? The linen, tobacco and cotton businesses did not depend on favours granted by nature, but on the energy, enterprise and imagination of the people involved. The Act of Union ensured access to the English market and freedom to trade with the American colonies, both of which were essential to the economy of the city. It also helped that labour was considerably cheaper than in England at the time. At the same time, Scotland intellectual life burst into bloom.

Education

From the 1740s to the 1820s Scotland was passing through a remarkable passage in its history, subsequently named the Scottish Enlightenment. Education had been a concern of Scots since the Reformation. Local elders of the kirk, rather than appointed officials from the crown or distant religious leaders or local landowners, were responsible for local practice. In 1698, it was determined that every parish should set up a school. This was extremely successful although the attendance of many children was limited by the parents' need for their labour, particularly at harvest time. Literacy was widespread and the ability to write and calculate fairly common. Education in the cities as they expanded rapidly was much less successful except for children of the middle classes who were educated to a high standard at schools, many of which were funded by public subscription. The classics, which remained the bedrock of a good English education, were ignored and replaced by mathematics and sciences. Scotland also had an advantage in its university structure. The Universities of St Andrews, Glasgow, Edinburgh and Aberdeen all had a long history and were comparatively cheap to attend compared with Oxford and Cambridge, but none had been particularly outstanding. The first sign of change happened in 1729 when Francis Hutchison became Professor of Moral Philosophy at Glasgow University. His appointment was strongly supported by a powerful and feared politician, Archibald Campbell, who prevailed over the wishes of the traditional clerical academics. Hutchison's appointment was a brilliant success. His first contribution was to teach in English, rather than Latin, which made his subjects much more accessible to his students. He proved to be not only a good teacher but a better organiser. He became powerful enough to appoint like-minded men to other chairs so that the University's reputation grew rapidly. He was succeeded by Adam Smith in 1751. Hutchison's personal philosophy, that men are created with an innate sense of goodness which motivated their actions, may have been the rationale behind the paternalistic attempts of David Dale and Robert Owen to conduct their business partly for the benefit of their workers. Sadly, this proved to be the exception and Lord Kames' idea that everyone behaves so as to increase their own wealth became the norm.

Hutchison was the spark that lit the Scottish Enlightenment which some think, perhaps grandiosely, invented the modern world. From Edinburgh and Glasgow and later from Aberdeen, a series of men used 'scientific' methods, which Newton had pioneered, to reflect on the causes of behaviour, the management of trade, the origins of the world as revealed by geology as well as advancing chemistry and medicine. The latter part of the Scottish Enlightenment in the early 19th century gave the world the historical novel and the *Edinburgh Review* which became hugely influential in the artistic and political life of Britain for many decades. Such was the fame of Scottish universities that they were used as a model for the new universities of the United States.

All this happened within a generation or two of the Act of Union. And that may not have been an accident since society became more peaceful (save for the Jacobite Rebellions), the law less capricious and government further away. The merchants and industrialists were left to their own devices with their security assured. The international reputations of local academics must have given them confidence to think radically about their businesses. However, there is not much evidence that the giants of the Enlightenment actually had a direct input into the development of industry or business. It is true that Joseph Black helped develop the process of bleaching described above and he and John Anderson encouraged the University's instrument repairer, James Watt, in his attempts to improve the steam engine. Yet Watt had to go to Birmingham to find engineers with the necessary skills to build his models. Adam Smith's description of the world of business may have influenced the legal framework for the conduct of commerce and industry. But the universities' major contribution was to change curricula in such a way as to encourage inquiry and observation leading to conclusions. This was rare at the time and did not happen in Oxford and Cambridge for several decades.

Political changes

There were two groups wielding political power in the city. The Campbell family (the Argyles) started their long period of political dominance in the early part of the century. It was one of them who insisted on the appointment of Francis Hutchison. It was another Campbell who represented the town in Parliament for many years. His support for the Malt Tax made him so unpopular that his house was burned down by a mob. They were a traditional landed family with important connections to government particularly when the Whigs were in power. The second power-base, which was of greater relevance to the city's development, was the City Council made up of businessmen. A City Chamberlain was appointed in 1755 to supervise the collection of taxes and monitor expenditure and the chief magistrate was promoted to Lord Provost twenty years later. The Chamber of Commerce mobilised support for business interests. Therefore, businessmen ran the town for business although the Argyll family had considerable power to influence decisions with which they were concerned. As the city's population grew, law and order were threatened. A weavers' strike in 1787 led to rioting and fear among the propertied classes. The following year, the magistrates appointed a police supervisor whose establishment was increased from eight officers in 1788 to three sergeants, nine officers and 68 watchmen a few years later. This force was sanctioned by Parliament in 1800 which also gave the council powers to raise rates and undertake the lighting and paving of streets and refuse collection. The functions of a well-ordered city were being put in place although some, such as the water supply, remained dire.

The French Revolution reverberated around Britain and nowhere more than in the movement for parliamentary reform. The merchant class believed that the increasing prosperity of Glasgow merited better representation than one MP shared with three other towns, all of which had conspicuously failed to match Glasgow's growth. Men of middling rank also thought that they deserved the vote. Henry Dundas, another Campbell, was Home Secretary at the time and completely opposed widening the franchise, citing the example of the French experience. He conspired actively to undermine the Scottish Association of the Friends of the People which had been formed as a pressure group for reform. In particular, Thomas Muir, a Glasgow lawyer, was charged and found guilty of sedition and sentenced to 14 years transportation. This effectively ended the agitation for the 20 years of the Napoleonic Wars.

It is difficult to know how prosperous Glasgow was compared to other British cities of the time. Certainly, Scotland as a whole remained less prosperous than England. At the end of the century drovers moved vast herds of black cattle from the Highlands and Islands to Falkirk Tryst where they were sold on to England to help satisfy the English demand for beef and to victual the vast appetite of the British Navy during the Napoleonic Wars. But at the same time:

> there were no butchers shops even in Edinburgh, and in the rural districts meat was seldom seen unless a beast died or a 'mart' was killed for salting for the autumn. In the northern counties, reported Sir John Sinclair in 1795, not five pounds of meat was consumed on a farm in a whole year and an egg was a luxury.
>
> *The Drove Roads of Scotland* ARB Haldane

However, Glasgow's growth and prosperity had undoubtedly increased more than other Scottish cities, let alone the rural North. At the end of the century, Glasgow businessmen probably looked forward to the next century with a fair degree of optimism and enthusiasm despite the Napoleonic war which closed much of Europe to trade. It is hard to pinpoint why Glasgow's economy took off in the 18th century. It may have helped that during the century repeated successful wars with France opened up the world to British colonisation and placed Glasgow at a geographical advantage, but the ambition of the City Council, the level of education of a significant proportion of the population and the can-do confidence of the business classes who seized the opportunities thrown up by the Act of Union must take most of the credit.

The comparative importance of the linen industry and tobacco trade to Glasgow's development in the 18th century is difficult to assess. In money terms, the tobacco trade was much the bigger of the two and earned capital which could be re-invested in the city. However, it died with American independence. The linen industry was more important in that it served as a model for a change into cotton which fuelled the next generation of business.

CHAPTER 2

THE 19TH CENTURY

If Glasgow's growth in the 18th century had been brisk, it accelerated spectacularly in the 19th century. Several major industries were developed or transformed. Railways were built to improve communications for both goods and passengers. The first, between Glasgow and Garnkirk, running alongside the Monklands canal, opened in 1831. It was very profitable and carried 354,000 tons of coal in its first full year, undercutting the rates charged for use of the canal. An unlooked for bonus was that it also carried 282,000 passengers during that year. The line between Glasgow and Edinburgh was completed in 1842. By then, Glasgow was connected to Paisley, Renfrew and Greenock, Kilmarnock, Ayr and the Ayrshire coalfields. In 1848, the year of revolutions in Europe, Glaswegians could travel to London in a sensational 9 hours 36 minutes. By comparison, 16 years earlier, it had taken 35 hours 50 minutes and 180 horses to get news of the passage of the Great Reform Bill to Glasgow. The railway raised the average speed from 11 to 42 miles per hour thus dramatically reducing Glasgow's geographical isolation. It is interesting that 150 years later the journey time has only been reduced to 5 hours 15 minutes.

Glasgow expanded eastwards absorbing some coal and iron villages (see later) and then southwards across the Clyde. This contributed to the huge increase in population from nearly 84,000 in 1801 to 275,000 in 1841, just under half a million in 1871 and 1 million at the turn of the century. The new Glaswegians came from starving Ireland and the changing Highlands. The speed of this increase led to some of the worst slums in Europe which have left scars that still survive. At the end of the century, some 700,000 people lived in indescribable squalor and over-crowding in about 3 square miles around High Street. This is more than the entire population of the city in 2001 which is spread over 70 square miles. The City Corporation and even British governments spent much of the 20th century trying to solve the resulting problems.

Cotton

The 19th century did not start well for cotton, at that time the unquestioned major industry of the West of Scotland, and its workers. First, the Napoleonic Wars interfered with continental trade as Napoleon tried to bankrupt Britain. Second, when the wars finished, the labour market was flooded with returning soldiers anxious for some form of employment. Third, the development of powered looms increased productivity considerably which inevitably meant that fewer workers were required. The first steam-powered mill was built in the east end of Glasgow in 1792 and there were 107 by 1831. It became harder and harder for families working in their homes as production was transferred to factories, often within the city. Wages fell dramatically because fewer workers were required and because of the ready availability of labour. For example, a weaver earned between 12s and 20s per week at the end of the 18th century but by 1810 it was down to between 6s and 15s per week. This led to a strike in 1812 in which the weavers tried to restrict access to their trade and to ensure a minimum price for their products. It failed. The effect on the workers, even those who were still employed, was exacerbated by the Corn Laws which subsidised (aristocratic)

farmers at the expense of manufacturing workers. This had advantages because the landowners were able to invest in land improvement which dramatically increased food production and
helped to feed the increasing urban population. At the time, however, hardship was severe for all
workers but particularly for those in the cotton industry in which the majority of Glaswegians
worked. Unfortunately, there were few other job opportunities so that the weavers had to hang
on desperately, even though there was work for only about one-third of the 45,000 in the West of
Scotland trying to earn their living this way. Those that survived concentrated on the production
of fine cotton products too complicated for the power-looms to produce.

The rapid changes in the cotton industry may have been catastrophic for the workforce but it
continued to make significant contributions to the income of the West of Scotland throughout
the 19th century, even during its decline in the second half of the century. The manufacturers
tried to undercut their competitors by investing in new heavy machinery imported from Manchester and elsewhere and bought on borrowed money. The results were that even more cotton had to be sold, but tariffs introduced to protect markets in countries developing their own
industries made that impossible. In 1837 the owners responded by trying to cut wages resulting
in a strike organised by the Cotton Operatives Union. Blackleg labour was brought in which
inevitably resulted in considerable violence. The police were instructed to implement the owners'
policies and the courts condemned the union leaders to transportation. The strike was broken
and thereafter management responded to all threats to their competitiveness by lowering wages.
To achieve this end, they used increasing numbers of children and women.

Some banks that provided funds for the mechanisation of the weaving sector were very exposed
to the success of a few companies. One such, the Western Bank, called in debts which could not be
paid. This caused a run on the Bank which 'closed its doors' in 1857. The ensuing crisis in confidence afflicted the whole industry and was compounded within a few years by the American Civil
War during which there was a severe shortage of cotton. These two events had a lasting effect on
the industry. Although the going had been getting more difficult as the century progressed, there
had been continuous expansion until 1856 even if the rate had slowed. After the 1860s, the number
of mills and spindles fell by a third within 10 years and the number of power-looms by a fifth and
labour by a quarter. Output is more difficult to measure but the use of imported cotton also fell by
about 30%. Therefore Glasgow faced the fallout from the decline of its premier industry.

Fortunately, other industries were emerging but the cotton industry continued to struggle for
survival. A minority explored niche markets by producing goods of higher quality and design.
David and John Anderson produced high quality and light fabrics in their factory in Bridgeton
and developed a world-wide reputation, exporting 75% of their production. Fine muslins were
another speciality much in demand in hot climates which included much of the British Empire.
Paisley firms supplied another niche market with their shawls which were worn around the world.
However, even this market proved susceptible to a change in fashion leading to closure of much
of the industry in Paisley in the 1870s throwing 10,000 out of work. The thread industry was
dominated by Paisley firms. James Coats was a weaver who made his first breakthrough when he
managed to imitate Canton Crepe which was silk based and imported from China. His product
was considerably cheaper and he cornered the market from about 1805. His next venture was to
set up a small mill producing thread in 1826. He retired four years later and his four sons took over
and the firm was named after two of them – James (junior) and Peter Coats. By 1850, J & P Coats
was the market leader exporting much of its product, particularly to the United States. In 1890, the
business was floated as a public company, being valued at nearly £6m and with an annual profit of
nearly £500,000. It was an enormous enterprise and got bigger when it amalgamated with another
successful Paisley thread manufacturer, Clark & Co and two English producers. At the end of the
century, it had 17 factories, including some in the United States, as well depots for storage and sales;

Statue of Thomas Coates in Paisley by William Birnie Rhind (Scotland's images)

it had about 21,000 employees worldwide with the largest group being in Paisley although the headquarters were in Glasgow. The enormous success of this business was partly due to the huge market created by sewing machines which were built over the river in Clydebank.

About 1860 it became possible to use power looms to produce cloth with a variety of designs, the jacquard patterning mechanism, which proved ideal for lace curtains. Several factories were built in the Irvine valley for their production which led to jobs for about 8,000 workers and they prospered until the 1920s. Other companies were less successful because they were unable to identify a niche to exploit and went under. Their supporting industries, not surprisingly, suffered a similar fate. Dyeing and calico printing were major employers and had concentrated around the Vale of Leven. Rationalisation was attempted but the businesses were closed one by one.

Glaswegians were not major pioneers in the cotton industry but were able to capitalise on developments elsewhere both in terms of methods of production and provision of some machinery. Eventually the cotton industry failed because local firms could not deliver bulk products more cheaply than rivals either in Manchester or abroad. The failure of the Glasgow cotton manufacturers to adapt to the conditions of the second half of the 19th century is puzzling. Oakley has suggested that the 'third and fourth generations of employers had lost interest in their industry… They became "mechanically minded instead of textile minded" and turned their attention to these fascinating industries where the work was so varied and interesting and the profits were so considerable'. By the end of the century, employment in the cotton industry was still about 30,000 but the future looked bleak apart from some highly specialised firms.

Coal

The industrialisation of Glasgow and its growing population meant that there was a shortage of coal and its price rose considerably in the first decade of the century. The problems associated with deeper mines – ventilation, drainage and raising coal to the surface – were being overcome with the use of steam power. Distribution remained a problem: it should have been solved by the Monkland's canal which opened in 1792, but the coalmine owners were reluctant to quench the city's huge appetite too completely, lest it impair their profits. No wonder that the first railway built in the region linked the coalfields with the city. It opened in 1831 and a dramatic reduction in the price of coal in Glasgow followed, from 3s 6d to 1s 3d per ton, and Glasgow was fully powered for the next generation of industries.

The supply of labour was another problem. Scottish colliers had been freed from servitude just before the turn of the century but it remained an unpopular occupation. With rising demand and labour shortages, wages inevitably rose – even as weavers were experiencing a reduction in their earnings. There is little evidence to suggest that weavers moved into coalmining if only because they considered themselves skilled workers, almost the antithesis of coalminers. Instead the influx came as a result of two developments elsewhere. Enclosures of land in rural Scotland, especially in Dumfries, Galloway and, later, in the Highlands, forced peasants off the land. Problems in Ireland, culminating in the famine of 1846, led to a halving of that country's population and many, both Catholic and Protestant, came to Lanarkshire. That county's population rose from 81,700 in 1755 to 523,800 in 1851 largely due to this immigrant labour. Towns and villages were built to accommodate them in close proximity to the mines and the countryside became industrialised. As a result, output soared from the coalfields of Western Scotland, from half a million tons at the beginning of the century to 5.6 million tons in 1854 and 12 million tons in 1870.

The mines themselves varied from one-man concerns to major companies like Baird & Co. which owned 26 collieries in 1870. In 1896, J B Atkinson compiled a list of 285 mines of all sizes in Lanarkshire alone, employing 34,000 under ground and 7,364 on the surface. As demand grew and some mines became exhausted, new ones were opened further south in Lanarkshire and in Ayrshire where the coal tended to be deeper. Conditions were harsh and the abundance of migrant workers drove pay down. Miners, like most workers of the time, worked a twelve-hour day with a half day on Saturday and Sunday off. Mining was also dangerous both in the short term as a result of firedamp and the risk of explosions, roof collapse or flooding, and in the long term as a result of silicosis.

Coal from Lanarkshire and Ayrshire was mostly used locally in the iron and then the steel industries as well as for domestic uses. Indeed, the iron works set up early in the century were deliberately sited to be near a supply of coal so that transport costs would be minimal. This led to the close alliance between the coal and iron industries. Only a small amount was exported to

Europe, using the canals to the east coast. Towards the end of the century there were signs that the seams were becoming more difficult and costly to operate, particularly in the Monklands area which had been exploited first.

Iron

In 1801, David Mushet, a founder of Calder Ironworks, discovered that blackband ironstone, hitherto regarded as poor quality coal, contained a high proportion of iron. There was therefore an abundance of local iron ore. This was brilliantly exploited once J B Neilson designed his prototype hot blast furnace in 1828. His key idea was to preheat the air used to blast the furnace. He had some difficulty in persuading the rather conservative ironmasters to try his new technique, but was eventually allowed to experiment by Dunlop and Wilson in one of their foundries in the Clyde Ironworks. Although his prototype was not particularly efficient, it was considered a success. After further improvements, he subsequently achieved a dramatic increase in efficiency so that the production of one ton of hot-blast iron required only 3 tons of coal, compared to 8 tons previously. At a stroke, the iron trade in the west of Scotland was changed from one supplying local needs with rather brittle and inferior iron to producing the cheapest good quality pig-iron in the world. The price per ton came down from £6 to £4 15s over 4 years. Heavy investment followed and output increased from 37,000 tons (5% of UK production) to 700,000 tons (25%) in the next 20 years and to 1,206,000 tons (about 30%) in 1870. Thereafter, it remained steady for the rest of the century. By 1885, there were 124 blast furnaces concentrated around the canal in the Monklands district of Lanarkshire and in Ayrshire. The West of Scotland became a major supplier of iron during the great

Girls working in a cotton spinning factory in Paisley 1905 (Glasgow University Archives)

expansion of manufacturing in the British Isles and abroad. Neilson thus delivered the means to found a huge industry, providing work for many who had been made redundant by the changes in the cotton industry as well as for a new flood of immigrants from Ireland and the Highlands. He deserves to be remembered as one of the great pioneers of Glasgow.

The captains of this industry were self-made men who founded family companies. Dixon, whose family operated three ironworks, and the Baird brothers who built the giant Gartsherrie works in 1828, were previously engaged in coalmining and became two of the biggest ironmasters. Their history helps to explain the close association which developed between the local coal and iron industries that had disastrous consequences in the 20th century. Henry Houldsworth had moved from Nottingham to Glasgow in 1799 to manage a small cotton mill by the Kelvin river. He and his sons started working metal for the machines in the factory and eventually diversified into iron and set up two ironworks, Coltness Iron Works near Wishaw in 1839 and Dalmellington Iron Company in 1848, financed largely from family sources. When he died in 1853, his family continued to operate these businesses.

By the 1870s, local iron deposits were becoming depleted and iron ore had to be imported in increasing amounts. The very advantages that had made Scottish pig-iron cheaper now started to work in others' favour, particularly those in the north-east of England and Wales which had good local supplies of iron ore and coal as well as larger, more efficient furnaces. As its advantages eroded, Scottish pig-iron became the most expensive in Britain. Radical measures were required if the local industry was to overcome the disadvantage of having to import its raw material. Instead, the ironmasters opted to adapt existing plants piecemeal rather than build anew. Surprisingly, local production remained stable at slightly above a million tons per year from 1850 to the end of the century. Nevertheless, the iron industry, like cotton, was condemned to slow decline in the second half of the century although both remained important contributors to the local economy.

It took some time before much of the pig-iron was used locally. To begin with most was exported for others to work. The conversion of pig-iron into end-iron merchandise was performed by the malleable-iron industry. Strangely, when it did evolve in the region, it was largely independent of the pig-iron producers, perhaps because they had such close links with coal. This new industry developed slowly until spurred on by the railway construction frenzy of the middle decades of the century. The switch from wood to iron in the shipbuilding industry also used significant quantities from the 1850s onwards and created a strong link between the malleable-iron industry and shipbuilding. Indeed, as early as 1842, Parkhead Forge was bought by Robert Napier, a marine engineer who fathered the shipbuilding industry (see below).

There were five malleable-iron works in 1849 and 14 by 1870. Malleable iron was used to construct a huge variety of items, decorative and functional, required by the New Iron Age. For example, the Saracen Foundry in Possilpark was famous for its production of ornamental cast-iron products such as bandstands, lampposts, clock towers and railings. It was founded by Walter McFarlane in 1850 near the Saracen's Head in Gallowgate but moved in 1872 to a green-field site in Possil where it spread over 24 acres and employed 1200 men. It became part of Federated Foundries and as such survived until 1965. Walter McFarlane had a town house in Park Circus which he decorated with some of the Saracen foundry's best work. The house still exists and is used as a rather stylish register office. The Dalmarnock Iron Works was set up by William Arrol in 1872. He began work in a cotton mill at the age of ten and then trained as a blacksmith, going to night school to learn mechanical engineering. He set up his company when he was 29 and became famous for his iron bridges which included the replacement railway bridge over the Tay (1882–87), the Forth Railway Bridge (1883–90) and, not least, Tower Bridge (1886–94) in London.

Even so, only a fraction of the pig-iron produced was used locally and more than half was regularly exported.

Steel

The iron industry had developed because of locally available deposits, the coal required for smelting and a major local invention, the blast furnace. Steel offered major advantages over iron. Production had been revolutionised by the Bessemer converter, patented in 1856, and then by the Siemens–Martin open-hearth furnace about 10 years later (Siemens was born in Germany but worked in England, while Martin was French). With commendable speed, Bessemer was invited in 1857 to set up one of his converters by William Dixon, a local ironmaster, but the steel produced was of such low quality that the attempt was abandoned. The reason was that the local phosphoric iron was unsuitable and the solution was to import haematite iron. The Atlas works in Springburn was the only company to operate the Bessemer converter successfully and started to produce steel in 1861. The Siemens–Martin process had three advantages: it was more prolonged and therefore permitted greater control so that the desired end point could be attained more predictably by regular analysis; it could use old discarded iron; and it was cheaper because it used pre-heated air. The ability to use discarded iron appealed to the owners of the Tharsus Sulphur and Copper Company. They had imported ore for the extraction of copper and had accumulated a huge store of non-phosphoric iron which was a waste product of copper extraction. The owners took the initiative to found the Steel Company of Scotland in 1871. Siemens was invited to construct a rotary furnace at Hallside in Cambuslang. The experiments with this source of iron failed and the company went on to build standard open-hearth blast furnaces at Hallside using imported iron from Spain and later Sweden. At first, the company specialised in producing rails but switched to supplying steel for the shipyards. It made its first profit in 1876.

Remarkably, only two producers of malleable iron changed to steel production; Beardmore's at Parkhead in 1879 (William Beardmore had joined Robert Napier in the 1860s and taken it over soon afterwards) and Colville's at Dalzell near Motherwell in 1880. One pig-iron producer, Merry and Cunninghame at Glengarnock, did so in 1884. Other pig-iron producers did not convert because their businesses were still reasonably profitable, or as Oakley put it:

> The Coatbridge firms were in the main unwilling to change their well established processes
> – it is remarkable how conservative the most liberal-minded people can become after twenty
> or thirty years – and the new steel producers grew up in another Lanarkshire district, Moth-
> erwell, where the manufacturers relied on imported pig-iron.

Scottish steel production increased rapidly to 240,000 tons by 1883 produced by 15 companies. Their major customers were the shipbuilders who preferred to use acid or mild steel, made in furnaces with an acid lining consisting of a siliceous refractory and under a siliceous slag. They assured the steelmakers' future while Clydeside shipbuilding flourished.

Marine engineering and shipbuilding

Glasgow's major success, in a century of several remarkable successes, was the shipbuilding industry. At the beginning of the century, the Clyde shipyards made a very modest contribution to the country's shipbuilding capacity but within 50 years the Clyde became the major shipbuilding river of the world. It was and remains one of the world's great industrial achievements, on a par with the domination of the computer industry by California in the late 20th century. The major reasons for its success were plentiful supplies of coal and iron and later local steel; it was a pioneering centre for building engines (there were already 14 firms producing steam engines in the city in 1835); and it had created access to the sea. This combination of assets was necessary for engineering skills to develop and flourish. The engineers involved had often trained as millwrights or blacksmiths. They had designed and built engines for industrial uses in factories of different kinds but particularly for the cotton industry. There was virtually no input from the universities once Watt had given his crucial initial impetus to improved engine design (and Watt was not an academic but an instrument repairer working for the university). It was not until 1881 that Glasgow University started a course on naval architecture and two years later a bequest from John Elder's widow endowed the first Chair. However, the graduates rarely went into the shipbuilding industry which was mature by that time. A second department was founded in 1909 at the Royal Technical College which subsequently became Strathclyde University. The universities, therefore, showed their interest almost exactly when the region's dominance in shipbuilding started to decline and their intervention did nothing to arrest that decline. Therefore, the industry was a home grown affair which started almost as a hobby for a few key individuals.

The story started with William Symington, an engineer with the Wanlockhead lead mine. In 1784, aged 20, he produced a model of a steam powered vehicle. This so impressed the manager of the mine that he arranged for it to be shown in Edinburgh University. One of the people who saw it was Patrick Miller of Dalswinton who was a significant shareholder in the Carron Iron Works. He was interested in powered boats but had no concept of how to generate sufficient power. They arranged to co-operate and Miller provided most of the capital. In 1788, the first powered paddle steamer sailed on Dalswinton Loch. The next year they launched a boat on the Forth and Clyde canal which achieved a speed of 6 mph. Miller then lost interest probably because of the expense of the project and, since Symington did not have the means to continue alone, the project lapsed until 1800 when Lord Dundas, Governor of the Forth and Clyde Canal Company, proposed that he build a powered boat for towing barges on the canal. Symington produced the *Charlotte Dundas* in 1801 which succeeded in all its tests, but the owners of the canal became worried by the effect of the wash on the structure of the canal and abandoned the experiment. Symington moved south and built more powered boats but eventually died destitute.

The *Charlotte Dundas* was seen by Robert Fulton who built the first commercial steam boat on the Hudson River in the USA in 1807. It also inspired Henry Bell to design the *Comet*, the first steam powered boat to serve as a passenger ferry on the Clyde between 1812 and 1820. Bell, who had trained as a millwright and builder, owned a hotel in Helensburgh and wanted a boat to bring customers down from Glasgow. The engine and boiler were built in Glasgow and the hull on the lower Clyde at Port Glasgow. The *Comet* was a huge success and led to a surge in marine construction.

Marine engineering rather than shipbuilding was the initial strength of Glasgow but the construction of the ships themselves followed soon afterwards. John Barclay opened the first shipyard in Glasgow itself only six years after the inaugural voyage of the *Comet*, in 1818 at Stobcross pool, but Robert Napier is usually considered the father of Clyde shipbuilding. He was born in 1791 into a family which was to figure so prominently in the history of shipbuilding on the Clyde. His mother was Jean Denny, whose family founded the family firm in Dunbarton which went on to build more ships than any other Clydeside company. His father's brother's son, David Napier, was born a year earlier and was probably an even better engineer. Both fathers of the Napier cousins were prosperous blacksmiths and both cousins started their training in their fathers' smithies. David helped design the engine for the *Comet* in his father's works at Camlachie and took over management of the business in 1814. His engines powered some of the first sea-going ferries running between Greenock and Belfast and Holyhead and Dublin in the 1820s. In 1821, he moved to Lancefield Quay to build complete ships including the first ship with an iron hull, the *Aglaia* launched in 1827. His cousin, Robert, took over the Camlachie Foundry from him.

The reason why Robert Napier became such a dominant figure in the history of shipbuilding on the Clyde was that he had three outstanding qualities: he was an accomplished engineer, although perhaps not as good as his cousin or one of his employees, David Elder; he was an entrepreneur of

The Comet, *first powered ship on the Clyde, 1812, now imprisoned in Port Glasgow*

some genius; and he succeeded in attracting quality people to work for and with him which ensured that the Clydeside remained dominant for the rest of the century. He worked his apprenticeship with his father during the Napoleonic Wars and narrowly missed being pressed into the Royal Navy. His marine career started in 1823 when he won a contract from James Lang of Dumbarton for the engine of a local steamer. This engine, built in the Camlachie Foundry, had a surface condenser which made it much more efficient in the use of coal because it kept seawater out of the boiler. (It was so good that it was later fitted to another ship.) He earned more fame when two boats powered by his engines won the August Regatta of the Northern Yacht Club in 1827 and gained serious attention when the East India Company asked him to make the engine for their ocean-going paddle sloop *Berenice* in 1836. This raced its sister ship, the *Atlanta,* powered by an engine designed by English engineers, to India and arrived a full 18 days before its rival which won him many admirers in the Admiralty. He went on to improve the efficiency of the driving system linking the engine to the paddle wheel. David Napier, then working with him, improved the shape of the hull by pioneering the sharp bow. Although David Napier built the first iron hull launched on the Clyde in 1827, it was Robert Napier who persuaded Lloyds to grant an A1 category to iron-hulled ships in 1844. The success of two iron-hulled ships, the *Royal Sovereign* and the *Royal George* built by Tod and Macgregor of Partick in 1838, undoubtedly helped. The seal of approval from Lloyd's accelerated the shift from wood to iron and ensured that the Clyde could compete successfully in building ships as well as the engines.

Robert Napier's relationship with Samuel Cunard, a Canadian businessman and ship owner, was another major factor in the development of the Clyde. Cunard planned a regular transatlantic liner service backed by a mail contract with the government. This contract was lucrative but there were stiff penalties for late delivery. Reliability was, therefore, crucial. The two men met in 1839 and Napier persuaded Cunard to modify his plans and increase the size of the proposed ships. This caused financial problems which Napier helped solve with a group of friends who together formed a company which became the Cunard Steam Ship Company. In essence, the shareholders were backing Napier's ability to build ships which could fulfil the contract with the government. He did, supervising the construction on the Clyde of four ships of about 1,150 tons and 420hp which proved fit for purpose and enhanced his reputation on both sides of the Atlantic.

The Admiralty were notoriously conservative and stuck with their Thames-side engine builder until questions were asked in the House. Investigations showed that Napier's engines were both cheaper and more reliable so the Admiralty were obliged to change and he became its main engine builder. Next he expanded his business by diversifying into shipbuilding itself. The reason was that the company with which he usually co-operated in Port Glasgow specialised in wooden hulls and Napier realised that iron hulls were the future. He set up a yard in Govan in 1841 where the *Vanguard* was built for the Dublin & Glasgow Steam Packet Company. Then he launched into building several iron-hulled ships for the Navy. Over the next few years he built bigger and bigger ships: the aptly named *Leviathan*, the first train ferry for the North British Railway Company in 1849, the year of the Californian God Rush, the *Persia* for the Cunard Steam Company in 1854 and then the *Black Prince*, the largest ship built up to that time at 9,800 tons, in 1861.

Perhaps Robert Napier's biggest contribution to the development of shipbuilding on the Clyde was that he trained the next generation of engineers. These included James and George Thomson, who later founded a Clydebank shipyard which became John Brown & Company and who, perversely, took away Cunard's business; John Elder (David's son) who founded another famous shipyard which became Fairfield's and A C Kirk who became famous for significant developments to the engine.

Glasgow's supremacy in marine engineering was maintained by a series of breakthroughs right up to the end of the century. Boilers capable of maintaining higher and higher pressures were produced until it was feasible to change from paddle wheels to propellers. Stevens, an American, was the first to point out the theoretical advantages of the propeller as early as 1802. By 1836, Smith and Eriksson, working elsewhere in Britain, had independently refined the mechanics and taken out a patent but could not apply them until a boiler capable of functioning at high-pressure had been developed. This was achieved by 1840 when the first screw driven steamer sailed on the Clyde. Thereafter, propeller driven ships quickly became the norm.

As boilers became more efficient, ships could sail further and carry more cargo. James Napier, another cousin, introduced the romantically named Haystack Vertical Boiler in 1830 which cut fuel consumption by 25%. Further pioneering work was carried out by the firm founded by John Elder and Charles Randolf in 1852 which took out fourteen major patents in as many years. The most important was the double expansion boiler which was first fitted into a commercial ship in 1855. The ship was for the Pacific Steam Navigation Company which operated along the coast of South America where coal was particularly expensive. It proved to be so much more economical (about 30%) that all the company's other ships were sent to the Clyde to have their boilers replaced with the new model. The developments continued up to 1874, when the triple expansion engine, designed by AC Kirk, who was the chief engineer of the company, offered still more efficiency in coal consumption. In 1862, James Howden introduced the Scotch Boiler which was significantly stronger than previous models and thus able to accommodate higher pressures. The increasing efficiency of these engine changes reduced the space required for coal thus making longer sea voyages practical and increasing the space available for cargo. This spelt the death of sailing ships. At the end of the century, the steam turbine engine, designed by CA Parsons of the Denny Yard, increased the speed of coal-powered ships, and was taken up by navies. This was the last major Clydeside development and heralded the high point of its domination. The next big development was the diesel engine which was a European discovery and which broke the monopoly of steam-powered propulsion, the strength of the Clyde.

The skills of Glaswegian engineers and workmen had beaten all competition for about 60 years. This was some compensation for the fact that James Watt had had to go to Matthew Boulton's works in Birmingham to find engineers who could make cylinders with the precision required for the development of his steam engines. It was a remarkable achievement.

If the Clyde began as a base for marine engineering, it quickly developed the skills required to build complete ships. There were companies that built wooden hulls on the Clyde as there were elsewhere in Scotland and around the coast of Britain. It had no natural advantage in this medium because wood was not particularly plentiful in Strathclyde. The change to iron was a wonderful opportunity because the local iron industry had just been established. Iron hulls had several advantages: they were stronger, lasted longer, could be used to build larger ships (the limit for wood was only 300 feet although the Chinese junks were said to be about 450 feet long) and, surprisingly, were lighter because the walls of the hulls were thinner. Nowhere else embraced the change as quickly or on the same scale. The first yard laid out for construction of iron hulls was that of Tod and Macgregor near Partick in the late 1830s and the last wooden Clyde liner was launched in 1852.

The ship designer who Robert Napier appointed to his yard in Govan was William Denny who could take much credit for the succession of marvellous ships that rolled into the Clyde from the yard. The Denny family had a pretty good pedigree of their own. William Denny (senior) established his yard at Dumbarton and started building ships early in the 19th century and brought three of his sons into the company. In 1844, they started to build iron hulls rather well. William Denny & Brothers' reputation for high quality owed much to their meticulous methods. They systematically recorded the results of all ship trials and were the first to use a test tank in which to assess the resistance of models pulled through the water at different speeds. Their main speciality was fast cross-channel ferries. In 1879, they launched the first ocean-going ship made of acid or mild steel. (This was only seven years after the Steel Company of Scotland was formed.) Steel was more tensile than iron, more elastic and above all stronger so ships could be built with less material, were lighter and thus more economical. Acid steel was favoured by Lloyds which was important because insurance was cheaper than for ships made of basic steel and this suited the local steel producers. Other companies adopted the technique and within ten years the output of ships built of this material had grown to 326,136 tons representing 97% of the tonnage launched on the Clyde in 1889.

These are some of the other famous Clyde shipbuilders.

James and George Thomson were marine engineers trained in the Napier school. They set up a marine engineering business at the Clyde Bank Foundry in 1847 and started shipbuilding in Govan in 1851. Twenty years later they moved to a green-field site down river and the subsequent development with its docks, works and houses became Clydebank. They rarely made a profit and were taken over in 1899 by their largest creditor, **John Brown** a Sheffield steelmaker. The yard became famous for its large liners and lasted longer than most of its rivals.

The company of **Randolf and Elder**, which had pioneered compound engines, started producing complete ships in 1860 and their yard became renowned as Fairfield's.

Scott's was an old shipyard which managed to ride the waves of the various innovations with unusual success. Another firm was set up in Port Glasgow in 1874 and, after a few changes of name, became **Lithgow's**. This company, more profitable than most, was unusual in that it built a large number of similar low cost, economical ships, which became popular for carrying cargo around the world. These tramp steamers were efficient enough with their triple expansion engines to drive the last sailing ships off the seas at the turn of the century.

Yarrow's was a Thames based company with a specialist interest in fast small naval vessels. It moved to Scotstoun in 1908 because of the high costs on the Thames and the shortage of available skilled workers in London.

As ships grew larger and some more sophisticated, yards began to specialise. For example, the three yards on the Cart river were unable to build ships of any size and, as a result, specialised in dredgers for which they became world famous. Others such as J & G Thomson and Fairfield's invested heavily and were able to build large liners and naval ships. Denny's specialised in fast light ferries and shallow draught boats for Burma.

In 1831, only 3% of British workers in the shipbuilding industry worked on the Clyde but by 1871 this had increased to 21%. That year, 250,000 tons of shipping was launched, about a third of the British total, showing the productivity advantage of the Clyde. Growth continued until 1913, when the shipyards produced 750,000 tons of shipping and employed 60,000 men in ship construction and marine engineering. It never achieved this output again. Much of the success of the Clyde might have been because, in the modern jargon, a cluster had been created. Firms fed off and competed with each other.

The Clyde must have been a spectacular sight, difficult to imagine today. It was lined by cranes over quays and docks for trade and over yards for shipbuilding, stretching from the centre of Glasgow down to Greenock. Ships tied up at the quay-side, often two or more deep, and ships under construction lay under the cranes. Ferries plied with passengers up, down and across the river. The sea dominated the economic life of the city.

But shipbuilding was by no means the only industry.

Railways and locomotive production

The railway age dawned with the opening of the Stockton and Darlington railway in 1825. This was a huge commercial success, slashing the cost of transporting coal by more than half. Yet, before this became apparent, some Glaswegians had already made a shrewd judgement about its importance. A bill was enacted in Parliament in 1826 sanctioning the building of a railway connecting the collieries of Lanarkshire with Glasgow. Funds were raised quickly and the line quietly opened in 1831 running from the Gartsherrie coalfield through Springburn to Townhead. The first two locomotives were built by Stevenson in Tyneside but, only a year later, the first Glasgow-built locomotives, named Glasgow and Garnkirk, came into service. The effect on the price of coal in Glasgow was as dramatic as it had been in Stockton. For the first time in history, it became practical to move bulk cargoes over long distances other than by water. This was the simple reason for the railway fever that led to the construction of thousands of miles of railway lines, first in Britain and then overseas.

Since the new industry was based on steam powered locomotives to pull the trains, it is not surprising that Glasgow grasped the opportunity: steam power was its strong suit. A new industry that was the younger and smaller brother of shipbuilding grew up in Glasgow. As with shipbuilding, the industry started in the engineering workshops of the city. The opening of the Glasgow to Edinburgh railway in 1842, to huge publicity, provided the opportunity to produce engines that had the capacity to pull trains. This was not straightforward because the journey out of Glasgow started with the Cowlairs Incline with a gradient of about 1:50. This was too steep for any engine in existence at the time and trains were towed up using ropes and a static winding engine built by Neilson (see below). The problem was that the ropes frequently broke which had a huge effect on punctuality. At the time, four trains a day went in both directions. The superintendent of locomotives for the Edinburgh & Glasgow railway was William Paton. He decided to build engines which could drag

City of New York under construction in 1888 by John Brown in Clydebank (Scotland's Images)

trains up the incline. In 1844, he produced Hercules, weighing over 26 tons, and followed it up with Samson later that year. Both were successful and reduced the cost of getting trains up the Cowlairs Incline by two-thirds. However, they were so heavy that it proved impossible to produce a track that could withstand their weight over prolonged periods. For that reason the directors were forced to return to the winding engines but replaced standard ropes with untwisted wire ropes which proved much more reliable and were used from 1847 to 1899.

Caledonian engine and train at Buchanan St Station about 1865 (Mitchell Library)

The Edinburgh and Glasgow Railway Company set up a workshop on a farm in Springburn at the top of the Cowlairs Incline from which it got its name. The Cowlairs Works became the centre of the company's operations. It was there that Hercules and Samson were built and trains were repaired and maintained. The dominance of the E & G Company was challenged by their failure to win the battle to build the north–south route from Carlisle to Aberdeen. This was won by the Caledonian Railway Company which was able to outbid the E & G in purchasing key connecting sections of the track. Services between London, Glasgow and Dubton, near Aberdeen, started in 1848. The company built Buchanan Station as their Glasgow base but their workshops were at Greenock until 1856 when they were moved to a purpose-built site in Springburn, which was called St Rollox. A third locomotive building company also moved to Springburn in 1861. This company was a spin off from a marine engineering business of which one of the partners was a young engineer called Walter Neilson, son of J B Neilson of hot blast furnace fame and nephew of John Neilson who built the Clyde's first iron ship. He was only 17 when he became a director of the family firm situated near the Clyde in Hyde Park Street, Finneston in 1836. At first, locomotives were built as a sideline but were so successful that they began to dominate the business. However, the factory beside the river was not ideal for serving the home market although exports were relatively simple to handle. Neilson decided to transfer to Springburn which he did in 1860. The new factory was called the Hyde Park Works after the street in which the company started.

In the 1860s, Springburn thus acquired three plants producing locomotives. Cowlairs was linked to the fading E & G railway company, St Rollox to the growing Caledonian Railway

Company which dominated the West of Scotland and the Hyde Park Street factory which was independent. This state did not last long. Henry Dubs, who was German born but who had worked in Lancashire, was appointed works manager at Neilson's in 1858, replacing James Reid. He had a personality clash with Walter Neilson and left in 1863 to start his own company on the south side of the city at Polmadie taking with him the brilliant designer, Sampson Goodall-Copestake. His new enterprise was called the Glasgow Locomotive Works and it quickly acquired an excellent reputation. Dubs died in 1876 and was replaced by William Lorimer who remained managing director until the firm merged with its Glasgow rivals in 1903.

Meanwhile, back at the Hyde Park Road Works, James Reid returned to his previous position and became perhaps the greatest figure of the Springburn Railway story. He must have been a dominating personality and a crafty politician because he ousted Walter Neilson from his own company in 1876. He ran the company very successfully and established his sons in the business which was renamed Neilson, Reid and Company in the 1890s. Walter Neilson had another attempt and set up the Clyde Locomotive Company, also in Springburn. Despite huge investment and modern workshops, it failed to thrive and was taken over by a Manchester company in 1888. This company, Sharp, Stewart had built their first locomotive in 1833 and saw a golden opportunity to expand into the state of the art workshops built by Neilson. Crucially, they served different customers from the other Glasgow locomotive builders and, unlike Neilson, did not depend on taking business from them. The workshop was named the Atlas Locomotive Works after their Manchester business.

In 1865, the E & G, which had started the railway boom in the city, was taken over by the North British Locomotive Company. This company dominated the lines in the east of Scotland and was desperate to gain a foothold in the west. In the process, it acquired the Cowlairs workshop. Therefore, for the last part of the century, there were five Glasgow based companies manufacturing locomotives: one for the North British at Cowlairs, one for the Caledonian at St Rollox and three independent companies, the Glasgow Locomotive Works of Dubs at Polmadie, the Hyde Park Road Works run by James Reid and the Atlas Locomotive Works, both in Springburn. The Atlas Works supplied their English customers while Henry Dubs in the Glasgow Locomotive Works and James Reid in the Hyde Park Street Works built engines on commission for whoever ordered them. Their clientele included several overseas customers. This proved awkward because the gauges for which they were built were often different from the local tracks. It was a huge logistical problem transporting these monster engines to the docks by road: management at the Hyde Park Road Works must have regretted the move out of Finneston! These five companies were so successful that in the 1890s they produced about 85% of the British output of railway locomotives.

Perhaps the most famous engine produced was the Dunalastair designed by John McIntosh for Caledonian and launched in 1896: it could go further, pull heavier loads and climb steeper inclines than any of its rivals. It helped to secure orders from Europe but oddly these were placed with Neilson's even though construction was supervised by McIntosh. When tried in Belgium, it was found that one engine could do the work of four local engines. So successful were they that the Belgian government replaced all their locomotives with Dunalastairs but built them locally. Holland bought Atlas built engines for some time. Outside Europe, some orders were received from several other countries, including Japan. The order books of the various companies were usually full and it was normal, except in depressions, for customers to have to wait. This gave an illusion of security, but the Americans started to make inroads into traditionally British markets. When Neilson's lost an order to supply 20 tank engines to Calcutta in 1900 to Baldwin's of America, questions were asked in Parliament. Baldwin's were able to undercut the price of Neilson's and to deliver more quickly. The British replied that their engines were of a superior quality which had been demonstrated, a little inconclusively perhaps, in trials run by the Egyptians among others. In terms of efficiency, however, Baldwin's won hands down: they could turn out 300 locomotives with a workforce of 1,400 men

Atlas and Hyde Park Works at Springburn : aerial photograph about 1930 (Mitchell Library)

but Neilson's could only produce 200 with 2,500 men. Baldwin's production increased from 313 in 1884 to 1,533 in 1902 while output of the British firms remained level. To respond to the American threat, a merger of the Hyde Park, Atlas and Glasgow Locomotive Works took place in 1903 to form the North British Locomotive Company, quite independent of the North British Railway, to try to achieve economies of scale. A grand headquarters was built in Springburn responsible for about 6,500 workers. Management was still confident about the future of the industry at the turn of the century, but the first signs of turbulence had already been felt.

Other activities

Fitting out ships required a whole range of skills, from furniture making to lifeboat construction. Catering and other services grew up to supply the ships using the port. For each man working on ship construction there must have been another supplying the necessary parts and services.

But do not imagine that Glasgow in the 19th century was limited to these industries alone. It had a portfolio of other manufacturing businesses, although none were on the same scale. **The chemical industry** was transformed by Charles Tennant. He began as an apprentice weaver in Kilbarchan where he opened a bleaching field in 1788. The bleaching properties of chlorine were already known, having been discovered by a Swedish chemist in 1776, but Tennant had difficulties in making it work. He collaborated with Charles Macintosh (he who discovered how to make cloth waterproof) and eventually developed a dry bleaching powder in 1799. The process required the production of sulphuric acid which interacted with salt to produce hydrochloric acid and sodium sulphate. The hydrochloric acid then became the source of chloride from which their bleaching powder was made. It reduced the time necessary for bleaching cotton from weeks to hours and moved the process indoors. It was a hugely profitable discovery. Tennant geared up to supply the textile industries of the world by building a large factory at St Rollox in 1800 where 52 tons of bleaching powder was produced in the first year and 9,251 tons per year 25 years later. St Rollox became the biggest chemical plant in Europe by the middle of the century and its chimney dominated the city's skyline. Some Lancashire cotton producers even sent their products north for bleaching. Sodium sulphate was a by-product of the reaction and was used in the production of soap from 1803, another profitable concern. Sulphur was required for the reaction and ore containing sulphur, iron and copper was imported from Sicily. This was the source of iron which others attempted to exploit for steel production although it proved too expensive (see above).

Charles Macintosh, his partner in the discovery of bleaching powder and a son of George Macintosh who had dye-producing businesses, was also a brilliant innovator. He set up factories at Hurlet in 1807 and Lennoxtown a few years later to produce alum for the dyeing industry. By 1835, production had risen to 2,000 tons. In 1824, he discovered his eponymous waterproof material and set up a factory for its production in 1834 but the tailors of Glasgow were strangely reluctant to work with it and he moved production south to Manchester in 1840.

Other companies in the chemical sector included: industrial acids and alkalis which were produced by Garroway's from 1819 and Hope's from 1843; White's produced chrome and chromates from 1808; Perry and Hope manufactured phosphates and its acid; and Cassel's started producing cyanide used in the South African gold mines in 1889.

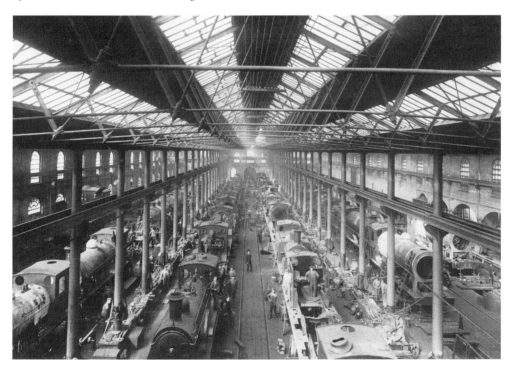

Cowlairs Locomotive Works 1921 (Mitchell Library)

Carpet weaving developed into a profitable but relatively small industry. The most famous manufacturer was an Argyll man, James Templeton, who commissioned work from weavers and became interested in a technique one of them used which he thought could be adapted to the production of carpets from wool. He exploited this so well that his carpets became famous for their quality and he had several major commissions among which was one to carpet the Royal Reception room in the Exhibition of 1851. This carpet was subsequently transferred to the British Embassy in Washington where it served for nearly 80 years and is now exhibited in the Smithsonian Museum. His factory in Bridgeton was destroyed by fire in 1856 and he hired a disused mill until he built his famous Templeton factory in 1892 which was modelled on the Doge's Palace in Venice. The design was chosen because the Council had rejected so many of his previous plans as being unsuitable for a building bordering Glasgow Green that he asked his architect to copy a building with a world-wide reputation. By 1900, he employed 2,000 workers.

Two major **publishing houses** were set up in the early years of the century and eventually employed thousands. Blackie and Sons was first in 1809. John Blackie had previously worked as a weaver but started selling books and two years later began publishing. His son joined the firm and became Lord Provost in 1863 and it was he who was largely responsible for the City Improvement Trust. The company flourished for the next century moving into a large site in Bishopbriggs and specialising in educational textbooks. Walter Blackie, one of his sons, commissioned Charles Rennie Mackintosh to design and build Hill House in Helensburgh in 1902. William Collins and Sons was founded in 1819. The original William Collins was a cotton mill clerk of an evangelical turn of mind who helped to attract Thomas Chalmers to Glasgow. Chalmers, in turn, provided financial help for Collins to set up as a publisher and, naturally, to publish Chalmers' best selling texts. The link with Christianity persisted and in the 1850s, the firm were printing 50,000 bibles a year. Like Blackie junior, William Collins' son became Lord Provost in 1877. The

Railway engine for export being hoisted on ship by a 70 ton crane at Plantation Quay.
Date not recorded (Mitchell Library)

Stately passenger communal room for the Duchess of Rothesay *1895 (Glasgow University Archives)*

firm continued to flourish well into the 20th century.

Brewing had begun in Glasgow in the 16th century and the Tennent family (not to be confused with the Tennants) had been engaged in it for several generations. John and Robert Tennent developed their massive brewery which still survives and was at one time the largest exporter of bottle beer in the country. Whisky, distilled in distilleries around the country, was stored and distributed from Glasgow.

High-tech companies were founded as spin-offs from the University. Lord Kelvin is the most famous scientist that Glasgow has produced even though he was born in Northern Ireland in 1824. He was appointed Professor of Natural Philosophy, or Physics as it would be known now, at the age of 22. He made some fundamental discoveries but was always interested in their practical application and started a company to manufacture scientific instruments many of which used electric power. He was also the driving force behind the laying of the first transatlantic cable. He took out 50 patents and his company exploited many of them. Another company came into existence in response to an advertisement from the War Office in 1888 asking for ideas for an efficient range-finder. Professors Barr and Stroud took up the challenge and Lord Kelvin's company made the prototypes. However, the two professors then opened their own manufacturing company in Byres Road and began production themselves. Subsequently, they diversified into vacuum pumps, periscopes and other high-tech items. These were perhaps, and remain, the most significant contributions of the University to the commercial developments in the city.

Exports increased hugely. In the early part of the century, coal and other goods were sent to

St Rollox from the air about 1930. The chimney was the tallest in Glasgow and the factory had been the largest chemical producer in Europe in the 19th century (Mitchell Library)

Southern Europe, North America and the Middle East. Pig-iron and its products went to Northern Europe. In the second half of the century a huge surge of all imaginable forms of metal manufactures from railway engines to prefabricated buildings were sent far and wide. Cotton products were still of major importance. Chemicals, oils and paints, whisky and beer went to the empire justifying Glasgow's claim to be the 'Second City of the Empire' after London despite stiff competition from Manchester and Birmingham. The title was appropriate because, in the last years of the 19th century, the population of Glasgow was second only to that of London in the whole of the empire and the sixth largest in Europe; but the cause of the population growth was business, much of it generated by the markets of the empire. Many of these enterprises were founded in the 1840s and 1850s just as shipbuilding surged and reflected both the demand initiated by that industry and the confidence it gave to local businessmen to try their hand in some other manufacturing venture.

Of all employed Glaswegians, 75% worked in industry of some form at the end of the century and Glasgow exported a greater proportion of its products than any other British city. Only 2% of the city's population worked directly in shipbuilding in 1900 (Partick and Govan were not part of the city until 1912). This gives some indication of the scale of other activities going on in the city although many of these were dependent on the continuing prosperity of ship construction.

In 1880, American companies started to move into the West of Scotland: Singer's Sewing Company paved the way (see below) then invited another American company, Babcock and

Sir Thomas Lipton's yacht Shamrock III *in the Clyde*

Wilcox to build the boilers for their factory in Clydebank. Their directors were so impressed by the business opportunities on Clydeside that they set up a factory of their own at Renfrew, completed in 1897. The Scottish end of the business eventually grew bigger than the American.

Service industries also developed, the most notable of which were the shipping lines. Glasgow became a major port and was home base for many shipping lines. Initially, the routes were confined to Ireland and the West Coast of Britain but quickly expanded into a world-wide web. The first off the mark were the Burns brothers. They had been traders of a fairly minor sort and bought their first small ship in 1823. They then expanded rapidly so that when Robert Napier was looking for financial support to set up his deal with Cunard, the brothers were two of the first he approached. They backed the deal and joined the board of Cunard's. George Smith conceived the idiosyncratic idea that he would like to sell his goods in India. He received no support from the shipping establishment and therefore set up his own line which traded with Calcutta and then Bombay and other eastern ports. He was so reliable and reasonable that his line monopolised the trade with these cities. He named his ships after cities (starting with Glasgow) and his line became the City line. The transportation of emigrants to the various parts of the empire and the United States was also a big business. The ships would return with the products of the colonies which, in 1882, included the first cargo of refrigerated meat from New Zealand.

The Burrells developed a world-wide network of ship-borne trade especially the highly profitable transportation of iron ore from Spain to Glasgow for the steel industry. William Burrell joined the company in 1860 and made a fortune by selling ships in times of plenty and buying during the regular periods of slump. He used his fortune to buy an eclectic collection of art which he bequeathed to the city and which is now on display in a purpose built building which did much to improve the image of Glasgow late in the 20th century.

Selling and marketing were a natural development in an economy dominated by industrial production from which more and more people derived incomes sufficient to indulge in luxuries. Many shopkeepers prospered. Two examples demonstrate what could be achieved. The first was local: John Anderson, starting with a small drapery shop in the Gorbals in 1837, expanded into an emporium in Argyle Street called the Polytechnic, selling a wide range of items including books, groceries and clothes. He was the first to realise the economy of scale achieved by bulk buying. His shop became the largest in Scotland at the end of the century but was sold to Lewis's after a 50 year run.

The second became a national and even international business: Thomas Lipton started life helping in his father's small food shop and then went to the USA for a period where he learned how a New York grocery store was run. He returned before his 21st birthday and opened his first shop in Stobcross Street. He copied the American methods of advertising and reduced costs by buying directly from farmers, usually in Ireland, and was thus able to undercut his competitors. His success led to rapid expansion all over Scotland and then into England. Irish farmers were not able to produce enough for his demands and he started to buy overseas. He began to specialise in the tea trade, at first buying directly from growers in Ceylon but then buying plantations so that he controlled the whole process. So successful was this that he is credited with converting the British into a tea-drinking nation! He became fabulously wealthy and financed a series of yachts of great beauty, all of which failed to win the America's Cup.

Growing Glasgow

Why did Glasgow become one of the first generation of industrial cities? It was clearly important that key natural resources were present in abundance. But that did not explain the first major industry, for after all cotton is not grown within thousands of miles of Glasgow. There was a certain amount of wealth available for investment thanks to the income generated by the tobacco trade and linen manufacture in the previous century and the latter established a template for the cotton industry. There was extensive investment in infrastructure – canals, railways and the newly dredged Clyde – thanks to the foresight of the City Council. Without them, there would have been no take-off in the 19th century. There was an apparently endless supply of cheap labour made available by the clearances of the Highlands and the suffering of the Irish, particularly in the years of the famine. (It seems almost incredible that the same sources helped to populate New Zealand, Australia, Canada and the United States at the same time.) Geography, rather surprisingly for a city on the edge of Europe, also proved an advantage because it was nearest to the United States. That country provided the tobacco and cotton which Glasgow exploited so well, but it also provided markets which the city was in an excellent position to service; for example, in 1849 61% of Scottish exports of pig-iron went to America.

But these factors, although necessary, were not in themselves sufficient. The contributions of key pioneers such as James Watt, J B Neilson and his son Walter, Charles Tennant and an élite cluster of engineers who developed engines to power the world's main forms of transport were essential. Skilled workers had been trained in abundance and were able to supervise the construction of intricate and large metal products that gained a reputation around the world. And lastly, the entrepreneurs of Glasgow had the confidence to spark off a virtuous cycle. They diversified and enlarged their companies so that they became world-beaters for much of the century – although as time progressed, others started to catch up.

As has been seen, the cotton industry ran out of momentum in the 1840s and started to fade in the 1870s; the iron industry developed conservative habits and started to run out of raw material from the 1870s; the chemical industry did not progress much after the key contributions of

Charles Tennant and Charles Macintosh: but the steel, and ship and locomotive building industries together offered hope. It was inevitable that the rest of the world would seek to force their way into the areas in which Glasgow had a strong and sometimes almost monopolistic position.

Management

Local management became less flexible because, as industrial units increased in size, the style of management had to change. It became impractical for the manager or owner to keep a close personal eye on production. Instead a system of supervisors was introduced. Skilled men were promoted in some industries to run facets of production. They were often hired on piece rates to produce defined items and given a free hand to hire workers who were paid at hourly rates. If that was not appropriate to the work involved, they oversaw the workers and had huge influence on who was hired or fired. Sometimes they were susceptible to bribery. The managers' main roles changed to marketing their products and controlling the terms of employment of their workforces. This system had two main consequences. Perhaps the more important was that it led to conservative practices. The prime interest of those who were supervising the processes of production was that the system that had treated them well should not be changed. The manager, who had in any case tended towards the conservative, became less interested in new methods of production. Glasgow was doing very nicely from their point of view and they were happy to keep the show going. This is, of course, a generalisation which may be unfair to many. The way in which Bessemer and then Siemens were invited to Glasgow to install their processes locally and the speed with which the shipbuilders adopted new techniques shows that innovation remained important in many companies. But they tended to belong to the newer industries of shipbuilding and steel which attracted the brightest of their generation. Managers in the older cotton, coal and iron industries tended to the conservative and, as a result, did not invest adequately; slowly these industries became less competitive. The second consequence was that the skilled respectable workers were used to police the less skilled and this reduced the power of both in confrontation with management. This in turn encouraged a low wage, low investment policy.

As Glasgow's industries began to feel the hot breath of international competition in the second half of the century, inquiries were set up to examine the structures of industry. Then, as now, a key question addressed was whether Scottish universities were giving the optimal training for the advancement of industry. It is interesting that the main European threat came from Germany and it was about this time that the Americans started remodelling their universities on German lines. As early as 1796, John Anderson, a professor of physics at Glasgow University, had bequeathed money to found an Institute to teach the subjects he considered necessary to improve industrial development. To begin with, evening lectures were given to those who wanted to attend but their value must have been appreciated because more donations were forthcoming and the Institute expanded and, after several metamorphoses, became Strathclyde University in 1963. The possibility that Scotland's and Glasgow's cutting edge was being blunted by poor university education led to two major inquiries. The Select Committee on Scientific Instruction reported in 1868 and a Royal Commission on the same subject produced eight reports between 1872 and 1875. Playfair of Edinburgh University noted that most foreign firms used their materials in carefully controlled ways so as to be as economical as possible whereas Scottish firms were hugely liberal with their resources because the industries had grown up without competition and in an area of abundant resources. As transport of even heavy goods became cheaper and local resources became scarcer, many companies started buying their raw materials overseas. He acknowledged that the universities had set up several new courses in technical subjects but there were also black holes. Attempts to set up a course in mining failed twice in Glasgow because the mine-masters and owners saw no need to change. This conservatism of the managers who worked by rules of thumb was identified as a major obstacle to the introduction of new methods. Macquorn Rankine, professor of civil engineering and mechanics at Glasgow, told the Select Committee on Scientific Instruction that his graduates occupied posts in India, Brazil, Liverpool and London but none in Scotland. Despite that, he and Lord Kelvin did not think that supplying industry with trained talent was a proper function of a university. In any case, the universities' representatives said that they were hampered by poor buildings and lack of funds. (Glasgow University, whose recent move to Gilmorehill was largely funded by a government grant, was the exception.) Another complaint was that the standard of students coming out of the schools was so low that much time was spent making good this deficiency. Some suggested that students should be selected by exam. Perhaps the main debate lay between those who thought that the Scottish tradition of teaching how to think (which had been so useful in setting up the Industrial Revolution) was not as useful a hundred or so years later when it was as important to learn basic scientific facts and methods. There was even a discussion of whether poor students were inhibited from a university education by the expense. The problems sound remarkably familiar to those of today.

The conclusions of these reports were nebulous. It was not recommended that science be taught in more detail. University status for Anderson's College was refused because:

> the proper function of the Institution is, we believe, to afford facilities for the education to those classes whose means or opportunities do not permit them to follow an university course….nor do we believe that an increase in the number of degree giving bodies in Scotland is desirable in the interests of the higher education of that country.

No changes were made in the curricula and an opportunity may have been lost.

The almost inevitable response of the managers of Scottish industries to foreign competition was to try and reduce costs by holding back wages. They were not particularly successful. Whereas Scottish wages were well below those of the English at the beginning of the 19th century and remained so until about 1875, they gradually rose to parity or near parity during the last quarter of the century. It should also be stressed that although foreigners were beginning their challenge, the local industries remained profitable for most of the century.

The workers' response

Attempts to reduce wages led to vigorous reactions by the workers. There were three types of response. The first resort was to the law. It was possible in the 18th century for workmen dissatisfied with their conditions of work to go to law, and JPs often upheld their complaints. For example, in 1799, wrights were granted an increase in wages because of a rise in the price of food. This caused anger among the owners and the law was changed in 1813 partly as a result of Adam Smith's ideas set out in *The Wealth of Nations.*

The second resort was to form unions which met with some initial success. The problems of the employees in the cotton industry at the beginning of the century have already been described – too many workers, not enough work. The government, spurred on by the industrialists, introduced the Combination Acts in England to try to prevent the formation of unions and these were used in Scotland to try the leaders of the Glasgow weavers' strike in 1812. At one time, the Spinners Union was powerful enough to determine who was employed (usually relatives) and even had some say in the level of wages. However, when the union went on strike in 1837 for almost pathetically mild demands, the employers responded by recruiting new workers and using the police and the military to beat off the strikers. Throughout the century, there were repeated attempts to form effective unions with only limited success. There were several reasons. First, workers' pay was not sufficient either to subsidise effective national unions which require offices and staff or to build up a nest egg for use during a strike. Thus the efforts made were often poorly coordinated, fragmentary and easily suppressed. Second, the skilled workers were jealous of their differentials and often stood aloof. Third, every recession threw thousands out of work with no means to feed their family so it was a brave man who became marked as a troublemaker. Even at the beginning of the 20th century, James Maxton was sacked from his job as a school teacher because of his political activities.

The third response was to agitate for political reform and in particular for universal male suffrage so that they, the workers, had some say in the legal framework of industrial relations.

Political activities: local and national

The end of the Napoleonic Wars was marked by industrial recession, particularly in the cotton industry, and by the introduction of the Corn Laws. These protected home produced food from foreign competition and thus increased the cost of food for the working poor who were already suffering. The main beneficiaries were rich landowners, some of whom were in the government. The poor were subsidising the rich. Glasgow's MP at that time, Kirkman Finlay, was also the Lord Provost. He was a supporter of free trade and was an early example of a Liberal. Yet he backed the legislation and this evoked widespread protest in Glasgow with his effigy being burnt by a crowd. The same year, Major Cartwright led a movement for reform of Parliament that attracted strong support in Glasgow. A meeting took place in the grounds of a tobacco baron's house, because the authorities denied access to public places, attracting a crowd of 40,000. Petitions signed by as many as possible were sent to Parliament but were ignored by Government. Not surprisingly, this provoked widespread unrest which affected many British towns and led to tragedy in Manchester where, in 1819, a rally was brutally broken up by unskilled militia resulting in several deaths. It became known as the Peterloo Massacre, news of which led to five days of rioting in the West of Scotland and local military forces had to be called in to restore 'the peace'.

The weavers considered themselves to be respectable workers. This term held huge importance for a considerable body of skilled and semi-skilled people in all industries. They were god-fearing, avoided debt and were able to feed their children who often received a basic education. It was these men who bore the brunt of the post-war recession and subsequent mechanisation. They blamed the system that made it difficult for them to feed their families. They formed Corresponding Societies in which political reform was discussed clandestinely. In 1820, *An Address to the Inhabitants of Great Britain and Ireland* was circulated throughout the West of Scotland and was apparently written by weavers from Glasgow. It called for armed rebellion to achieve reform. It is unlikely that respectable workers thought it proper to resort to violence but thousands went on strike to show their approval of the reforms demanded. A curfew was proclaimed in Glasgow and troops concentrated in the city. An attempt to march on the Carron Iron Works to secure arms was called. Only 50 people answered the call and were easily dealt with at the 'Battle of Bonnymuir'. If this was a half-baked insurrection, the response of the government, both local and national, was not so squeamish. Of the 19 captured, three ringleaders were executed as traitors and 16 transported. It is likely that *agents provocateur* played an important role in this deadly farce. The result was a temporary success for the ruling élite and the West of Scotland quietened down for a few years.

Even so, reform remained on the national agenda and many groups participated in the increasing ferment which was promoted in articles in the *Edinburgh Review*, perhaps the major Scottish contribution to the debate. Eventually the Great Reform Bill was passed in Westminster in 1832 and was greeted in Glasgow with much celebration: it increased Glasgow's parliamentary representation from one MP shared with Rutherglen, Dumbarton and Renfrew to two MPs of its own but it only extended the franchise to males whose property was worth £10 or more. Only 7,204 men qualified in a population of about 200,000 but this was better than the previous system when 33 men voted for a quarter share of one MP. The small proportion of men who qualified for the vote was a reflection of the uneven distribution of Glasgow's wealth. The subsequent election led to the serving Lord Provost, a Tory called James Ewing, heading the poll with a Liberal gaining second place. Municipal reform followed in 1833. The new qualifications were applied to local elections and the city was divided into five wards each returning six councillors. The Dean of Guild and the deacon Convenor were *ex-officio* members. The resultant election swept away the old Tory crew and voted in 27 Liberals most of whom were connected with business, particularly cotton. But, at first, they were little different to their predecessors.

Disillusion soon set in particularly at times of economic slow down and was compounded by the reluctance of Parliament to legislate to improve conditions in the factories or to reduce the length of the working week. The Chartist movement, which was a genuinely national movement given vigorous support by the middle classes and by the skilled workers of Glasgow as elsewhere, followed in 1838. The main demand of Chartism was for universal male suffrage; the movement was most active during the periods of recession with high unemployment. The depression of 1837 had been accompanied by the bitter cotton spinners' strike in and around Glasgow that had been suppressed perhaps a little too vigorously for those with any sympathy for working men. This may have prepared the way for Chartism which was strongly linked, at least in Scotland, with religion, usually of the dissenting variety, and abstinence from alcohol. Indeed, Chartist churches were set up in several towns in Scotland including Bridgeton, Paisley and Hamilton in the west. The members were solid citizens who eschewed violence and sought to persuade by argument and petitions. There was another group in England headed by Feargus O'Connor who believed in national strikes and armed force but it had little backing among Glaswegians. O'Connor came to Glasgow during an economic downturn and attacked the 'saints of the Glasgow Chartist Synod' for their timidity. He declared a 'Sacred Month' which was to be marked by a general strike. Support was minimal. During this time, two mammoth petitions were sent to Parliament without noticeable effect. The economy picked up in 1843 and militancy was abandoned and only the Chartist churches remained.

The next significant event was the repeal of Corn Laws in 1846. Cheaper food could be imported which benefited the city worker at the expense of the landowning aristocracy. However, a further economic slowdown in 1847 precipitated renewed interest in the struggle for reform and the Chartists collected signatures for a third massive petition which was sent to parliament only to be rejected once more. This last burst of activity involved the unskilled Irish workers and both skilled and unskilled Scottish ones working together for the first time. Once the petition had been rejected, widespread rioting broke out in several cities including Glasgow. This frightened the middle class and property owning members into abandoning the movement and Chartism died, but not before it taught many activists how to organise. The restrictive franchise of the Reform Act was no accident. The ruling élite believed, in Hobsbawm's words, that the masses were:

> numerous, ignorant and dangerous; most dangerous precisely by virtue of their ignorant tendency to believe their eyes, which told them that their rulers paid too little attention to their miseries and the simple logic which suggested that, since they formed the bulk of the population, government should primarily serve their interests.
>
> Hobsbawn *Age of Revolution* 1977

To the middle classes and even the skilled working classes, it seemed self-evident that a feckless worker who could not keep his own family in food should not have an equal input into government as a colliery owner who had a far bigger stake in the country.

The disruption in the Church of Scotland of 1843 had significant consequences on the political structure of Glasgow. The Tories backed the establishment's decision to continue with the appointment of ministers by patronage whereas the group that became the Free Church wished the appointments to be made by elders. Most influential Glaswegians backed the Free Church as did the Liberals. Perhaps as a result, Tory influence in Glasgow waned and the city became a stronghold of the Liberals and of Gladstone in particular.

However, attitudes to the grievances of workers remained hard line. Strikes in the coal industry were not infrequent; one happened in 1850, allegedly provoked by English militant miners who told their Scottish colleagues that they were underpaid and should have 4s per day instead of 3s 6d; it lasted 10 weeks until the miners were forced back at a rate of 3s 3d per day. The dispute was investigated by a Commissioner, Robert Brown, appointed under the 1842 Mines and Collieries Act. He wrote a letter to the Duchess of Hamilton which included the following passage:

> As usual, this contest ended in the failure of the attempt to coerce employers to give a higher rate of wages than men of fair dealing and unexceptionable character find they can afford. Unfortunately, all experience on this subject seems hitherto to have been thrown away upon the great mass of the colliery population. No sooner is one set of 'delegates' from some distant coal district discredited by the failure of their promises or by their pecuniary delinquencies, than the colliers are ready to listen to others. The want of discipline, of due control over their own servants, is an anomaly in these vast concerns, where such great capital is embarked, that demands all the efforts of the most able among those wealthy and intelligent masters to correct. There is at present an element in their great industrial and commercial enterprises that occasionally baffles all their skill and destroys all their calculations. In vain they display the greatest judgement in selecting the field of their operations, the greatest ability in arranging their extensive works, the most accurate scientific knowledge in erecting their powerful machinery; their labours and their skill are liable at any moment to be foiled and set at nought by an ignorant population.

Clearly there was little sympathy for workers in general among the ruling classes and political reform would be required to change the balance.

Changes in Glasgow

The city boundaries were widened in 1846 to include Anderston, Calton and the Gorbals. Significantly, the new City Council took over some of the functions of the Police Board which included what would now be termed Public Health. The City Council was very conscious of the city's image and began to work to improve it. Lord Provost Orr talked about making it a model municipality and, ironically, one of his first acts was to purchase the art collection of Archibald McLellan for £44,500 from city funds in the 1850s. Of much greater significance was the investment in a decent water supply. The private water company did not have the resources to supply the quantity or quality of water required by the huge expansion of the city. Although the link between clean water and prevention of diseases such as cholera was not clearly established by 1850, the City Council decided to take over the service and to invest hugely. The reasons for doing so were partly demographic because the population had outgrown available supplies, partly commercial in that industry was a major user of water and inadequate supplies could put a brake on expansion and partly the empiric belief that clean water was good for you. Loch Katrine was chosen as the reservoir for Glasgow and was connected to the city by huge pipelines built within a few years. Water flowed by gravity with no pumping required despite the distance involved and the topography of the countryside traversed. The new system cost the enormous sum of £1 million and was opened in 1859 by Queen Victoria with much publicity. The curse of recurrent epidemics of cholera killing about 3000 of rich and poor (but mostly poor) at each visitation was

Bridge in Singapore built in 1868 by P&W Maclellan, Engineers of Glasgow

over. A medical officer of health for the city was appointed and the position was held by James Russell between 1872 and 1898. His was a powerful voice using detailed statistical evidence in presentations such as 'Life in one room' and 'The children of the city'. He discovered that:

> 25% of the people of Glasgow were living in houses of one apartment, that lodgers were living in 14% of the one-room houses and in 27% of the two-room houses and that only 8%…were living in houses of five or more rooms.

From CA Oakley *The Second City 1948*

One reaction to these findings was the assessment of each apartment and the certification of how many people might live in it. The number was posted on the door and inspectors were instructed to visit at night to count the number sleeping there. The pressure on housing and the need to increase income were so great that it was a difficult regulation to enforce. However, Russell's commitment had some effect. For the first time, the middle classes began to appreciate that the working classes might benefit from recreational facilities other than pubs, so parks were opened and sports clubs formed. But a building programme large enough to alleviate the problem was conspicuously absent.

The transport system within the city was revolutionised. The first horse-drawn tram went from St George's Cross to Eglington Toll in 1872. Initially, the Council owned the track but private companies ran the trams. More track was added year by year and Glasgow Corporation, as it had become, took over the whole enterprise in 1894 and changed to electric-powered cars in 1898. Fares were reduced, trams ran frequently and the network was extensive, eventually consisting of 135 miles of track linking Paisley in the west with Airdrie in the east, and from Balloch beside Loch Lomond to Rouken Glen in the south. The system was enormously popular and carried 300 million passengers per year before the First World War and employed 5,000 workers in 1900.

The Underground was opened in 1896 and an extensive suburban rail network was built. This investment in public transport gave Glasgow one of the best city transport systems in the world. At that time, Glaswegian workers reversed the usual flow, living centrally and travelling out to their places of work; only the more prosperous travelled in from the suburbs to offices in the centre. The City Corporation also ran the gas and later the electricity systems. It was one of the most active and progressive city councils in the country with the single and vital exception that it ruled over some of the worst housing conditions imaginable – the nearest suburb to hell.

Social conditions

The huge immigration into Glasgow was not associated with a building programme to match. Much of the accommodation was in the form of badly built tenements in the back gardens of older tenement buildings. There was no ventilation and little light in these closely packed wynds (alleys). The wealthier citizens moved out, usually westwards but some to new developments on the south side of the river. All buildings in the city centre were subdivided to create as many dwellings as possible resulting in the infamous single end – a one room flat. There were no facilities and the sewage was dumped in the communal close at the back of the block. This excrement became the property of the landlord generating extra revenue when sold on to farmers.

Why was so little done to improve these grim conditions? Perhaps one of the main reasons was the perception that the middle classes had of the poor. The poor were the workers flooding in from Ireland, as many as 1000 per week in the 1840s, the Highlands and the surrounding countryside as the Agricultural Revolution reduced the need for labour. These workers had nothing except low pay from unskilled work when times were good and they were the main victims of the trade cycle when times were bad. Indeed, the trade cycle was a much more vicious problem to them than industrial relations. Recessions were frequent – one occurred on average every seven to nine years between 1822 and 1879. The century's biggest boom was in the late 1860s and early 1870s which led to a shortage of labour, so wages soared and workers were able to negotiate improvements in working conditions. However, the bust came in 1878 with a general economic recession causing a slump in orders for ships and the collapse of the City of Glasgow Bank which led to the liquidation of many firms and massive unemployment. The Bank had debts of £6 million (compare that with the £1 million cost of building the Loch Katrine water project) and left 1,200 shareholders, who had unlimited liability, bankrupt. There was much sympathy in the city for those who lost their savings and Lord Provost Collins, one of the publishing family, organised a fund to alleviate their distress and collected £400,000. The lending policy of the bank had been reckless and the directors were tried and found guilty of fraud and imprisoned. The shock to the city's élite was considerable and their values of temperance and thrift, which they had been preaching loudly, were seen to be hypocritical. The pulse of the economy of the city slowed while the effects spread around businesses with connections to the bank. Eventually 18s in each pound was repaid, and life resumed.

The plans of the City Corporation remained grand. Within a few years they spent £590,000 on building the imposing City Chambers which was opened in 1888 to house the bureaucracy necessary for running the services. In the same year the first of Glasgow's Exhibitions was held to 'promote and foster the sciences and arts, and to stimulate commercial enterprise'. A record (excepting London's) 5,748,379 visited it and a profit of £46,000 resulted which was used to build the Kelvingrove Art Gallery in the west and the People's Palace in the east, both to improve the city's reputation. The Corporation's campaign for a Greater Glasgow was also successful with the incorporation of Crosshill, Hillhead, Kelvinside and Pollokshields which almost doubled the population of the city and increased its income even more. Therefore, lack of funds was not the reason for not tackling the housing problem.

Neither was lack of information. Edwin Chadwick's *Report on the Sanitary Condition of the Labouring Population of Great Britain* published in 1842 picked out Glasgow as 'possibly the filthiest and unhealthiest of all British towns'. Even in good times conditions were bad but during recessions they were fearsome. They were a time of belt tightening for the skilled worker and of near starvation for the unskilled who were the first to be thrown out of work so that companies could cut costs to weather the storm. In the early part of the century, when wages were so low that saving during good times was almost impossible, it is hard to know how the poor survived. Epidemics, particularly of typhus, carried by lice in dirty clothing, and water-borne diseases such as cholera, were relatively common and killed thousands with each outbreak.

As the century progressed and some of the huge profits generated in Glasgow trickled down to the ordinary worker, saving during good times became possible. For the last 40 years of the century, wages may have grown by about 1.5% per year while prices remained stable. However, to enjoy prosperity, the demon drink had to be avoided. Alcohol permeated the workplace for the first few decades of the 19th century. When an apprentice was taken on, he had to buy drinks all round; to get a job, it was commonplace to bribe the foreman with alcohol; if the manager wanted to reward a worker, he did it with whisky. Absenteeism was so rife on Mondays that it was named St Monday, a day when workers recovered from the excesses of the weekend. Attitudes to alcohol distinguished respectable from unrespectable workers. The latter often drank and their families suffered. For them, food would be less plentiful, domestic violence more probable and schooling less likely. When laid off, there would be no reserve to tide the family through until the next job appeared.

This was not a problem exclusive to Glasgow but was a feature of most European industrial towns. It cannot have helped that Glaswegians lived in the most densely populated city in Europe and that a single room was often shared by more than one family. There was no privacy and little else to do except visit the pubs. The response to this had a unique Scottish flavour. Thomas Chalmers set out to solve the problem. He was a charismatic clergyman who did not believe that drunken labourers had become useless individuals because of the desperate circumstances in which they had to live but because they were feckless. It was his task to stiffen their moral backbone so that they were strong enough to resist the temptation of alcohol. It was the duty of the faithful and fortunate to give their time and money to help redeem the lost. He started work in the slums of Glasgow in 1815 and during the next seven years of hectic activity enjoyed some success and considerable popularity and fame. He set up several Sunday schools in his parish; he helped to reform the parish poor-relief system; and he encouraged adults to seek refuge and support in the societies attached to their local churches which sometimes even ran savings banks to encourage thrift. He was an immensely talented man whom people trusted and even loved. Many were devastated when he left to become Professor of Moral Philosophy in St Andrew's in 1823. It is remarkable what a strong impression he made in Glasgow in such a short time. When he died, thousands followed his funeral cortege.

Thomas Chalmers' analysis of the causes of poverty made it easier for the authorities to ignore the atrocious conditions in the slums and to blame drunkenness, brawling and other sorts of disorderly behaviour on the undeserving poor. Samuel Smiles' book *Self Help*, published in the middle of the century, reinforced the idea that 'God helps those who help themselves'. It was generally believed that society had the capacity to heal itself without any state-directed action if only the weak would listen to the just. Even the early socialists such as Keir Hardie thought that drunkenness was the fault of the individuals and tended to exclude the unskilled from his plans and party because of it.

In the last half of the 19th century, the middle classes realised that they ought to offer some facilities to the poor so they had somewhere else to go other than the pub. Theatres and other cheap forms of entertainment were encouraged. The drink culture at work gradually faded. Bosses no longer endorsed it and some foremen encouraged their team to join temperance societies. However, even at the turn of the century, the main streets of the East End were best avoided:

> 'In 1889', said Sir John Hammerton in his *Books and Myself*, 'Glasgow was probably the most drink-sodden city in Great Britain. The Trongate and Argyle Street, and worst of all, the High Street, were scenes of disgusting debauchery…where there were drunken brawls at every street corner and a high proportion of the passers-by were reeling drunk: at the corners of the darker side streets the reek of vomit befouled the evening air….Jollity was everywhere absent: sheer loathsome, swinish inebriation prevailed'.
>
> CA Oakley *The Second City* 1948

Education of the poor

The huge increase in Glasgow's population overwhelmed the ability of the parishes to provide schools for the children of the immigrants. At the beginning of the 19th century the Grammar School or High School existed only to educate the sons of those who could afford it. During the century, about 300 schools were founded: of these, 200 were the so-called adventure schools which had little to recommend them; 100 schools were run by the church or charities and gave some sort of education with a heavy religious emphasis; about 40 were serious schools but charged fees and were not therefore accessible to the poor. Some heroic efforts were made by some, among whom David Stow was the most successful. He, with the help of Thomas Chalmers and money from the righteous, set up a school for 100 pupils in the poor Drygate area in 1824. He introduced new 'natural' methods and banned physical punishment. This was considered outrageous by many traditionally minded citizens but his results were extraordinary and persuaded others to set up similar schools. He addressed the shortage of skilled teachers by founding the Normal School for Training of Teachers in 1836 which was admired nationally and described as 'the most perfect school of this description'. Even so, before 1872, perhaps one-half of Glasgow's young (and two-thirds of the children of Irish immigrants) did not go to school. That year the new Education Act came into force requiring all children between the ages of 5 and 13 to attend school regularly. The influx of new pupils was so large that the new School Board of Glasgow, which was directly elected, found that the schools could accommodate only about two-thirds of the number eligible. It tackled the problems energetically and built new schools, one of which was the Scotland Street School designed by Charles Rennie Mackintosh. The Board also extended the curriculum. From that time, children were to learn how to behave. Discipline was vigorously enforced not only by tawse-armed teachers but by ex-soldiers who taught the children military style drill, doubtless with a view to filling the army that empire required. The hope was that this discipline would improve the behaviour of the working class when the children grew up. The quality of the education was also good, especially for those who attended the five Higher Grade Schools which were all in operation by 1893. They were sited around the city so that any child could attend. Bright children, who had previously been without much hope, had a serious chance of succeeding. Increasing numbers of these turned to Socialism with major consequences in the 20th century.

Housing

None of this fully explains why a Council so active in almost every other department allowed the worst slums in Europe, with the possible exception of Naples, to exist for so long. Why was so little done? There are several possible reasons. First, the influx was so large and so prolonged that it was impossible to build adequate housing quickly enough; nor was sufficient land available. Second, the landlords supported the Radical Liberals who ran the Council most of the time and several sat on the Council. Their income depended on the system and acted as a break on change. Third, the belief that the conditions were due to the feckless nature of the poor was widespread. Fourth, the solution would be very expensive and the middle classes and even the skilled workers, who would have to pay, were relatively well housed and had the votes.

Slowly the pressure for improvements built up. Eventually in 1866 at the instigation of John Blackie, then Lord Provost, Parliament passed the City of Glasgow Improvement Act to try and produce solutions. It created the City Improvement Trust which had the power to raise money to solve the housing problems. It started by demolishing 15,000 slum flats in the centre – as well as the beautiful buildings of the old University site after it moved to Gilmorehill in 1870. Unfortunately, the Trust was not as successful at rebuilding. The railways used much of the space cleared to build stations and a huge marshalling yard replaced the old university buildings at Townhead. This was good for transport but made overcrowding worse. Many felt that it was not the Corporation's job to supply housing for the poor but private builders were reluctant to take the initiative, especially after the failure of the City of Glasgow Bank. A few municipal model blocks were built at Drygate to set a precedent and encourage private developers but without much success. Model Lodging Houses were built for single people. But the sum total of the reconstruction did not succeed in re-housing the 50,000 people displaced by the initial demolition. Inadequate housing projects became a recurring theme in the city and explain why housing remained top of the political agenda throughout the 20th century.

Political changes

The housing issue became the flank that the Independent Labour Party used to break the Liberal stranglehold on the West of Scotland. The rise of the ILP was also helped by the unease felt by skilled workers at the increasing mechanisation of production that downgraded their skills. In time, it marked a change from a Glasgow designed for business and wealth creation (Liberal values) to a Glasgow trying to undo the social damage spun off from that policy (Labour concerns). Many blamed the business culture for the social ills afflicting the city, with dire consequences for the future. At first the programme adopted by the ILP was not so different from that of the radical wing of the Liberal Party. The Liberals had had the support of the electors of the West of Scotland since the 1832 expansion of the franchise which was extended again in 1867 – by Disraeli whose motive may have been to steal Gladstone's thunder. This Act enfranchised men who had paid their rates and increased the electoral roll from 18,361 to 47,854 in a population of about half a million, about one in five men: no women yet, of course. Glasgow was given three MPs but an individual voter only had two votes, a move designed to increase the probability of one being Conservative. The city voted as an entity with no subdivisions until the third Reform Act in 1885 which increased the number of MPs to seven and, for the first time, divided the city into separate constituencies. This change fundamentally altered local politics because the new constituencies had differing priorities. Seven Liberals were returned but the party was fracturing along various lines, of which the most important was Gladstone's conversion to Home Rule for Ireland. This pleased the Irish in Glasgow but alienated the business sector which largely supported Empire, the source of much of their wealth. Joseph Chamberlain's conversion to the Conservatives prompted a revival of the Conservative Party in Glasgow under the title of Unionism which meant much more than keeping Ireland. It also stood for the maintenance of Empire and business. However, Chamberlain lost support when he campaigned for tariff reform.

The Liberal Party had selected no working class representatives for any seats. An ex-miner, Keir Hardie, attempted to correct this and stood as a socialist candidate for Mid-Lanark in 1888. He was unsuccessful and the Liberal candidate was returned even though the electorate was overwhelmingly working class and included miners. He set up the Scottish Labour Party with a group of like-minded zealots but it performed badly in the election of 1892 and foundered. It had, however, devised a programme of widespread nationalisation, an eight-hour day, reform of the House of Lords, home-rule for the constituent nations of the UK and full adult suffrage. This programme was adopted by the Independent Labour Party founded in Bradford in 1893. The Scottish ILP differed from the English section in some ways. It stressed temperance and believed that the state should control access to alcohol. Hardie, like Chalmers before him, believed that poverty resulted from the habit workers had of 'pouring their incomes down their throats in intoxicating drink'. Most of the early members were also devout non-conformists. These two aspects reflected the values of the skilled workers of Glasgow who were inspired by the Christian message rather than that of Marx. The party encouraged the formation of rambling and cycle clubs, art and musical societies and debates. It was a rather exclusive party: unrespectable workers were not welcomed particularly if they drank; Irish Catholics were not particularly at home in a party dominated by non-conformism; women were allowed to help with social functions but were not expected to take part in serious work. In 1900, there were only 1,250 members and the importance of these early moves only becomes significant after the First World War.

CHAPTER 3

THE 20TH CENTURY

Glasgow was a confident city at the beginning of the 20th century. It was the sixth largest in Europe and the most populous non-capital city. It chose to celebrate the new century with its second International Exhibition which was held in 1901 in Kelvingrove Park. The theme of the exhibition was the civilising influence of empire and trade. Patriotism was given full voice as the Boer War was in progress. This time some foreign countries built pavilions to exhibit their achievements, the most exotic of which was the Russian contribution. Over 11 million visitors attended and the profits were spent on restoring Kelvingrove Park and improving the Art Gallery. The city received the plaudits of the critics who recognised the quality of its industrial, commercial and civic triumphs.

For the first decade of the century, all the heavy industries of the region survived but with increasing difficulty. It was a period when some of their weaknesses became increasingly obvious and only partial solutions implemented. Significantly, no major new industries took root.

Glasgow: changing ethos

There was a serious recession in 1908 which, as usual, resulted in large numbers being laid off. Although this was part of the cycle of industrial life in Glasgow, something different seems to have happened to the mood of the workers. Did attitudes change because of the teaching of socialists or was the confidence of the working class rising? It was probably a mix of the two: workers had the time and inclination to listen to the message of socialism so the popularity of the ILP and more left leaning parties increased and changed the thinking of increasing numbers, among whom even the unskilled had become literate. But there remained two main obstacles to the acceptance of socialism. The Roman Catholic clergy warned their parishioners that it was evil and exerted considerable pressure to ensure that their advice was followed at election time. Home rule for Ireland was their main political demand which they thought the Liberals most likely to deliver. The second problem was that skilled workers had a tendency to be Masons, Orangemen and Liberals or even have a sneaking regard for the Tories with their emphasis on Empire. It still took some courage to think of becoming a socialist or trade union member because they were the first to be laid off when work was slack and the last to be taken on again, no matter how good the quality of their work. There was no unemployment pay and able-bodied men had to go to the workhouse in order to receive relief, which was minimal and given with as large a dose of humiliation as could be managed. Interestingly, the recession of 1908 was so bad and so many were affected that the City Corporation started work schemes and even provided food vouchers for the first time to ease the suffering. Clearly, those that did the suffering must have thought that there were better ways to run the world.

The 1908 recession turned out to be a good recruiting sergeant for the socialist parties such as the ILP, the Social Democratic Federation (SDF) and the Scottish Labour Party (SLP). Speeches and debates were held at weekends on Glasgow Green as well as more formal presentations in halls and theatres to vast audiences often addressed by visiting speakers. Several socialist newspapers appeared about this time. Debates centred on whether reform should be achieved through parliamentary action, championed by the ILP, or whether extra-parliamentary activities including local actions, usually industrial, were necessary – an approach championed by the SLP and SDF. Some groups were openly Marxist and much effort was spent in educating the working class in their doctrines. John Maclean, a schoolteacher, ran Sunday classes on the economy attended by several hundred people in the City Halls. He printed pamphlets which were eagerly read. He believed that the workers should understand the principles of economic management by which the ruling classes exercised their control. A new militancy developed and a wave of strikes hit the country from 1910 onwards. Glasgow was only one centre of unrest: dockers in London and Liverpool were the vanguard of this particular wave. But there was one strike in Clydebank which was particularly significant.

The Singer Company made the first major overseas investment in Clydeside. It was the world's leading producer of sewing machines. It had started mass production in the USA in 1872 in the largest factory in the world devoted to the manufacture of a single product. It built a major plant in Clydebank in 1884 to supply the Western European market and employed 11,000 workers in the first years of the century. Attempts to introduce scientific methods of management in 1911 sparked an all out strike because the outcome was, in effect, more work for less pay. The strike was suppressed when the company threatened to move the factory elsewhere. The ringleaders were hunted down and dismissed. Although it failed, the strike was significant because it was the first dispute in Clydeside in which all workers, skilled and unskilled, male and female, Catholic and

Typical Glasgow scene with chimneys belching smoke. This is of Solway Street in 1910 where Carson's made confectionery (Mitchell Library)

Feeding the swans on the canal Firhill 1960 (Mitchell Library)

Protestant, joined together to fight management. Whether this newfound unity was the result of the activities of socialists, particularly the Scottish Labour Party, or the consequence of the skilled recognising that they had common cause with the unskilled is unclear. There were several more disputes in the four years before the war both local and national as labour started to resist yet another series of attempts by management to reduce wages in a bid to become more competitive. The most famous was the Dublin tramways strike of 1913 which lasted four months and was bitterly fought. There was immense sympathy in Glasgow for the strikers and collections were made and other support offered. That strike also failed.

It is easy to sympathise with the workers' case during this period but disruption for unworthy reasons, which was to plague British industrial relations later in the century, also occurred. Harry McShane describes his work at Weir's, an engineering company, which he thought a fair and just employer with a well-developed shop steward's system. The workforce was treated well, paid well, had a generous bonus system and were rarely laid off when business was slack. Nevertheless, when one shop steward was sacked because he ran a betting syndicate at work, a strike was called to reinstate him. It lasted a fortnight before the men voted for a return to work without him.

The productivity of Scottish workers compared to their English equivalents has proved difficult to study. There were two censuses of wages in 1886 and 1906. In 1886, Scots were usually paid less than English workers in the same trade with the exception of miners who earned the same. Cotton workers did particularly badly, receiving on average only 78% of the English salary. Shipbuilders fared a little better with 92%. By 1906, the situation had changed with the Scots receiving approximately the same wages. Productivity in 1907 was higher in the Scottish coalfields but lower in iron and steel production and almost the same in the shipbuilding industry. This reflected the amount of investment in the industries rather than the amount of work contributed by the labourers. Therefore, at the beginning of the 20th century, Glasgow was no longer a low wage economy in British terms (but remained so compared to America) and there were concerns that its major industries were less productive than elsewhere in Britain and abroad. Subsequent censuses in production were not associated with labour costs and therefore it is difficult to discern trends.

The Labour group were beginning to experience success at the polls and had 19 councillors on the City Corporation in 1914. The number of workers joining a trade union affiliated to the Scottish Trade Union Council increased from 129,000 in 1909 to 230,000 in 1914. Thus there were clear signs of a change in political loyalty and of increased industrial organisation among the workers.

First World War

The outbreak of war in 1914 completely changed the whole industrial climate. Suddenly the country needed everything that Glasgow's industries could produce. Unemployment disappeared. The shipbuilding and engineering industries expanded to produce as many ships and as much ammunition as possible. The attritional war of mass armies on the Western Front and the battle to supply the country from America, and in particular during the unrestricted U-boat campaign of 1917, stressed all industries to the utmost. Beardmore's, for example, supplied a huge variety of products which necessitated major expansion. It alone built 73 warships of all sizes, 50 tanks, 516 aircraft and more than 800 six-inch howitzers during the war.

Once again workers poured into Glasgow to provide the labour required. A severe shortage of accommodation developed even though large numbers of men also left to serve in the forces. This presented a golden opportunity for the landlords to raise rents. The resultant rent strike may have been the event which turned Glasgow from the second city of Empire devoted to business into Red Clydeside with its insistence on the rights of the common man. The change was so dramatic that Lenin, as well as members of the British Cabinet, thought that the British Revolution could start in Glasgow. Of course, the rent strike of 1916 would not have been sufficient by itself. The work of a few visionary and now legendary figures who sacrificed all for their political beliefs, such as John Maclean and James Maxton, had developed a following in Glasgow among both skilled and unskilled workers. Their socialist views and powerful oratory may have helped trigger the new militancy and cohesion in the workforce immediately before the war but their principled objection to the war itself, leading to terms of imprisonment, was admired even if their views were not widely shared. Soldiers returning to a city with precious few jobs after the war must have been hugely disillusioned after their extreme experiences and were therefore ripe for socialism. However, it was probably the way that the women of Glasgow fought the Rent Strike that symbolised the change to active opposition of the business orientated culture of the Liberal tradition.

The law allowed landlords to evict tenants from their homes if they fell behind with their rent and also allowed them to seize the tenants' possessions to make good their losses. The squalor of many of the tenements in the centre of the town was not much changed from when Owen Chadwick had condemned it 70 years before. The women of Govan and Partick, where the densest concentrations of munitions production were sited and therefore where there was most pressure on accommodation, arranged a rent strike. This quickly spread to other districts. The ILP supported it and the men came out on strike. It was easy to portray the landlords as war profiteers extorting rent from women whose husbands were fighting and dying for their country. The

Government, faced with the loss of Glasgow's industrial input to the war, had no option but to order a settlement much to the advantage of the women, since rents were fixed at pre-war levels. When you remember that these landlords were also a significant part of the ruling Liberal Party, it is easy to see why their opportunism discredited the City Corporation and inflamed the passions of soldiers and workers alike.

More industrial unrest followed, this time triggered by the management at Weir's who refused their employees a cost of living increase while paying significantly more to American workers brought over to help with production. This led to a strike organised by the local Labour Withholding Committee (LWC) rather than the official union shop stewards because the unions had given an undertaking to the Government at the beginning of the war that no action of theirs would undermine the war effort. Radical local militants felt no such restraint. Many believed the war was unjustified and in the interests of capitalists. The strike lasted three weeks and involved 10,000 engineers. The settlement was not particularly helpful to the workers and the fallout was even worse. The Government, worried by interruptions in output, introduced the Munitions of War Act in 1915. This supported the employers to such an extent that the workers regarded it as a Slavery Act. No one was allowed to change employment without the permission of their employer or to refuse overtime or new work. A tribunal was appointed to settle disputes which the employers used eagerly, submitting about 70 cases a day. It was not long before three workers at Fairfield's were imprisoned for failing to pay a fine for supporting some sacked workers. This led to another confrontation with the official union representatives asking for an investigation and the LWC proposing a strike. In the end the three were released after their fine was paid. People suspected that the unions had paid up in order to defuse the issue.

There was another confrontation in 1916 over the principle of dilution, or the replacement of skilled by less skilled workers – often women. Managers hoped this would lead to an increase in productivity. Once again the official trade unionists were conciliatory but the LWC took up the challenge which led to unrest. The authorities scotched it by exiling the leader, David Kirkwood (to Edinburgh!) together with some of his colleagues. They were abandoned by their unions and the LWC was broken for a time. This may have been because Kirkwood was considered somewhat compromised by his attempts to increase production at Parkhead Forge and his close association with Sir William Beardmore, its owner. The Defence of the Realm Act enabled the Government to imprison its critics and it duly entrapped anti-war activists, communists such as John Maclean (who later became the Glasgow Consul for the Soviet Government of Russia) and members of the ILP like James Maxton. Lloyd-George came to Glasgow to try and enthuse the citizens for their role in production but, to his surprise, met a hostile reaction. The LWC was reborn as the Clyde Workers' Council and met every week to discuss tactics. The skilled engineers' representatives turned up with bowler hats and furled umbrellas. This was a key sign that militancy was shared by the skilled workers. The old divisions, which had served the industrialists well, were breaking down. The advent of the November Revolution in Russia galvanised the activists.

> When Lenin called for all power to the Soviets it meant that they had discovered a system of working class self-Government through which the old crowd could be completely destroyed. We began to realise what was meant by revolution. We had only known working class revolt: now we could talk about working-class power.
>
> Harry McShane No Mean Fighter 1978

The last year of the war was marked by weariness, long hours at work (12 hours per day Mondays to Fridays and six hours per day on Saturdays and Sundays), rising prices and a re-

Jewish cap making factory in the Gorbals about 1910 (Mitchell Library)

lentless drain on manpower as even skilled workers were conscripted. Anti-war meetings were well attended but often led to violence as 'patriots' sought to disrupt them. The end of the war came suddenly and was hugely welcomed. It was quickly followed by the khaki election when only a solitary member of the ILP, Neil Maclean, was elected from Glasgow. John Maclean, the hero of the anti-war struggle, was beaten by a Tory– a surprising result for a city regarded as the revolutionary capital of the country. It is partly explained by the low poll caused by inadequate electoral rolls.

1918–1945

The new militancy carried on after the war when the Clyde Workers' Committee (CWC) rejected a national agreement for a 47-hour week (compared to 54 hours before the war) but insisted on a 40-hour week. They were backed by the Glasgow Trades Council (GTC) led by Emanuel Shinwell and the Scottish TUC. (The GTC had been founded about 60 years earlier and was designed to coordinate action between the various unions of the West of Scotland. It had been taken over by the left towards the end of the 19th century.) The main objective of the demand was to try and reduce unemployment and thus the number of unemployed on which employers could call to break strikes. A general strike in the West of Scotland followed. The shock troops were the engineers and 40,000 stopped work supported by many miners. All businesses and industries on Clydeside were affected. Flying pickets were used for the first time to encourage or enforce support. There was a giant rally with a march on George Square and members of the CWC met the provost and asked for a resolution. The provost said he would have to consult and agreed to give a response on Friday, 31 January 1919. When the rally returned on that day and the strikers' committee were in discussions within the City Chambers, some angry support-ers attacked a tram, infuriated that the system had continued to run. The police intervened and a giant battle rolled up and down the streets around George Square. The leaders were arrested. The army was called out, backed by tanks and machine guns. The strike limped on for another 10 days before a return to work based on the 47-hour week was implemented. Shinwell, Gallacher and Kirkwood were among 15 charged and received prison sentences of some months. Support from other centres had been limited to Newcastle, Belfast and London. Glasgow was undoubtedly the centre of industrial and political unrest in the country at this time and its reputation changed abruptly. It was no longer the city devoted to business but a place where businesses had to fight their workforces.

The ILP was the main beneficiary of the new militancy and of improved electoral rolls. It won 10 of Glasgow's 15 seats in the election of 1922. Four of the new MPs were James Maxton, John Wheatley, David Kirkwood and Emanuel Shinwell. They had a huge send-off and promised to represent the interests of their people which they had done so much to define. They kept their promise but did not achieve power in, or even much influence on, the subsequent Labour admin-istrations. The major exception was the achievement of John Wheatley in steering through the 1924 Housing Act which introduced the first programme of large-scale council house building 2.5 million homes throughout the UK to ease the plight of those living in appalling and ex-ploitative accommodation. The Red Clydesiders were widely respected both in Westminster and Glasgow but the main result of their advocacy may have been to accelerate the change in outsid-ers' perception of Glasgow: away from a city of industrial prowess and towards a city of slums, violence and their attendant problems. A book, *No Mean City* written by Alexander McArthur,

Grenade production during the First World War at Elbank Foundry, Possil (Mitchell Library)

an unemployed worker in a Glasgow slum, with the help of Kingsley Long, a London journalist, describing life in the Gorbals had a large circulation and reinforced the change in the city's image during the interwar years. Businesses may have become reluctant to invest in a city with such overwhelming problems so the indirect result of the election of the Class of 22 may have been to make Glasgow a city for outsiders to avoid.

After the war, the ILP was the Labour Party in Scotland. It had a major fault line which was defined by the way its members reacted to the process of reform by Parliament: Ramsay Macdonald believed that the Party should concentrate on building up a consensus in Parliament with which to introduce reform: others, such as James Maxton, believed that would take too long and that all reasonable methods should be used to accelerate reform. The Red Clydesiders returned to Parliament in 1922 probably never believed in armed revolution and the setting up of Soviets but they did believe in the use of industrial muscle. The failure of the General Strike typically struck both sides as evidence that they were right. The Labour Party in England and Wales moved towards the Parliamentary route. The ILP cracked open over the issue. Maxton succeeded in persuading a majority in the party to secede from the Labour Party in 1932; others left the ILP and either joined the Labour Party outright or formed another affiliated party, the Scottish Socialist Party (SSP) led by Tom Johnston and Patrick Dollan. The Labour Party appointed Arthur Woodburn and William Elger to re-build the party in Scotland virtually from scratch; they did so autocratically without any local consultation. Their creation was a bureaucratic and centrist structure dependent on the National Executive Committee. Labour Governments during the interwar years were not viewed with any affection by Glaswegian activists although some remained loyal to Macdonald even while regretting his policies.

But the alternatives were doing even more badly. The SSP folded just before the Second World War and the ILP was dead on its feet and only kept in existence by the will of James Maxton. Whereas the ILP had sought to represent the interests of the working classes and to educate and enrich them, the new Labour Party concentrated on the second task alone.

The industrial unrest of 1919 to 1926 would have been bad enough if industry had been prospering but the end of the war left Glasgow firms with excess capacity. A peace dividend had been expected as countries, including Britain, rebuilt. This only lasted a few years and then the world experienced a period of slow growth throughout the later 1920s followed by outright slump from 1929. Only rearmament in the run-up to the Second World War plus the New Deal in the USA pulled industry at home and abroad out of the slump. There were at least two factors that made matters worse in Britain. One was the Government's desire to return to the gold standard which they believed necessary to secure international financial stability and healthy economic growth. In order to do so, prices had to be nursed downwards. Success was achieved by restricting credit so prices fell by half and wages by 40% between 1920 and 1922. When the pound was put back on the gold standard in 1925, it was overvalued which meant that German and American products tended to be cheaper. The second problem unique to Britain, and Glasgow in particular, was that the country had had an enormous share of world trade before the war which was always likely to diminish as other countries caught up. This was compounded by the effect of slow growth in the world economy. Even worse, several countries protected their markets by tariffs and there was a clamour for the British to do the same. Glasgow's major industries were mature and suffered from excess capacity partly caused by the expansion that occurred during the war. For all these reasons, it is not surprising that the interwar years were horrendous on the Clyde with unemployment averaging about 20% and production in shipbuilding, coalmining and pig-iron falling substantially. Only steel manufacture managed to maintain production.

The misery of huge unemployment scarred the West of Scotland throughout the interwar years and its effects lingered on for decades. One-third of the registered workforce was unemployed in Lanarkshire and Renfrewshire in the early 1930s; in 1932, fully one-half were out of work in Dunbartonshire. That year, unemployment in shipbuilding was 75% and over 40% in the engineering, iron and steel industries. Benefits were insufficient to pay the rent and to feed a family adequately so the unemployed formed a union which campaigned for the right to work and for better benefits for those out of work. Hunger marches were dispatched regularly to London or Edinburgh. A sullen hopelessness seems to have been the most common reaction which may have been why the General Strike of 1926 was a subdued affair in Glasgow. The miners were involved in a prolonged battle but the ten days of the General Strike was marked by an absence of the trams and other municipal services but little else. For example, the engineers were not called out until the strike was nearly over. The main effect on Glasgow was a shortage of fuel as a result of the miners' strike.

After 1926, the burst of militancy expressed in strikes in and around Glasgow was effectively ended. There was a movement to join or rejoin national unions even accepting London leadership in some. Work practices also became less confrontational as both sides of industry joined to try and find solutions to the dreadful state of the economy. Management did, however, cash in on their earlier victories to take further measures to improve efficiency. In industries which could be rationalised, the role of the foreman was reduced and supervision of the workers by a junior layer of management intensified. Workers were fined for leaving their benches or even talking to their mates. Quotas were set higher to increase efficiency and workers were rewarded under the Premium Bonus System. This was a complicated arrangement between management and workers which could be individualised thus making it difficult for the unions to interfere. Industries needing specialised skills were much less suitable for these changes. In some, the foreman held information vital to the manufacturing process, such as in the production of steel and, naturally, he was too important to upset. In others, such as shipbuilding, some tasks were so specific that the foreman was the only one who could oversee the task. In these industries, the importance of the trained worker was difficult to discount. Nevertheless, wherever possible, new methods of working, particularly specialisation, were introduced which tended to reduce the value of fully trained workers capable of doing all relevant tasks; their bargaining position was weakened as a result. Union activists were weeded out easily in a time of high unemployment so it is not surprising that industrial peace broke out. However, the economic pick-up before the Second World War led to a surge in union membership suggesting that all was not well between management and workers.

The poor performance of the local economy in the 1920s was due to a mixture of structural problems in the core industries and cyclical ones resulting from the slow rate of growth in the economies of the world. The structural problems were acknowledged by local business leaders who knew they should diversify into new industries for which there was greater demand and a more secure future. Beardmore's tried by moving into car production, buying Arrol-Johnston, and started manufacturing planes and aero-engines. As a major company, it could have provided the link between the old and the new industries. Unfortunately, the state of the world economy made these attempts futile and, as times became tough, Beardmore's retreated to its core that was the traditional heavy industries. It stopped work on the aircraft projects in the late 1920s and failed to invest further in its car plants.

Government reactions to the recession fell into two categories. On the one hand, it tried to reduce the cost of unemployment to the state as much as possible. On the other hand, it became increasingly active in trying to reshape the region's economy. In the short term, the granting of credit to build Cunard's giant liner, the *Queen Mary*, brought temporary relief and there were other projects on a much smaller scale. In the longer term, it tried to plan the region's economy. Economic management was a major feature of the rapid development of the Soviet Union where their Five Year Plans appeared to produce results and were held up as an example of new methods by some on the left. The Soviet Union was a beacon of hope for socialists and a lurking menace to the

Establishment. It is possible that this fear was one reason why the Government turned to regional planning which was an almost unknown skill to British governments of the 19th century. The first steps were timid and inexpensive. Measures were introduced in 1928 to encourage the unemployed to move to areas where work was available. They were quite without effect – as they were later in the century when Norman Tebbit advised the unemployed to 'get on your bikes' to find work.

The next move was to make it cheaper to set up businesses in the region. In 1929, rates were waived on businesses in deprived areas. Again this had virtually no impact. In 1931, the Scottish National Development Council was formed with a remit to encourage the growth of new industries and to encourage exports. The local big hitters, Sir James Lithgow and Sir Stephen Bilsland, were appointed to it. In 1934, Distressed Areas were identified. Much of the West of Scotland was so designated but Glasgow itself was excluded despite having 136,331 unemployed at the time, probably because local politicians did not want to see their mighty city being classified as distressed. A Commissioner was appointed to identify and implement possible solutions but was only granted £2.5 million to work with. Some public works were undertaken and the sewage system improved. Only £500,000 was spent on industrial development and the total yield between 1934 and 1937 was 16 factories employing a few hundred men.

In 1936, the Scottish Economic Committee, responsible to the Scottish National Development Council, was charged with developing a master plan for the development of Scotland's industries. The Treasury also gave financial assistance to any firm moving to a Distressed Area. The Special Areas Amendment Act was passed in 1937 which, for the first time, made significant funds available. The Commissioner was empowered to build and rent factories on modern industrial estates and to assist with payments of taxes. The Scottish Economic Committee recommended that such an estate be built at Hillington. This was accepted and rapidly implemented. The Commissioner set up a Board of Directors under the chairmanship of Sir Stephen Bilsland. An area of 320 acres was identified and flexible factory units, each of 5,000 sq ft, built. Roads and other facilities were quickly installed. This was the most successful venture in central planning in the West of Scotland since the linen industry 200 years before. By the outbreak of war, 67 of the 103 factories were occupied and production of goods ranging from chemicals to garments and biscuits had started. Less than £1 million had been spent but although the results were gratifying, only 4,000 were employed, which was a drop in the ocean. One of the attractions of the estate was that it was considered safer from air raids than the South of England which helped to attract Rolls-Royce, producer of vital aero engines, in 1940. Encouraged by these results, similar but much smaller estates were set up in Carfin, Larkhall and Chapelhall.

Glasgow institutions also tried to offer help to the distressed and find solutions to the industrial implosion. The Lord Provost's Relief Fund helped some of the unemployed with their rents; it raised money by, among other ways, selling tickets on the trams. In 1930, the Development Board for Glasgow and District was set up with the support of the City Corporation, the Chamber of Commerce, the Navigation Trust, the Trades House, Glasgow Trade Council and Merchants' House. Once again little money was made available and the Board started by logging available sites and vacant factories as well as promoting the city as a place to locate a business. More significantly, the Clyde Navigation Trust made land available at Shieldhall for the construction of another, if smaller, industrial estate, which was quite successful. The success of Hillington and Shieldhall led to a third industrial park being set up in 1938 at Dalmuir's redundant shipyard. It became a centre for the laying of submarine cables for the Post Office and for breaking up of old ships. Modern factories were built on nine acres.

The Corporation itself was a major employer having 34,000 workers on its books, about 15% of the male labour force in the city, compared to 18.5% in shipbuilding and the metal industries. For Glaswegian women, service in richer families and in the retail trade were the main growth

The Queen opening Hillington Industrial Estate in 1938 (Mitchell Library)

points in employment. Remarkably, during this period of misery, there was strong growth in retailing as Hugh Fraser established his empire and Marks and Spencer opened a store.

The fundamental problem was that the fading industries had been responsible for the surge in population in the region and without them many people were bound to be jobless. The small projects outlined above, worthy in themselves, were incapable of replacing the jobs lost in the ageing industries. That would have required something on the scale of what had happened in the West Midlands where a motor industry had been born with an integrated network of manufacturers and suppliers. There was no sign of anything like that happening around Glasgow. The area's economy which had moved seamlessly from linen to cotton to coal and iron production to steel manufacture and shipbuilding and metal engineering had no new industries that could begin to replace the dying ones. The Second World War provided a temporary solution for exactly the same reasons as had the First.

Second World War

Clydeside had a privileged position being further away from German bombers and nearer to American help than any other major centre in the country. It was bombed comparatively lightly compared to other major industrial areas except for one horrendous 48 hours. In Churchill's words, with a customary sting in the tail:

> On the 13th and 14th (of March 1941) the Luftwaffe fell for the first time heavily on the Clyde, killing or injuring over 2,000 people and putting the shipyards out of action, some till June and others till November. At John Brown's shipbuilding works large fires caused stoppages, and normal production was only restored in April. This firm had been affected since

March 6th by an extensive strike. Most of the strikers had been bombed out of their homes, but the raid sufferings and perils bought them back to eager duty.

The Grand Alliance, Volume 3, Winston Churchill

The scale of the destruction in Clydebank was awesome: only seven houses out of 12,000 were undamaged. The industrial infrastructure of the town was obliterated. This included not only Brown's and Singer's, the two largest employers, but a huge Admiralty oil depot which burned for a fortnight. Forty-eight thousand people became homeless and were dispersed around the country; in nearby Milngavie, the incomers' descendants can still be distinguished from the 'true' locals. Glasgow too suffered but the concentration of damage was less even if more people were killed. That Clydeside escaped further punishment was due to Hitler's decision to invade the Soviet Union and take much of the Luftwaffe east.

The Clyde had huge strategic importance not only as a centre of production but also as a port receiving aid from the United States. The east coast ports were almost non-operational so that the west coast ports were the main centres of distribution of all kinds of goods needed by a nation at war. Keeping up a sufficient supply of merchant ships to carry these cargoes was a major problem. Many were damaged but managed to return to port. Their repairs were given priority since it was usually quicker than building a new ship.

As in the First World War, the need for ships, munitions and raw materials rekindled the dying industries and production of all types shot up except that of coal which remained at its pre-war level. Steel output increased to 1.9 million tons and pig-iron production was up 60% to 659,000 tons. The tonnage of ships launched leapt to nearly 500,000 tons each year, a rise of a third on pre-war levels. Despite the strike at Brown's before the raid, industrial unrest was much less marked. Pat Dollan, who had been a campaigning pacifist in the First World War was Lord Provost and encouraged support for the war effort. It may also have helped that the communists became enthusiastic supporters once Hitler invaded Russia. The only significant strike was by women working for Rolls-Royce who believed that their skills were ignored and their pay too low compared to their male counterparts. They were successful. Above all, the Second World War was fought using centralised planning and it was seen to work. These lessons were well learned by Labour politicians determined to apply them to post-war recovery, after victory in the election of 1945.

1945 and after

How much planning contributed to the remarkable post-war boom that lasted up until the oil shocks of the 1970s is debatable. The immediate aftermath of the war in Europe ended with a landslide election victory for Labour. Rationing, introduced during the war, continued for several years and the hunt for food was a major preoccupation among housewives. Perhaps the most morale-sapping problem was the lack of housing. Immediately after the war ended, there were 94,000 names on the Glasgow housing list of whom 40,600 were actually homeless. Those with homes were little better off: half of all homes in the city consisted of one or two rooms, compared with only 5.5% in Greater London. The population density was 163 per acre, compared to 48 in Birmingham and 77 in Manchester. In the Gorbals it was an unbelievable 564 people to the acre. The council faced a housing problem without parallel in Britain. Not only was there overcrowding but the properties themselves were run down. Private landlords owned the majority and had been unable to raise rents easily. Several simply abandoned their properties and most failed to make necessary repairs let alone improvements.

The end of American subsidies in the form of Lend-Lease meant that the country was not only worn out by the struggle but almost bankrupt. It was not an appetising homecoming for returning soldiers. The home country reminded many of the horrors that followed the First World War. Almost immediately, the new Government tried to negotiate a gift or a loan from

America. Keynes was sent to arrange it and was confident that he would succeed by reminding the Americans quite how much Britain had sacrificed in the war. To his dismay, the Americans were unimpressed – perhaps expressing American disapproval for the new Labour administration's nationalisation plans. The *New Statesman* thought that the Americans were 'nearly as hostile to the aspirations of Socialist Britain as to the Soviet Union'. It may simply have been that they did not believe that a country that had so vigorously prosecuted the war was in danger of bankruptcy. Eventually, Keynes was successful but at a terrible price: he secured a loan of $3.75b but agreed that the pound should be made freely convertible into dollars. This, in effect, gave the US access to all British markets and led to a balance of payment crisis as American goods replaced British exports. The Labour Government reacted by reducing imports even further and thus intensifying the shortages. A run on the pound inevitably followed which eventually led to devaluation in September 1949, reducing the rate from $4.03 to $2.80 to the pound.

The first two or three years after the war were tough for most Europeans, and for the Germans most of all. Their average diet provided about 1,000 calories per day so that the German nation was slowly starving. In Britain, shortages of some foods were actually worse than during the war; for example, rationing was extended to bread, which had never been rationed during the war. The winter of 1947 was so severe that mining and moving coal became impossible. Since most houses were heated by coal, there was considerable suffering. Misery hung over the whole of the country and indeed over all Europe, all but destroyed by the war as it was. Then in 1947, the Americans reversed their policy and offered aid to European countries that would accept their terms. This proved impossible for the Soviet Union so the aid was concentrated in countries of Western Europe (and, indeed, the plan was designed to prevent impoverished European countries being forced into the Soviet sphere of influence). Between 1948 and 1952, the US delivered about $13b of aid, $3.3b of which came to the UK. This Marshall Plan, named after the Secretary of State who initiated it, is often credited with setting the tone of European recovery. European industrial production increased by 35% between 1948 and 1952 and huge increases in agricultural production were enough to feed the populations. The scene was completely transformed. Of course, much of the aid was spent on American goods but investment in local manufacturing also became possible. Austerity measures were relaxed and life seemed more hopeful.

Thus there was plenty of work to be done rebuilding the shattered infrastructure. Unemployment remained low rising only briefly to about 50,000 in the West of Scotland in the late 1940s. There were severe shortages of coal and steel and a hungry market for ships so it was not long before the people in the West of Scotland began to enjoy the advantages of steady growth which persisted throughout the 1950s. Altogether, the recovery of the global economy from the Second World War was completely different to the First.

The Labour Government of Clem Attlee energetically pursued a regional policy for slower-growing regions. The Distributions of Industries Act was passed in 1945 defining development areas which would receive central support. One was the West of Scotland and this time Glasgow was included. The Board of Trade was given powers to acquire land, build factories and equip them with basic requirements such as power and roads. Firms were also entitled to grants to help with capital investments. The Town and Country Planning Act of 1947 required firms setting up a factory of more than 5,000 sq ft to seek planning permission which gave the Government some influence in where investments were made. Scottish Industrial Estates was set up as an executive company to run the industrial estates in Scotland on behalf of the Board of Trade with an initial grant of £10 million for the West of Scotland. A large building programme followed, leading to an eleven-fold increase in factory floor space. Industrial estates were set up Newhouse, Blantyre, Carntyne, Queenslie, Port Glasgow and Vale of Leven. The Government's main aim in the West of Scotland was to attract new industries, to broaden the industrial base and to reduce dependence on the traditional heavy industries.

There were signs that the local economy was responding and 13% of investment into Britain came to Scotland, including 10 American firms by 1949. Unfortunately, this promising development policy was blown off course as the terms of the American loan of 1947 started to bite and the Government was forced to cut back investment in the regions. The new policy was to encourage exports and to replace imports with home produced goods. Then in 1950, Britain sent an expeditionary army to Korea as part of the United Nations attempt to reverse the invasion of South Korea by North Korea. Paying for this war soaked up any spare money that might otherwise have been invested in continuing the regional policy. It also helped to prolong rationing. Not surprisingly, despite popular welfare reforms, Labour was voted out in 1951 and the Conservatives reduced regional aid further. The management of the industrial estates in the region responded by attempting to attract private investment and were quite successful. There were 41 American firms in Scotland by 1960 and they owned or partly owned a further nine companies. Altogether these 50 companies employed 25,000 workers about 70% of whom were in the West of Scotland. They brought in industries new to the region and helped to rebalance its economy. Heavy earth-moving equipment, tyres, electronics and computers were some of the new products. This represented a considerable achievement. But the nicest surprise was that indigenous local industries turned out to be more robust than expected. Steel production and shipbuilding continued to flourish until 1960 and still dominated employment. The newly arrived companies accounted for 18% of all manufacturing employment – some 65,000 employees.

Therefore, in the 1950s there was near full employment; the traditional industries had not imploded and new industries were being introduced. Surely the corner had been turned. But even then, warning signs of future decline were present. Britain grew less quickly than the rest of Western Europe and the West of Scotland grew less quickly than Britain. Shipbuilding held steady but did not expand. Wages, which had fallen to about 90% of the British average in the 1940s, started to catch up so the competitive advantage of setting up a factory in the region diminished. This was partly because many wage deals won by national unions applied nationally yet local productivity was lower in many industries than in the rest of Britain. This was attributed to lower investment but also to an increasing reputation of the workforce for cussedness and a proneness to strike. The number of days off work each year per thousand workers in some of the main industries between 1947 and 1959 was 448 in Scotland and 226 in Britain as a whole. Although both were surprisingly good in international terms (Japan: 671 days and USA: 1473 days, but Germany: 75 days), it did not help foreign investors to choose to locate in Scotland rather than elsewhere in Britain and did not encourage investment by indigenous firms. How much of this absence from work was due to strikes is not clear. For whatever reasons, the region's share of inward investment into the UK started to fall about this time. Furthermore, unemployment, although low by the standards of the interwar years, was always higher than in the rest of the UK despite the fact that the West of Scotland started to lose population. There is one other reason why the region may have performed less well. The post-war era up to the 1990s was the period of the stop–go economy. Governments managed the economy to protect jobs, manipulate the balance of payments and, especially towards the end of the period, to dampen inflation. Interest rates were one of the main clubs in their bag used to achieve these goals. Since the region was growing more slowly than the South of Britain, interest rates were usually too high for the local economy even though they may have been appropriate for the faster growing regions with larger populations. An interest rate rise of 1% is equivalent to knocking 0.3% off growth. Assuming that the North of Britain had interest rates that were too high by 1–2% for them, this must have reduced growth by a considerable amount over these decades. Therefore, despite the rosy appearances at the end of the 1950s, problems remained.

The businesses in the region had changed significantly from being locally owned with locally sited headquarters to being subsidiary companies. By the 1960s, fully 60% of firms in the area employing more than 250 workers were owned by companies with their headquarters elsewhere. In times of recession, it was likely that these peripheral factories would be the first to close. The firms in local control tended to be the older firms engaged in metalworking. Their skilled workforce could do a great variety of tasks and were famous for producing bespoke metal products. Mass production methods inevitably led to a dilution of the skills of the workforce and were resisted. This may have been a major reason that no process requiring mass production flourished in the area with the possible exception of Singer's at Clydebank.

The fight to maintain the old industries was not helped by the antipathy between a heavily unionised workforce and management trying to hang onto market share. Most of these old companies were large concerns and, for historical reasons, were seen as the enemy; the union was regarded as the means of getting the workers their just rewards. Their attitudes were remarkably unsympathetic to their company's problems. If times were good and wages moved ahead, there might be a strike if profits advanced more quickly than wages. If times were bad and the company was in difficulty, the workers could still strike because they knew that Government could be relied on to provide the necessary support. Nationalisation was seen as a long term solution by many workers, who envied their comrades in the nationalised industries.

Governments in the 1960s and 1970s were remarkably sympathetic and did indeed sustain companies in times of trouble. This did nothing for the management of companies in difficulty trying to restructure or downsize. Edward Heath, who won the election in 1970, tried to initiate a policy of letting lame ducks disappear but was forced to make a U-turn when Rolls-Royce threatened to go to the wall. Both Labour and Conservative administrations provided generous support for the shipbuilders. Margaret Thatcher, prime minister from 1979, was determined to change this policy of rewarding failure. Huge battles were fought between the union barons and their workforces against industries backed by the Government. They were noisy and generated much heat but the Government won each one. The mining industry came to a virtual end when the miners were defeated in 1984. The shipbuilding industry limped on in a vestigial form from order to order, often saved by the Admiralty. No large liner was built on the Clyde after the launch of the *QE2* in 1969 and the *Queen Mary 2* was recently built in France. Workers in the steel industry also fought the rationalisation plans of Ian McGregor, an American of Scottish descent with experience of managing steel production, and lost. Steel production was consolidated around the integrated works at Ravenscraig until it too was shut in 1993. The fourth of the region's main industries of the 19th century – pig-iron production – is now a distant dream.

The loss of regional jobs in these industries was on a huge scale, perhaps 40,000 miners, 30,000 shipbuilders and 70,000 engineers of different sorts as well as 30,000 steelworkers in the period after the Second World War. A further 7,000 were made redundant when Singer's closed their factory in Clydebank in 1985.

Perhaps the most ambitious attempt to regenerate the industrial base of the region was made by Harold Wilson's Labour Government in the 1960s. A major car manufacturer was persuaded to set up at Linwood but the project foundered on the dual rocks of poor management and a reluctant workforce. The discovery of oil in the North Sea would not seem of immediate advantage to Glasgow but the Government hoped that the Clyde shipyards would be used to build many of the platforms and other infrastructure needed. This did not happen to any significant extent although Marathon, an American company, bought John Brown & Co in 1972 for £1.5m for the purpose, encouraged by a grant of £12m. The Government did, however, have one plum in its gift. It needed a company to run the development of the new oilfield, to arrange the sale of blocks of the seabed for exploration and to deal with the companies who had bought the blocks. It set up the British National Oil Corporation (BNOC) in Glasgow. It created jobs for a large number of managers and executives which had a noticeable effect on house prices in the more desirable suburbs. In the 1980s, BNOC consumed about half of the UK's manufacturing investment and generated annual revenue of £12 billion. It was indeed a magnificent plum for Glasgow to be offered. However, it was a Government Agency and, therefore, privatised as Britoil by the Conservative Government which took over in 1979; it remained independent for a few years until taken over by British Petroleum in 1988. The Glasgow office was closed soon afterwards. Thus, all efforts of Government to help the West of Scotland failed. It became widely accepted that Government directed efforts were always a waste of time and that markets alone should decide.

If Government could not help, and if the people of the West of Scotland had misplaced their appetite for creating businesses, Clydeside would have to depend on inward investment. The days when successive industries were set up by local talent using local finance were over. It is not quite clear why. Bad luck played a part in that attempts to move into the automobile and aviation businesses were made but did not succeed, perhaps because not much succeeded between the wars. The older generation became too conservative and perhaps the younger generation simply left Glasgow for London or North America to get the freedom to experiment. The city's reputation for bad industrial relations, poor productivity and irrelevant skills made it unattractive to would-be incomers.

However, some inward investment did occur, setting up new light industries in the region. The electronics industry, encouraged by Scottish Enterprise (see Chapter 8), moved into the Central Belt creating large numbers of jobs in the 1980s and 1990s. Factories poured out chips, transistors and TV tubes. The jobs were mostly assembly work and there was little product development or research involved. They were welcome at a time of high unemployment, occasioned by an over-valued currency and the demise of the coal and steel industries, but were always likely to be temporary, providing goods for a buoyant market and closed when the market contracted or transferred to countries where production was even cheaper. They made a very important contribution to Scottish manufacturing output for a short time but, once the bubble burst in the late 1990s, many were shut and consequently Scottish manufacturing output tumbled by about a quarter at the turn of the century.

The service sector did not fare much better. By the mid-1980s, Glasgow city was actually losing service jobs in shops, hotels and restaurants although they increased as a proportion of the employed because of the greater fall in manufacturing. In 1951, 41% of employed workers in the region worked in manufacturing and 53% in the service industries and this remained little changed until 1960. By 1975, only 30% of employment was in manufacturing and 61% in the service sector. All the huge industries that changed Glasgow from a small regional centre on the edge of Europe to a manufacturing giant had been closed or become vestigial. The speed with which these industries collapsed between 1960 and the end of the century is amazing. It led to a period of high unemployment and hopelessness when Glasgow was seen as the invalid of Britain. This phase lasted until the late 1980s, when Glasgow began to present itself as a resurgent city, fun to live and do business in. By 2000, manufacturing accounted for only 14% of employment compared to the service industries' 78%. This represents a considerable repositioning of the economy which has brought increasing prosperity once more.

Reconfiguration of Glasgow

The population of Glasgow increased to a little above 1 million in 1921 and remained above that figure until 1965 after which it declined to about 600,000 in 2001. Part of the expansion was due to boundary extensions. The area of the city increased between 1891 and 1938 from 6,111 acres to 39,725 acres which included the addition of some neighbouring burghs – Govanhill,

Pollokshields, Hillhead in 1891 and Maryhill and Pollokshaws, Govan and Partick in 1912. By the end of the century, the total area of the city was 50,111 acres with the addition of Rutherglen, Cambuslang and Mount Vernon in 1978.

The huge social problems of Glasgow at the end of the 19th century were hardly improved before the Second World War. It is astonishing that after 1910 virtually no houses were built by the private sector and some projects ground to a premature halt. Some attributed this to the landmark Budget of 1909 which put a 20% tax on the increased value of inherited property. In 1919, the Coalition Government empowered local councils to build municipal houses subsidised by central grants (the Addison Act). A housing department was immediately set up by the City Corporation with a target to build 57,000 new houses which was just about achieved by 1939. The plan was to build three types of estates. The first was for those who could afford an economic rent. Estates of detached or semi-detached houses were built in a ring around the city from Riddrie in the east, Mosspark in the south and Knightswood in the West. These were allocated to skilled workers and remain attractive. Only 1,510 houses were constructed and so did little to reduce overcrowding which was aggravated when 18,000 homes were declared unfit and pulled down in the centre of the city. The second type was for those who could not afford full rents but were not from the slums of the city. This type included the Drumoyne Estate and a total of 800 houses were completed. The third tier was designed to provide modern houses at greater density and in significant numbers for unskilled workers and the unemployed. The most infamous example of this type of estate was built at Blackhill on ground previously occupied by Glasgow Golf Club. It was built cheaply but large enough to house 980 families and opened in 1935. Since it had few amenities and was filled with the families of unskilled workers including a large number of problem families, it looked and felt like living in a ghetto. Its reputation was never good and became dire. Although numerous houses were built for private use just outside the city boundaries in the south at Giffnock and Newton Mearns and in the north in Bearsden and Milngavie, virtually no private houses were built within the city boundary. This gave the Corporation power to organise the distribution of tenants by any system it chose and it segregated the skilled and unskilled, the worthy from the feckless. At the start of the Second World War, although the Corporation had achieved its target of 57,000 new houses, overcrowding persisted with nearly half of the inhabitants living in one- or two-roomed apartments, and only half having access to a bath and a third sharing toilets.

The City Corporation and the Government knew that fundamental solutions to the housing problems of the city were required and planning started during the Second World War. Two basic solutions were offered. The first was to decant a significant proportion of the population so that the remainder could fit in comfortably and the second was to build upwards within the city's boundaries. The first was the basis of the Clyde Valley Plan of 1943 written by Patrick Abercrombie who had won fame for his plan for Greater London and seemed to have a finger in every urban post-war plan. He proposed the creation of new towns at East Kilbride, Cumbernauld, Irvine and Stonehouse. The numbers involved would be sufficient to reduce the hideous overcrowding within the city limits and would also provide the workforce for industries attracted to the region under the Development Area project. The Scottish Office favoured this plan. The second approach was to build suitable housing within Glasgow thus retaining its population. To do so required both the creation of new estates and the use of new techniques in construction by building upwards, converting horizontal communities into vertical ones. This formed the basis of Robert Bruce's reports of 1945 and 1946. He was the City Engineer and obviously more in tune with what the local councillors wanted. They emphatically did not want the city to lose population. Bruce essentially planned to rebuild Glasgow over 50 years, moving the excess population to estates built on the borders of the city but within its boundaries. The spaces vacated would then be rebuilt with modern accommodation. The plan included reworking Glasgow's communication system and redeveloping the banks of the Clyde.

Elements of both plans were adopted. Plans for East Kilbride were approved in 1952 and for Cumbernauld in 1956. Both were built and filled with younger and perhaps more ambitious Glaswegians than those who remained. Cumbernauld had a population of 18,400 in 1965 and 48,000 in 1980 and has remained about that level. East Kilbride grew progressively to become Scotland's sixth largest town with a population of 74,000 in 2001. Many more prosperous Glaswegians moved just outside the city's boundaries to suburbs where private housing was available, such as Newton Mearns and Bearsden. Partly as a result, the city's population fell from 1.1 million in 1951 to 765,000 in 1981 but the population of the conurbation was also falling slowly as others headed south to England or west across the Atlantic.

The Corporation's favoured plan also went ahead with the construction of very large peripheral estates on green-field sites and comprised mostly three- or four-storey buildings. In the west was Drumchapel, in the east Easterhouse and Cranhill and in the south Castlemilk, Nitshill and Pollok. Each accommodated about 30,000 and by 1980, 60% of all Corporation administrated housing was in these vast schemes. The new towns became prosperous and attracted employment whereas all the new housing estates suffered from high unemployment and a variety of social problems. The vacated slums were then torn down and replaced with buildings which were mostly flatted including 160 huge high-rise buildings; some were the tallest in Europe with 31 stories. Council homes were built at a cracking pace at a time when the number of houses completed each month was announced on the main news. It became a symbol of renewal after the traumas of the war. Unfortunately, the obsession with the headline figure blinkered planning for communities such as the provision of shops and leisure facilities. For example, Easterhouse did not have a town centre: it was in the original plans but was omitted because of bureaucratic problems in the departments of the City Corporation and was added later in 1973. Pollok also lacked shops, recreational facilities and even primary schools. Decanting led to a loss of neighbourliness and communal ties. Allocation of accommodation by the Housing Department tended to zone families according to a ranking system of worthiness so some areas quickly acquired bad reputations. Once gained, they were difficult to lose as the most problematic families were drafted in and the most deserving promoted out. The high-rise buildings were recognised to be particularly difficult places for developing decent communities and none were built after 1974.

By the time the rebuilding was complete with the provision of 100,000 units, Glasgow had changed from a city of private landlords with huge overcrowding and miserable buildings to a city of which perhaps 70% of the housing was owned by the Corporation and much of it modern but substandard. Glasgow's rainfall is about 1000 mm per year and houses built with the designs and techniques for drier climates proved inadequate. It was not long before damp and its consequences became a common bugbear for the occupants of the new properties. The Housing Department became overwhelmed with organising repairs, collecting arrears of rent and, in the 1980s, reduced budgets. Some of the new high-rise buildings were demolished within 20 years of construction. The fall in the population in the 1970s accelerated, with an estimated loss of about 25,000 each year. Glasgow was not alone in this but the loss of population between 1971 and 1981 was 22% compared to 10% in London and 17.5% in Manchester. Over the same decade, unemployment doubled from 7.5 to 15% in Glasgow and was, of course, much higher in disadvantaged areas of the city. From 1969 to about 1986, central Government set about trying to rescue the more precarious areas. One problem was created by the number of agencies involved: the cabinet set the policy, the Scottish Office tried to implement it, Glasgow City Corporation wanted to have its input and, between 1975 and 1996, Strathclyde Regional Council existed to coordinate plans at regional level. During this time, Strathclyde Regional Council was responsible for strategic planning, education, major roads, police, fire services, sewerage, personal social services and regional parks; Glasgow City Corporation managed housing, environmental health, local planning and city parks. The Scottish Development Agency and the Scottish Special Housing Authority also had some responsibilities. By the time the Health Board, the Social Work Department and other specialised bodies had made their input, the task of coordination was formidable.

Planning went through three phases after the end of the sixties.

1969–76: the social work approach The underlying reasoning was that people were poor because of their own incompetence and the locality would improve if they were given a bit of grooming, much like Chalmers' approach a century earlier. This stage began and ended with a Labour Government but the Heath administration contributed between 1970 and 1974. Areas of deprivation were identified and limited resources given to establish a better environment with provision of community services providing advice to families, nursery schools and help with the education of ethnic minorities. However, the rising tide of unemployment and the poverty of pensioners argued that people could be victims of circumstances beyond their control.

1976–79: the holistic approach A white paper, *Policy for Inner Cities*, introduced a much more ambitious attempt to reverse the tide of impoverishment. The diagnosis now added poor facilities, bad housing, derelict land and erosion of economic activity to the low educational achievements and poor motivation of the people. Treatment would require all problems to be addressed in a coordinated approach involving Central and Local Government as well as relevant agencies. The Government made little extra money available but re-directed existing funds to urban problems. It was hoped that private investment would follow and complete the job. Results were not immediate and in 1979 the Government changed. The Glasgow East Area Renewal (GEAR) project was set up during this phase (see below).

1979–86: the market approach The new Conservative Government wanted to reduce the role of the state. This would, in theory, free the private sector to generate wealth which would lead to urban regeneration through the trickle-down effect. Economic regeneration thus became the main objective from which other benefits would flow. The Urban Programme was still funded but the amount did not keep pace with inflation and one-off grants for business projects were more likely to be funded than ongoing social projects.

Enterprise Zones were the flagship of this programme. These were designated areas into which businesses would be enticed by 'deregulation', or cutting red tape to a minimum, and by financial inducements such as a 'rates holiday' of 10 years and tax concessions for investment in industrial and commercial property. This, it was hoped. would set the entrepreneurs free. There were 11 zones throughout the UK in which 8,065 jobs were 'created' at an apparently excellent rate of £16,500 per job. Subsequent evaluation showed that nearby firms often moved into the Enterprise Zones to take advantage of the tax breaks and that many of the new firms may well have started up in any case. Clydebank was selected as the area for the West of Scotland. It led to significant construction. The Scottish Development Agency (SDA) invested £85 million in Clydebank, so the state did not rely entirely on private initiatives. By 1984, it was realised that Enterprise Zones had not unleashed a surge of new economic activity.

The next initiative of the Government, faced by rising unemployment, was the introduction of Urban Development Corporations (UDC). In 1981, the London and Merseyside Docklands Development Corporations were set up. They were quangos whose task was to cut through red tape and harness whatever means were necessary for the economic development of their area. The London Docklands Development Corporation adopted a plan to develop the area as an overspill for the City of London providing new buildings with all the necessary facilities. Land was purchased from the local council at rock bottom prices and developed for offices, including the massive Canary Wharf, and houses for the well-off. Fleet Street decamped there early to escape the grip of their unions. This was a success. The Liverpool project led to an improvement in the appearance of the area with only a modest increase in economic activity.

The main initiative in Glasgow was the Glasgow Eastern Urban Renewal (GEAR) project which aimed at the economic and social transformation of an area in the East End of Glasgow. This area had suffered severe depopulation from 140,000 in 1951 to 45,000 in 1981. The residual population tended to be older, less skilled and more handicapped as people with initiative left. In 1977, only 40% of heads of households were working compared to 60% in the Strathclyde region. Extraordinarily, this was not due to a shortage of jobs but a shortage of workers with the necessary skills: there were 2.5 jobs per worker in the East End compared to 0.9 in Clydebank. Because of facts like these, Glasgow as a whole was seen to be on a downward spiral, with loss of population and skills, an increasing proportion of unskilled, old or incompetent workers and a city that looked and felt unattractive to outsiders. The GEAR project was set up in 1976: Central Government was determined that it should be taken out of the hands of the City Corporation, which had manifestly failed over several decades, and the Scottish Development Agency (SDA) was asked to manage it. City planners, who had been due to work on the plans for Stonehouse, were transferred to the project. New housing was built to more sympathetic standards than in the dash for houses of the early post-war period. Firms were encouraged to move into new business premises and given financial incentives. Derelict land was landscaped. Even so, the results of GEAR and the Clydeside Enterprise zone were disappointing for a variety of reasons. Analysis found that many of the firms moved from elsewhere within the Strathclyde Region and that few of the workers taken on were long term unemployed. Although 75% of the new workers in the GEAR area came from the ranks of the unemployed, most had been unemployed for short periods and were recruited by personal contacts with the person starting up. Some of the new businesses were the rump of old ones that had collapsed and were restarted by employees, using existing networks, in a scaled down form. Overall, the number of new jobs created was small (404) and was less than twice the continuing rate of job losses (220). Furthermore, the type of new business was in the service sector, such as bicycle repairs, rather than businesses with potential for major growth.

Although the number of jobs created was disappointing, other less tangible advantages accrued; large areas of derelict land were landscaped, new pleasant housing was built and the morale of local businesses seemed to have been boosted. However, the overall returns were sparse for such a major investment.

One initiative of the Thatcher years did transform the face of Glasgow and was essential for the successful re-branding of the city. In yet another attempt to reduce unemployment, grants were made available for cleaning buildings. This provided temporary work for many and transformed the initial impressions of visitors to Britain's northern industrial towns, none more so than Glasgow. For the first time in years, some even considered Glasgow to be a good looking city.

While the appearance of Glasgow was being transformed, plans were also made to improve the communication systems. The city had been well served by canals, railways and ports largely built before the beginning of the 20th century. Glasgow ceased being a port of any significance in the early 1970s as containerisation revolutionised sea transport and Greenock was developed to handle it. Roads, always important for local commerce, became increasingly important for long distance trade. Motorways came to Britain quite late: the first linking London and Birmingham was opened in 1959. Glasgow was congested with the slowest average speed of traffic (7 mph in 1957) of any of the major cities of Britain. Plans to drive a motorway through the centre of Glasgow were carried through and opened in sections between 1968 and 1972. This removed a significant proportion of the traffic from the city streets. North–south traffic was improved by the Clyde Tunnel, opened in 1963 and carrying 65,000 vehicles per day, and by the Kingston Bridge, opened in 1969, which carried the motorway across the river and became the busiest commuter bridge in Europe being used by 180,000 vehicles per day. The two were linked by the new Expressway on the north side of the river.

The motorway system extended westwards towards Greenock, eastwards to Edinburgh and southwards to Carlisle, although it was several years before all these links were converted to motorway. Indeed the link between Edinburgh and Glasgow must be one of the most inadequate roads linking cities of equivalent size and proximity in Europe. The M77 was built in the 1990s and improved access to Ayrshire.

Attempts to improve the rail links with English cities were frustrated time and time again. Electrification of the west coast line from London to Glasgow was completed in the 1960s reducing the journey time to a little over 5 hours and remains the last significant development. Britain's answer to the TGV of France was the tilting train, which was designed to use existing track at speeds of 150 mph because it leaned into the curves. It was launched on a bitterly cold day in December 1981 and was a technical failure and quickly withdrawn, never to reappear. The line is currently the centre of a political battle on whether it justifies expenditure of billions of pounds. Meanwhile the trains are full and frequently late.

Glasgow Airport was built at Abbotsinch which had previously been developed by the RAF in 1932. It was taken over by Glasgow Corporation in the 1960s and construction completed by 1966. It was run by British Airports Authority (BAA) from 1975. Until BAA was privatised in 1988, Prestwick was the international airport for the West of Scotland and Glasgow was used for local or national services. Air links with London were revolutionised by the introduction of the shuttle by British Airways in the early 1970s. This was an hourly flight between Glasgow and Heathrow taking one hour. Passengers could turn up and be guaranteed a seat, another plane being provided if necessary. It proved popular and was well used by business people for whom it made Glasgow easier to reach from London than several nearer cities. Subsequent developments have concentrated on low cost flights, which, together with the need for greater security, have changed the service somewhat, but Glasgow airport is now linked to most of the major British cities and a handful of European cities. Passenger numbers are increasing, albeit slowly.

Twentieth-century Glasgow was no longer a rich city. Wealth generation declined with the industries that had sparkled in the preceding 150 years. In the period between 1960 and 1990 it had become the sickest city in Britain. This economic decline highlighted the social problems that had always been present but the most harmful change was that a city and region that had been innovative and resourceful became an economic backwater with scant hope and a growing culture of apathy, social dependency and antagonism towards wealth creation. The city was scarred by dereliction, closed factories and new poorly constructed housing estates.

Shipbuilding

At the turn of the 20th century, this industry seemed to be doing well. Production was increasing, John Brown bought J & G Thomson in 1899, Yarrow's moved up from the Thames in 1908 and the steam turbine was introduced by Denny's in a Clyde steamer, the *King Edward*, in 1901. This type of engine proved ideal for ships requiring speed such as naval ships but was less useful for the tramp steamer. The output from the Clyde was about 400,000 tons each year and reached an all-time high of 750,000 tons in 1913. Continued prosperity seemed assured. However, there were signs that all was not well. Orders were not abundant and there was a trend for contracts to be less profitable as competition increased and shipbuilders quoted lower prices to win orders and thus keep their core workers together. They used up some reserves of capital in the expectation, hallowed by precedence, that trade would pick up and prosperous contracts return. Naval contracts were usually profitable but were insufficient to keep all yards busy even after the race to produce Dreadnoughts started.

To add another dose of anxiety, a major advance in engine technology happened elsewhere and threatened to devalue the Clyde's expertise in marine engines. Rudolf Diesel patented his engine in 1892. It was smaller, ran on different and cheaper fuel and offered major advantages for tramp steamers around the world. It was developed on the continent and first installed in a large ship by a Danish shipyard in 1912. Clyde businessmen, however, reacted quickly and by 1914 had the first works in the world specially constructed for building large marine diesel engines on licence.

Over the last years of the previous century, Clyde shipyards had changed from being a supplier to most of the world to supplying a relatively few influential customers. Brown's was linked to Cunard for whom large liners were built; they also specialised in passenger ferries for railway companies. Denny's had strong links with Henderson and Co and through them supplied ships for trade with Burma and the East. Fairfield's built passenger liners and ferries for a few customers. Thus, the activity of these yards depended on orders from a relatively small number of companies which made periodic bouts of under-activity inevitable. Some companies, particularly Brown's and Fairfield's also had commissions for naval vessels, mostly for the Royal Navy. The profitability of these undertakings decreased from the turn of the century until the outbreak of war. For example, 7% of Denny's contracts were unprofitable between 1893 and 1909 but this rose to 28% in the immediate pre-war years even though the number of ships built only decreased from 27 per year to 23 per year in the two periods. Beardmore's (which had diversified into many different forms of manufacture) made an overall loss on its ships in the years leading to the First World War even though its naval contracts were profitable. Fairfield's fared better, helped by a profit of 20% on the *Lusitania* launched in 1906. Therefore, shipyards were signing contracts which were as near the bone as they could justify. The position seemed to be worsening immediately before the war and there were five fewer shipbuilders on the Clyde in 1913 than in 1870. This was not necessarily a bad sign but did show that the years of expansion were over.

Shipbuilders expected busy times when the First World War ended as countries and companies re-equipped their merchant fleets after wartime losses. They were anxious to have sufficient supplies of steel to meet the expected demand and some acquired steel works as insurance. Several re-equipped their yards. A new company, the Blythswood Shipbuilding Co, set up at Scotstoun in 1919 as a specialist builder of oil tankers.

The good years only lasted until 1922 and were followed by the leaner years when output was maintained but competition hardened. The years following the crash in 1929 were the worst that the Clyde had experienced leaving many companies with unused capacity and large debts. One exception was Lithgow's, whose management had avoided the expense of expansion because they believed that there was excess capacity in Britain. There were few orders from the Admiralty because countries undertook not to build warships for ten years at the Washington Conference in 1922. In 1913, the Clyde had turned out 750,000 tons of shipping and about 500,000 tons per year in the 1920s except during the miners' strikes. By 1932 only 66,000 tons were launched and in 1933 just 10,000 tons. These were particularly bad years but the average for the 1930s was little more than half of the average for the 1920s. Clearly, too much capacity remained. Although the Clyde was still dominant in Britain with about a third of the total tonnage launched, the British share of world supply fell from 45% in the 1920s to 36% in the 1930s as other countries, notably Holland, the Scandinavian countries, the USA and Japan developed their own capacities. Therefore, the fault was not necessarily with the Clyde, either management or workers, but with the ability of others to do what had once been uniquely well done on the Clyde.

Sir James Lithgow instigated the founding of National Shipbuilders Security Ltd in 1930 to take out excess capacity. This organisation was financed by the shipbuilders, the Government and the Bank of England and supervised the closure of eleven Clydeside yards over the next six years including the modern Beardmore yard at Dalmuir. However, it did nothing to alter the uncomfortable fact that very few new orders were coming in. The only yard making money was

Lithgow's whose management took over Beardsmore's and Fairfield's yards as well as buying a large stake in Colville's, the steel manufacturer.

The high unemployment on Clydeside was not alleviated by Government creating demand as Roosevelt did in America. There was one large exception called Project 534 and it became a symbol of hope for the Clyde. Cunard had ordered a very large liner and Brown's won the contract in 1929. Work started and went on for a year before the Bank of England announced that it would no longer continue to underwrite Brown's overdraft. Work stopped at the end of 1931 and for two years the monster's hull lay silent.

> Ships in the making throb with more activity and vitality than at any other time during their lifespan with men yelling, hammering, sawing, drilling, slicing through steel… men scaling ladders and men clambering on skeletal stages. Men everywhere, like feasting ants on some vast carcase… Then as dramatically as though someone had thrown a switch, everything is stilled.
>
> Burrows *Great Glasgow Stories* 1998

After two years the Government relented, faced with the huge social problems of Clydeside in recession, and agreed to underwrite Brown's debt. Work restarted involving about 100,000 people directly or indirectly. They made engines, anchors, lifts, cables, staircases, furnishings and all the things required for a luxury liner. The ship was launched in September 1934 by Queen Mary after whom it was named. It had been hoped that resumption of work on 534 signalled the end of the recession on the Clyde but this was premature and it was not until re-armament began that recovery was assured. In the short term, once the *Queen Mary* sailed away, many went back on the dole. It is worth stressing that it was a wonderful investment that the government made. Not only did it help a substantial number through some of the worst years of the recession but the *Queen Mary* and the *Queen Elizabeth*, also built by Brown's and launched in 1938, proved wonderful troop ships in the Second World War carrying huge numbers of American soldiers across the Atlantic at speeds that meant that they could do so without escorts.

The Second World War created huge demand again. Any firm with experience in working steel was asked to build ships of all sizes and classes as Britain fought the crucial Battle of the Atlantic. Just how close the result was is highlighted by comparing the 645,000 tons lost in one month, April 1941, with the Clyde's average output of 500,000 tons per year during the war. Even the combined shipbuilding might of Britain and the USA had difficulty in keeping up.

The boom that followed the war kept the shipyards busy – too busy to modernise. Besides, the owners, remembering the events following the First World War, were understandably cautious. Meanwhile European countries were building or rebuilding modern yards. Competition was keen, first from Scandinavian countries and Germany and then from the Far East with Japan leading the way, followed by South Korea. The world economy grew at about 7% per year between the end of the war and 1960 and there was an insatiable appetite for ships with a doubling in the size of the world's merchant fleets. During this time, the Clyde launched an average of 400,000 tons each year but its share of the tonnage launched in the world fell from 18 to 5%. Shortages of steel and skilled labour prevented further expansion. By 1960, the glut of orders was coming to an end and success depended on ability to supply credit and to deliver quickly at fixed prices. The Clyde fared badly on all counts compared to other countries which offered state subsidies in one form or another. The small yards on the narrow Clyde found it impossible to introduce the flow line production methods used by their competitors, although improvements were made with greater use of prefabrication and heavy lifting gear. Lithgow's and Brown's were the most successful yards and launched 30% of the Clyde's output during these years.

Two events had a crucial and damaging effect on the prosperity of the industry. First, the Suez crisis of 1956 blocked the canal and threatened the supply of oil to Europe. The response was to construct ever larger tankers to sail around the Cape. Unfortunately, they became far too large to be constructed on the Clyde. Therefore, the only growing point in the industry was unavailable. The second event was that the first jet passenger aircraft crossed the Atlantic in 1958. Within a few years, no one thought of sailing the Atlantic and the demand for passenger liners fell quickly. Some yards took the opportunity to modernise belatedly but the market had changed for good. Once again, ships were built at or below cost price and the consequences were dire. In 1963, Denny & Brothers called in the receiver. Two years later Fairfield's did so. The Government stepped in and brokered a deal at the end of 1965 setting up Fairfield (Glasgow) Ltd. The Government hoped that the new company would introduce new work practices which were more flexible, responsible and productive so that it could compete with overseas shipbuilders. The experiment was too short lived to succeed because the Government also set up the Geddes inquiry which reported in 1966 recommending amalgamation of the upper Clyde firms of Brown's, Fairfield's, Yarrow's, Stephen's and Connell's as the Upper Clyde Shipbuilders. Scott's and Lithgow's on the lower Clyde were also to amalgamate. The UCS had a short life, dominated by the building of the liner *Queen Elizabeth 2*, before going bankrupt in 1971. The two were connected because the liner was built at a considerable loss and its engines broke down on the trial voyage which was not good for the firm's reputation. (Yarrow's, with its naval connection, managed to escape into independence.) The announcement of bankruptcy by UCS provoked the Upper Clyde work-in which grabbed the attention of the world. A group of trade unionists, many of whom had insisted on practices so arcane that it was difficult to achieve even the simplest task without prolonged consultations, now put the men to work without orders to fulfil. They were led by Jimmy Reid, Jimmy Airlie and Sam Barr, all communists. In publicity terms, the work-in was a huge success and Jimmy Reid was elected Rector of Glasgow University in 1971. The attention it generated put huge pressure on the Heath Government to find a solution. It had announced that it was not going to bail out lame ducks so it became a test of strength of resolve. Jimmy Reid declared that they were not going to allow some Whitehall mandarin to close 'our' shipyard. The Government desperately tried to find private buyers and, remarkably, succeeded to some extent. Brown's was bought by an American firm, Marathon, and Fairfield's and Connell's merged to form Govan Shipbuilders. Both were given large subsidies: a total of about £100 million. However, the 1970s was also the decade of two oil shocks which provoked high inflation and recession. Orders were almost non-existent and Labour (elected in 1974 as a result of the miners' strike) responded by nationalising the industry only for the Conservatives to privatise it again when elected in 1979. Scott-Lithgow's closed soon afterwards. Only three yards survived to the end of the century: Yarrow's kept alive by a drip feed of naval orders, was bought by General Electric and then by BAE in 1999; Kvaerner which took over the Fairfield yard of Govan Shipbuilders until it was also bought by BAE; and Ferguson's, a small yard at Port Glasgow. The sorry post-war story is summarised in Table 3.1. Only 12.7 million tons of shipping was launched in the 50 years that followed the war. Figure 3.1 shows that the annual output of about 400,000 tons per year was maintained until 1960 but thereafter decreased year by year to virtually nothing despite all the subsidies and reconfigurations. This was associated with a loss of some 36,000 jobs in the industry itself and perhaps twice as many in the support industries. The shipbuilding industry, which started the great leap forward in 1840 effectively died in 1971. During those 130 years, it had contributed massively to Glasgow's wealth but that contribution declined drastically and progressively in the 20th century. At the beginning of the 21st century, only 2,500 workers were employed in the industry, about half as many as work in Glasgow Royal Infirmary.

Table 3.1   Fate of shipbuilders on Clydeside after the Second World War

Shipbuilder	Location	Output Since WWII		Peak Employment	Closed
		No of Ships	Tons		
William Denny & Bros. Ltd.	Dumbarton	101	280,321	1,500	1963
Scott & Sons (Bowling) Ltd.	Bowling	82	28,800	200	1979
John Brown & Co. (Clydebank) Ltd.	Clydebank	115	1,498,042	5,000	1987
Yarrow & Co. Ltd.	Scotstoun	166	212,766	2,000	Active (1)
Blythswood Shipbuilding Co. Ltd.	Scotstoun	48	490,835	1,000	1964
Chas. Connell & Co. Ltd.	Scotstoun	89	915,198	1,000	1980
Barclay Curle & Co. Ltd.	Whiteinch	51	513,065	3,000	1968
A. & J. Inglis Ltd.	Pointhouse	60	33,897	600	1963
Harland & Wolff Ltd.	Govan	54	504,481	2,000	1963
Fairfield Shipbuilding & Engineering	Govan	158	2,330,652	4,000	Active (2)
Alex. Stephen & Sons Ltd.	Linthouse	89	603,540	2,400	1969
Simons-Lobnitz Ltd.	Renfrew	99	114,468	2,000	1964
Fleming & Ferguson Ltd.	Paisley	48	41,848	400	1970
James Lamont & Co. Ltd.	Port Glasgow	73	52,011	400	1979
Ferguson Bros. Ltd.	Port Glasgow	127	165,046	700	Active (3)
William Hamilton & Co. Ltd.	Port Glasgow	57	454,974	1,000	1964
Lithgows Ltd.	Port Glasgow	180	2,764,628	4,000	1988
George Brown & Co. (Marine) Ltd.	Greenock	46	34,462	300	1983
Greenock Dockyard Co. Ltd.	Greenock	70	649,942	800	1980
Scotts Shipbuilding & Engineering Co	Greenock	93	845,994	2,000	1984
Ardrossan Dockyard Ltd.	Ardrossan	35	33,202	700	1965
Ailsa Shipbuilding Co. Ltd.	Troon	111	141,913	800	1988 (4)
Totals		1,952	12,710,085	35,800	

Notes:
(1) Yarrow's is now the Scotstoun division of BAE Systems plc and is still building frigates.
(2) Fairfield is now the Govan division of BAE Systems plc and is building naval amphibian vehicles and auxiliaries.
(3) Ferguson's is independent (again) and is building OSVs, ferries and similar small ships.
(4) Ailsa stopped shipbuilding in 1988 but never actually closed and later began small-scale shipbuilding again: in July 2003, it was reported to have closed again.
Source: www.coltoncompny.com/shipbuilding/statistics/clyde.htm

Steel

Steel depended on shipbuilding and survived reasonably well while ships were being built even if profits were minimal. There were, however, several structural problems. The local steel plants were smaller and less efficient than those in the north-east of England. They were separated from the pig-iron producers with only three of the 15 steelmakers being on the same site as iron production. In the others, the iron had to be cooled down, transported to the steel mill and then reheated. This was the price paid for the link between coal and iron on the one hand and steel and ships on the other. Local raw materials were being depleted rapidly with only 25,000 tons of iron being mined in 1929 and with a shortage of suitable coking coal for the furnaces. Producers in Cleveland and even in Germany could sell plate steel to the shipyards more cheaply than the

Ship's engines made by Beardsmore being moved to the Yard at Dalmuir 1911 (Mitchell Library)

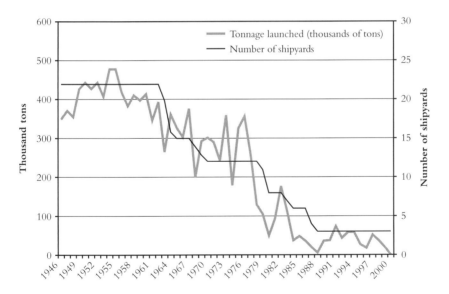

Figure 3.1   The decline of shipbuilding on the Clyde

Source: www.coltoncompny.com/shipbuilding/statistics/clyde.htm

Safe for Bank of Greece 1935 (Glasgow University Archives)

local producers. Two reactions averted disaster for the industry. Firstly, piecemeal modernisation was undertaken, adapting existing plants and secondly, discounts were offered to loyal customers who used only one supplier. Beardmore took this to the logical conclusion by building a ship-building yard at Dalmuir so there would always be a market for his steel. The firm had undergone radical change under the leadership of William Beardmore. He joined the family firm in 1877 when it was a relatively successful supplier of boilers to both the ship and railway industries. He restructured the company on a grandiose scale after the retirement of his uncle a few years later. In addition to Parkhead Forge, he bought a shipyard at Govan in 1899, a steel plant at Mossend, the Arrol-Johnston car company as well as building the new shipyard at Dalmuir. He also went into construction, building houses for its workers. He was wealthy enough to subsidise Shack-leton's 1907 Antarctic expedition and thus have a glacier named after him. Immortality comes in strange ways. Altogether, his company employed about 40,000 men in the run up to the First World War when it contributed hugely to wartime production.

The abrupt decline in shipbuilding over the interwar period meant that steelmakers had to find

Empress of Britain being built in 1931 by John Brown showing how tight space was for the larger ships
(Scotland's Images)

new markets. Since the world was gripped by a prolonged recession, this was almost impossible. The structure of the industry was too fragmented to be really efficient and required major investment. A significant proportion of it was owned by shipbuilders who considered it a secondary business and, in any case, did not have the necessary funds to modernise. Furthermore, several producers believed that the major problem was that foreign steel manufacturers dumped their excess production on the Scottish market. Whether this was true is not clear, but it was believed and the industry lobbied for protection. They thought that without it, there was little point in investment because they could always be undercut. Another problem was that most of the plants were on sites that would not allow major expansion. The Steel Company of Scotland had actually opened a second plant at Blochairn because the original site at Hallside was too small for the desired expansion. To try and work out a communal solution, several companies including Baird's, Colville's, Dunlop's, Stewart and Lloyds' and the Steel Company of Scotland commissioned an inquiry. The resulting Brassert Report was published in 1929. The main recommendation was that a single integrated plant should be built on a site on the south bank of the Clyde consisting of a blast furnace, a coke plant and steel works. This would have several advantages including easy access both for imported iron ore and to its main market, the shipyards. The hot gasses emitted could be used for heating the homes surrounding the works. Iron and steel production would be on one site producing economies by reducing transport costs and the expense of reheating iron for use in the steel works. It would also achieve economy of

Cameronia at Finneston Docks 1930 (Glasgow University Archives)

scale. Unfortunately, the plan was not implemented not least because the magnates quarrelled over their share of the new company. Also Beardmore's was in financial trouble by this time and the others were reluctant to be saddled with its debts should it take part in the merger. It was duly declared bankrupt and its several businesses were dismembered under the direction of the Bank of England. Their naval shipyard at Dalmuir was closed in 1930 and Sir James Lithgow, a lower Clyde shipbuilder, took over the Parkhead Forge. In 1932, Stewart and Lloyds took matters into their own hands and moved their works and workforce to Corby in order to be near the abundant ore fields of that area. Another company, Colville's, effectively scuppered the Brassert plan by beginning a series of acquisitions at the end of which it was in a dominant position and implemented piecemeal changes which were cheaper but did not give the required boost to efficiency. Steelmakers also shifted from the production of acid steel to the cheaper basic steel which had become acceptable to the shipbuilders. Unfortunately pig-iron production did not make the equivalent change so reliance on imports increased. The industry shed 5,000 workers, doubled productivity and was protected by tariffs, which measures were sufficient to maintain Scottish steel production between the wars. However, the failure to implement the Brassert Report was an opportunity lost. Scotland had produced a little less than 25% of British steel up to 1920 but its share fell progressively to 15% in 1937.

After the Second World War, the management of the post-war iron and steel industries was a political ping-pong match between nationalising Labour governments and denationalising Conservative ones. Nationalisation came more slowly than to the coal industry and it was not until 1951 that the Government took control. That was the year of the change in Government and denationalisa-

The half built Queen Mary *lies idle in Clydebank in 1932 because John Brown's credit with the Bank of England was withdrawn (Glasgow University Archives)*

tion followed in 1953 and the Scottish plants were back in private hands by 1955. A Plan For Steel in 1946 proposed the expansion of Scottish steel production from 2 to 2.3 million tons. Once again it called for an integrated plant at Erskine. However, so much was happening in so many sectors that the delay in nationalisation prevented implementation. The political uncertainties made owners reluctant to invest in major projects so, since demand was high, all existing plants geared up to maximum production. The Government did authorise major investment at Clydebridge and Clyde Iron and Motherwell. Production of pig-iron increased to slightly less than 0.9 million tons and steel to 2.1 million tons in 1952 both of which were near the targets set in the 1946 plan.

The steelmakers then drew up another plan which was approved by Government in 1954. This called for the building of an integrated iron and steel works at Ravenscraig near Motherwell, controlled by Colville's. Unlike the Brassert plan and the 1946 plan, the site chosen did not have access to the sea which increased transport costs. Ravenscraig did, however, have the advantages of combining iron and steel production on one site and it was large enough to achieve economies of scale. It cost £22.5 million and was built on time and opened in 1957. It produced 400,000 tons of steel in its first year raising Scottish production to 2.6 million tons which was above target. As demand remained high, a second plant was proposed for Ravenscraig. However, 1958 proved to be a turning point in the demand for steel world-wide. Whereas before the Government issued export certificates to prevent too much steel going abroad, now it had to act to protect the British steel industry from imports. Prices started to fall. Scotland's production had become much more efficient with the introduction of Ravenscraig. Clyde Iron (where new furnaces were constructed) and Clydebridge were partially integrated, as were Gartsherrie Iron Works and Coatbridge steel mill which were owned by Baird's and Scottish Steel. All were able to use the hot metal process in steel production with the consequent gains in efficiency. There was a switch from coal- to oil-firing of the furnaces. However, despite meeting targets, the contribution of Scotland to British steel production fell from 15% post-war to 11% in 1960.

The era of closures started in 1975 when the Parkhead Forge was closed followed by Clyde Iron, Clydebridge, Tollcross and Hallside, all of which were closed by 1983. Ravenscraig, the last flagship of this key industry of the old order, was finally shut in 1993 as it could not compete with the Welsh and Northern English plants.

Iron

Production continued to dwindle from its peak of 2.2 million tons in the 1870s to only 0.6 million tons in 1913. Much of the ore used was imported and when the particular type of coal required for the furnaces began to run out, this too had to be imported. Altogether, the rationale of the industry based on local resources was gone. It was also unfortunate that the links with the steel plants were usually poor.

There was a bounce in production during the First World War and, by its end, production had increased to about one million tons per year. However, the increasing scarcity of raw materials, antiquated plants, the reluctance to switch to products suitable for the production of basic steel, which had become the preferred choice of shipbuilders, and the failure to build modern plants integrated with steel production all worked against it. By the start of the Second World War, production had halved and only five pig-iron producers were still in business.

After the Second World War, production at Park Forge was increased again as the Government sanctioned much needed investment but this proved to be only a temporary reprieve.

Coal

Output doubled in the West of Scotland between 1870 and 1913, when 22.4 million tons were mined by 79,000 miners. The contraction of the pig-iron industry meant that coal was switched to steel production and an expanding local market. Mechanisation was introduced using mechanical coal cutters and conveyor belts but they were not particularly useful in coal-fields that were nearly worked out. This was reflected in the price: Lanarkshire coal was 11s 5d a ton in 1913 compared to 8s 10d in Linlithgow and a Scottish average of 9s 8d. The West, which produced 80% of Scottish coal in 1870, only produced 50% in 1913 and productivity had slumped from 345 to 283 tons per worker per year over the same time. These were por-tents of trouble ahead.

It became clear after the First World War that most mines were making a loss. Management insisted on trying to reduce wages, for which there was some justification because output per employee in Scotland fell progressively from 301 tons per worker per year in 1913 to 269 in 1918 and 211 in 1920. A prolonged strike occurred in 1921. Complicated formulae relating pay to profits were used to try to achieve fairness but, since the mines were not making profits, they were unsatisfactory. A second strike in 1926 sparked off the General Strike. The miners lost after much hardship and their wages were reduced so that the proportion of wages in the total cost of coal production fell from 70% to 65%. This did not help much as demand remained poor because of improving efficiencies in the use of coal in the iron and steel industries and by the change to oil and gas which started about this time. Furthermore, the owners had miscalculated and the guaranteed minimum wage increased wage costs at times of reduced production. The mines remained unprofitable until demand improved in the late 1930s as industry recovered due to rearmament. By then, the industry in Scotland had contracted considerably. Employment had fallen from 154,500 men in 1923 to 81,600 ten years later. Total output fell from 38.5 million tons in 1923 to 32.25 million tons in 1937. The changes in the West were even starker because of the exhaustion of many of the seams. Output fell from 19 million tons to 14.5 million and employment fell from 79,000 to 45,000 over the same time as the least profitable pits were closed and others were mechanised. Therefore, the contribution of the coal industry to the economy of the West of Scotland diminished.

The war years, once again, required maximum output with a guaranteed market for everything mined. This demand continued after the war when there was a severe shortage of coal. The mines were nationalised by the new Labour Government in 1947 and one of the first acts of the National Coal Board was to audit their resources. The startling finding was that half the Scottish coalmines were in severe straits and it was proposed that they should be phased out over 20 years. The NCB rejected this advice and made a decision to increase output at whatever cost. Coal production in Scotland was only 22.5 million tons in 1946 and the planners estimated that 35 million tons were needed. Investment was poured in, even more than had been planned. New coalmines were opened, four of which were in the West of Scotland; surface coal was extracted in drift mines but the amount of coal recovered fell from a post-war maximum of 24 million tons in 1948 to 18 mil-lion tons in 1960. The production of the Western region fell from 13 million tons to 8 million tons over the same time. Perhaps fortunately, the demand for coal went into reverse in 1958 because of the increasingly rapid change to oil and gas and the railways' change to diesel. The mines remained unprofitable over the whole period and productivity remained stagnant partly as a result of over-manning but also because the seams were becoming more difficult to work.

Once demand fell, the NCB started to close unprofitable pits and this hit the coal industry in the West hard with the loss of 100 pits and a reduction of 14,000 in the workforce. Efforts were made to improve efficiency despite which the industry required subsidies throughout the post-war period. Attempts at reform were made but the National Union of Mineworkers consisted of the crack troops of the union movement and, under the leadership of Joe Gormley, defeated Edward Heath's Conservative Government in 1972. He lost the subsequent election called on the slogan 'Who governs Britain?' The Labour Administration of the 1970s took no decisions on the future of the industry, perhaps in fear of the power of the NUM. Even the Conservative Government of Margaret Thatcher, elected in 1979, followed suit for a few years. She bided her time until she thought she had a reasonable chance of winning and took on the NUM under Arthur Scargill in 1984. She won a bitter and prolonged dispute. Thereafter, all the remaining deep mines in the West of Scotland were closed within a few years and the only coal recovery occurring in the region is now from open-cast mining in Lanarkshire. Although the manner of the end of this once mighty industry was traumatic, it had been in decline in the region for the whole of the 20th century and would not have survived long whatever the circumstances.

Locomotives

The formation of the North British Locomotive Company in 1903 from the merger of the independent locomotive makers produced the largest company of this type in the world before 1914. The future looked secure. All went well until the downturn in the world economy in the late 1920s when the number of orders decreased and all but ceased in the early 1930s. As with the shipbuilders, contracts were signed which were unlikely to make any profit. Between 1921 and 1929, the company accepted 106 contracts to build 1,133 locomotive engines of which only 18 contracts for 154 engines were profitable. Activity even of the unprofitable sort was drastically reduced in the 1930s. In 1920, 307 locomotives were built, 197 in 1925 and none in 1932.

The story was much the same as the experience in shipbuilding. Managers tried to secure work on any terms to keep their skilled workforce together; financial reserves were run down; and attempts were made to try and remove idle capacity. This time the discussions foundered on the personality of the chairman of the company, Sir Hugh Reid. He believed that the main fault lay in the subsidies received by foreign competitors, particularly in Germany and even at home where the Bank of England had supported Beardmore's entry into the locomotive business. He preferred to hunker down and ride out the storm. The company survived until 1962 when it closed. Once again, a major Glasgow engineering industry based on the steam engine failed to evolve.

Other industries

The contraction of the traditional heavy industries and closure of several yards in the interwar period had a knock on effect on many engineering firms supplying the shipyards and several ceased trading. Unrelated industries, such as brewing and whisky distilling, were hit, this time by the introduction of prohibition in the United States. Furthermore, the unemployed did not have money to spend so that most companies dependent on local trade also suffered. And the recession went on for years, deeper and longer than any before.

The dependency of Glasgow and its region on steam engines, whether on the sea or on rail, was all too clear to the businessmen of the time. They knew that other industries ought to be developed so that the dependency on heavy engineering could be lessened. Furthermore, attempts were made to introduce the industries which were to be vital for post-war prosperity – the automobile industry, the manufacture of household goods and the aviation industry.

Automobiles

The first motorcar was imported into Scotland in 1895 by George Johnston, a minister's son living in Springburn. He was born in 1855 and trained as an engineer in the Hydepark Locomotive Co of Springburn. He had to teach himself to start his car and to drive it. He was also the first Scot to commit a driving offence when he drove in a proscribed area. Not content with owning a car, he set out to build them. He teamed up with Sir William Arrol, famous for the construction of the Tay

Workers at Beardsmore's Parkhead Forge 1909

and Forth bridges, to form the Arrol-Johnston Company in 1899 which was partly financed by the Coats family. The cars were produced at Camlachie, until the factory was destroyed by fire in 1901 and thereafter in a disused thread mill in Paisley. Sir William Beardmore bought the company and Johnston quit. Thomas Pullinger was appointed manager and moved the factory to Heathhall near Dumfries so that production was nearer the English market. The timing was unfortunate because the First World War broke out a year later and production was switched to shells and aero engines. The company enjoyed some success after the war but their hand-built cars became comparatively expensive as mass production was introduced elsewhere. In 1928, the Model T Ford cost £150, the Morris Oxford tourer £315 and the Arrol-Johnston 15.9 tourer £385 (reduced from £625 eight years previously). In 1927, the firm merged with Aster Engineering Co but went into liquidation two years later. William Beardmore successfully used the Paisley factory to produce taxis, light vans and engines for heavy vehicles. By 1928, there were 6,000 of his taxis in London alone.

The Argyle Motor Co was founded by Alexander Govan in 1899 in Bridgeton. The first model was produced very quickly and bore a striking resemblance to a Renault. Thereafter, the company energetically developed its own designs and produced the Argyle. Production rose to 15 cars per week bringing in appreciable profits. As a result, the company outgrew its premises and moved to a 53-acre site in Alexandria in 1905. A model and expensive factory was built for the huge sum of £500,000. Govan took the health and comfort of his workers seriously. There were recreation rooms, washrooms and lockers as well as a restaurant. The factory soon had its own orchestra, magazine and sports clubs. Plans projected an output of 1,200 cars a year and by 1905 had achieved 800 cars per year which made it the largest volume of any car manufacturer in Europe. The cars were hand-built, well designed and tested. Unfortunately, Govan died suddenly in 1907 and the company did not manage to replace his vigour and vision. A year later it was declared bankrupt with debts of £360,000. The receiver managed to keep a reduced workforce employed under the management of Colonel John Matthew. A new and successful engine was developed and the new Argyle won prizes in motor sports. However, the company did not survive long partly because it was bled by an expensive court case with Daimler (which it won) and by a venture into aero engines. It collapsed in 1914 and the factory was used by the Admiralty to make torpedoes until 1969.

The third Glasgow venture into the automobile industry was to prove the most successful. Two of the team that George Johnston had assembled for the Arrol-Johnston Company became disenchanted with his style and left to set up the Albion Motor Car Co. Norman Fulton and his brother-in-law Thomas Murray established their own company at the end of 1899 in an attic of the Clan Liner repair shop. They won a prize for their car at the Glasgow International Exhibition of 1901 and their machines proved popular in a remarkably short time and were sold around the empire. In 1903, they moved to a factory in Scotstoun and continued to expand production of cars and trucks. Their light vans became popular with almost all British retail companies – Harrods alone had a fleet of 100. Trucks and buses followed and the directors decided to specialise in heavy vehicles, so car production was gradually tailed off. The A10 truck proved a great success with the armed forces which bought 6,000 during the war. The company survived the depression and employed 1,650 people in the late 1930s. The Second World War also provided plenty of orders but the post-war era proved more difficult. It was taken over by Leyland which invested heavily in the factories at Scotstoun and Yoker. Work was plentiful and the workforce increased to 3,500. The factories turned out both completed vehicles and parts for the whole Leyland range. In 1972, the company changed its name to Leyland (Glasgow). Leyland's were also asked to take over the British Automobile Company by the Government and suffered thereby. In 1980, the Yoker factory was closed and the Scotstoun factory converted to producing axles only. The workforce was down to 1,100. Even this

Men working in Parkhead Forge 1932 (Glasgow University Archives)

was unviable in the context of the British motor industry of the time and the company collapsed. The receivers constructed a rescue by the local management team led by Dan Wright. He renamed the firm Albion Automotive and persuaded the creditors to invest in the company. The main work was again supplying axles and it continues in business although it is now part of American Axle & Manufacturing.

The final, and much later, venture into the automobile industry was made at the request of Government. The Rootes Group wished to build a small car to rival the Mini. It needed a new plant and the Government offered inducements to build it at Linwood, a centre of high unemployment. It had the advantage of a good supply of local pressed steel made by Coleville's at Ravenscraig and, of course, there was no difficulty in finding workers. However, only parts of the engine were made at Linwood. The block and cylinder heads were sent down to Coventry where they were fitted to the main engine which was then returned to Linwood where the car was completed. This was not an ideal production line. The factory was opened in 1963 and employed 3,000 workers producing 850 Hillman Imps per week, well below maximum capacity. The venture was handicapped in almost every way. The parent company was in a poor financial condition and was acquired by Chrysler. The car suffered technical problems which tarnished its reputation. Lastly, industrial relations were awful from the start, reflecting the antagonism between workers and their bosses so prevalent at the time. There was a further investment in the factory so that the Hillman Hunter could also be produced there. By 1972, it was turning out 2,400 cars each week. The Imp was replaced by the Avenger and the workforce reached a maximum of 8,400 turning out 2,800 cars per week. This was still below target. Chrysler sold their European wing to Peugeot/Citroen which closed the plant in 1981 after only 18 years.

Therefore, the hope that a new industry would take root in the West of Scotland was frustrated. The home-grown efforts of the pioneers produced high quality cars but failed to respond to the move to mass production. Whether Alexander Govan would have managed this transfer had he lived is a tantalising question but the suspicion is that the prevailing culture in the Clyde was geared to quality craftsmanship rather than production lines. The second attempt to import a car plant foundered for a variety of reasons, not the least of which was the antagonistic attitude of the workforce and management, confirmed by conversations I have had with patients who used to work in the plant.

Conclusion

The first three-quarters of the 20th century saw the slow demise of those industries that had made Glasgow the second city of Empire and the biggest non-capital city in Europe. Social issues, particularly housing, dominated the agenda of the City Corporation. It succeeded in building enough houses but produced new estates which failed most other tests. The vigour of local entrepreneurs seemed to run out although times were tough particularly between the wars. Inward investment contributed significantly after the Second World War but mainly in the region rather than Glasgow itself. Emigration of talent started after 1950 and the number of jobs fell progressively. Attempts by Central Government to halt the slide were unsuccessful. In 1975, Glasgow was indeed a gloomy place.

PART 2
THE RECENT PAST: AFTER 1975

CHAPTER 4

1975 TO 2001: THE REGION

The West of Scotland entered the last quarter of the 20th century in a state of bereavement for past glories, unsure of the future and poorly regarded by the rest of the country. Bereft of its traditional industries and with no obvious replacements, the local economy was in a dire condition. The UK entered the European Union in 1972 and the West of Scotland was designated an area for which significant development funds were available. Mrs Thatcher was elected Prime Minister in 1979 and slowly introduced the reforms for which she became renowned throughout the world and hated in most of Scotland but with particular intensity in the West. Her monetary policies led to periodic overvaluation of the pound to the great detriment of manufacturing industry. She planned the demise of the coal industry as carefully as a general does his battles. The reorganisation of the steel industry vastly improved productivity but lack of demand led to the closure of the last significant Scottish steel plant. The destruction of large segments of manufacturing hastened the switch to service industries throughout the UK and, surprisingly, Glasgow became attractive to inward investors.

The first and perhaps most important reason for this change was a successful attempt to portray the city as an attractive place in which to work and live. The outside world had continued to perceive Glasgow as a rough, tough city permeated by reds and gangs and had given it a wide berth. The leaders of the City Council deserve most of the credit for changing this perception. During the 1980s, Central Government made money available for cleaning the buildings in cities. Emerging from its grim, sooty persona, Glasgow appeared clean and sometimes elegant to visitors attracted by the slogan with its deliberate ambiguity 'Glasgow's miles better.' This catchphrase was proposed by John Struthers in 1983 and enthusiastically taken up by the Lord Provost, Michael Kelly. It, together with Mr Happy which was chosen as the logo, became world famous and is said to have been nearly as well recognised as New York's description of itself as The Big Apple. However, slogans alone would never change peoples' minds. There were other developments to act as persuaders. The Burrell Collection, which had been bequeathed to the city in 1967, was opened to the public in 1983, housed in a bespoke gallery set in a handsome park; the combination of collection, building and background were stunning and widely appreciated. Burrell's collection was truly catholic and had something of interest among its 9,000 items to everyone. Pollok House, the 18th-century mansion of the Maxwell family and gifted to the city in 1966, is also beautiful and contains some wonderful Spanish paintings.

The Scottish Exhibition and Conference Centre (SECC) opened two years later. It was built on derelict land in the old Queen's Dock site. This marked the beginning of the regeneration of the Clyde Corridor on which Glasgow had turned its back since the ships stopped docking and the cranes became idle. The choice of a conference centre was astute. Only Birmingham had one to rival it in Britain and even within Europe there were not many which could host the largest conferences. It then became clear that Glasgow lacked sufficient quality hotels and these were subsequently provided, adding considerably to employment opportunities. An extension of the Conference Centre, capable of seating 3,000 people in one hall, was added in 1997. Its design was rumoured to have been inspired by the Sydney Opera House and it resembled a giant armadillo, substantially altering the skyline of the riverside.

The next event that drew visitors to the city in large numbers was the Glasgow Garden Festival in 1988. It was also sited on derelict dockland, south of the river opposite the SECC at the old Princes' Dock. A new pedestrian bridge was built across the Clyde so access was easy from either bank of the river. One hundred and twelve gardens were laid out on the 25 hectare site in six themes. The Festival attracted 3 million visitors who, the City Council claims, spent £100 million pounds in the six months that it was open. The site was subsequently used for the building of the Science Museum and an IMAX cinema whose designs complemented that of the SECC's armadillo opposite.

Perhaps the greatest fillip to the acceptance of Glasgow as an attractive city in which to live and work came in 1990 when Glasgow became the European City of Culture. The City Council showed foresight and ability in recognising this opportunity. Glasgow was an unlikely city to be selected: in the previous five years the cities had been Athens, Florence, Amsterdam, Berlin and Paris and Dublin followed the year after, all with international reputations. For Glasgow, it was different; the opportunity had to be used to create a reputation among other Europeans who knew little about it. The year was an outstanding success both culturally and economically. Indeed, the way in which Glasgow exploited that year of opportunity became a blueprint for the use of culture in regenerating a city in decline. The EU Commission was so impressed that members rethought their ideas about the role of culture in economic regeneration. Perhaps more than anything else, it transformed Glasgow's reputation and, for a time, pushed the problems of Glasgow's deprivation into the background. One assessment wryly commented:

> the best proof of the positive impact of 1990 was that afterwards French artists did not have to be persuaded to come to Glasgow but actually put themselves forward.
>
> French Cultural Attaché in London, quoted in Myerscough
[web site Department of Culture. Media and Sport.]

The event was huge; during the year 3,400 entertainments from 23 countries were staged including plays, dance, sport and exhibitions. Forty major projects were commissioned specifically for the festival and there were 60 world premieres. Venues were built or adapted for the occasion; a new Concert Hall, of which the design was functional rather than attractive, was opened by the Princess Royal in October 1990; the McLellan Galleries were expensively renovated; and a great barn, previously used to house tramcars, was converted to an unlikely theatre using tiered seats supported by scaffolding. The year was hailed as a great success, rivalling the Glasgow Exhibitions of the previous century.

In 1996, the Gallery of Modern Art was opened in a paradoxically classical building which was designed by David Hamilton and built in 1778. It became the second most visited modern art gallery in Britain outside London, with 530,000 visitors in 2005. At the end of the 20th century, Glasgow boasted four art galleries or museums of distinction all housed in memorable buildings, four orchestras with two concert venues, the acoustics of the City Halls being the envy of most other British concert halls, an ailing opera company as well as a ballet company shared with Edinburgh.

A profusion of places to eat, drink and be entertained accumulated in or near the city centre from the Merchant city in the East to Byers Road in the West. Glasgow was widely seen as a place with buzz. Even the French started coming for mini-holidays. Therefore, the first reason for a surge of inward investment was that Glasgow was no longer regarded as a city to avoid. It was fun.

The second reason for the change in the perception of Glasgow was that there was a wealth of talent available for hire. The banks, call centres and other business services could recruit relatively skilled workers for less than the rates applicable in the South of England. Graduates from Glasgow's universities poured into these new jobs. Thirdly, buildings in the

Plate 1   *The Glasgow Arc or the Squinty Bridge framing the Finneston crane (Neil Guthrie)*

Plate 2   *The Armadillo of the SECC (Neil Guthrie)*

Plate 3 *The M8 makes an S shape slash through the city taking much of the traffic off the streets.*
(Neil Guthrie)

Plate 4 *View of the Clyde from Glasgow Green to the Suspension bridge*

Plate 5   *The city chambers, seat of local government (Neil Guthrie)*

Plate 6   *Thomas Graham who discovered the principle of dialysis that had a major impact on my life*
(Neil Guthrie)

Plate 7   *Glasgow Cathedral (Neil Guthrie)*

Plate 8   *James Watt and Christmas lights (Neil Guthrie)*

Plate 9   *The new flats on the riverside viewed from the Squinty Bridge (Neil Guthrie)*

Plate 10   *Glasgow University from the south (Neil Guthrie)*

Plate 11   *Kelvingrove Art Gallery and Museum (Neil Guthrie)*

Plate 12   *Lord Kelvin, Glasgow's most famous scientist (Neil Guthrie)*

Plate 13   *Queen Street Station Low Level 2004*

city centre were upgraded to offer good office space at reasonable prices. Lastly, transport around the city was better than in almost any other British city although road, rail and sea links to the rest of Britain (with the exception of the air service to London) and the continent remained relatively poor. Happily, this was of less importance to service industries than good telecommunication links.

For these reasons, the economy of the West of Scotland started to show the first signs of lusty growth since the catastrophic loss of jobs in the decades after the war.

Recent performance of the economy of the Glasgow Region

Detailed statistics for the region are available for this period. I have used three sources which have different definitions of the region (see Table 4.1) which are important as they explain some variations in the data.

Table 4.1   Definitions of the region used by different organisations

Source	Title of region	Extent of region
Cambridge Econometrics	Glasgow Region	Glasgow city East and West Renfrewshire East and West Dunbartonshire Inverclyde North Lanarkshire
Audits	Glasgow Metropolitan Region	As above + South Lanarkshire
Office of National Statistics (ONS)	Southwest Scotland	As above + Ayrshire Dumfries and Galloway

Definitions

The Office of National Statistics (ONS) divides the country into NUTS (Nomenclature of Units for Territorial Statistics) areas. Scotland is one of 11 NUTS 1 areas in the UK, Southwest Scotland one of 37 NUTS 2 areas and Glasgow City one of 133 NUTS 3.

GVA (Gross Value Added) and GDP (Gross Domestic Product): Wealth created in a region or country is measured by adding the value of all products, whether services or manufactures, from that area. This is the GVA which is used in the estimation of Gross Domestic Product (GDP). Basic GDP excludes taxes and subsidies and is equal to GVA. Market priced GDP is basic GDP plus taxes minus subsidies on products. The term GDP used in this text is the basic GDP and equates to GVA, which is also used. The two are therefore interchangeable. **Gross National Product** (GNP) is usually very similar to GDP but measures the current account rather than the balance of trade. If a significant amount is earned by a foreign company and repatriated, then the GNP falls compared to the GDP. This affects Ireland most.

The Glasgow Region's wealth increased over the period between 1975 and 2001 in a surprisingly healthy manner, virtually doubling in real terms in 26 years (Figure 4.1). According to Cambridge Econometrics European Service (2003), between 1991 and 1995, it grew at 2.1% per annum and between 1995 and 2001 it accelerated to 3.7% per annum, outperforming the UK as a whole. During these years, which were nothing if not turbulent, the Gross Domestic Product (GDP) fell in only six of the years compared to the year before.

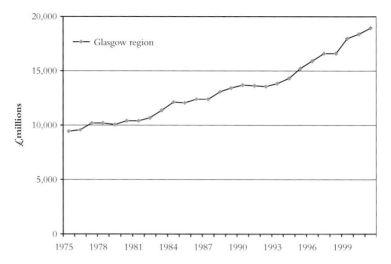

Figure 4.1   Changes in wealth creation in the Glasgow Region. Results for Glasgow region are expressed as Gross Value Added in £m at 1995 values

Source: Cambridge Econometrics

Cambridge Econometrics divided the economy into four sectors: manufacturing, market services, non-market services and construction. Manufacturing, the traditionally dominant sector of the region, includes mining, food and drink, textiles, electronics and energy production. Market services include banking, call centres, entertainment, tourism, shopping and transport. Non-market services, such as education and health, are under the control of Government. Construction is as it sounds. The contribution of the various sectors to the wealth generated in the region is shown in Figure 4.2.

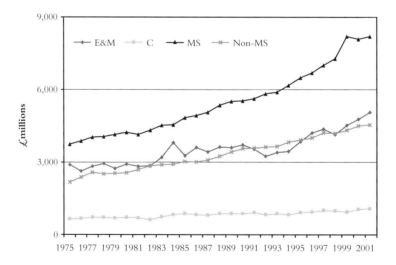

Figure 4.2   The contribution of different sectors of the economy of the Glasgow Region to wealth creation between 1975 and 2001 expressed as Gross Value Added in £ millions at 1995 values. E&M is Energy and Manufacturing: C is Construction, MS is Market Services and Non MS is non Market Services.

Source: Cambridge Econometrics

Thus all sectors contributed to the growth in the economy, but the service sectors contributed most. Interestingly, the contribution of Government-provided services is almost exactly the same as that of manufacturing although employment in manufacturing fell almost as quickly as it rose in non-market services. The values and proportions of these sectors in 1975 and 2001 are shown in Table 4.2, as is the amount they grew over the last quarter of the century. The proportion contributed by energy and manufacturing fell from 31% in 1975 to 27% in 2001 although its value increased by 75% in real terms over the 26 years. Construction had a 62% increase in value over the same period but the leader was the market services sector which increased in value by 120%. The data in Figure 4.2 show that output from the manufacturing and the market service sector increased more rapidly between 1993 and 2001. The other two sectors grew linearly.

Table 4.2   Shows the amount contributed by different sectors of the regional economy in 1975 and 2001 together with their share of the whole.

	Value 1975 (£ x10⁶)	% contribution to GVA in 1975	Value 2001 (£ x10⁶)	% contribution to GVA in 2001	% change in value
Agriculture	23	(0.2)	42	(0.2)	83
Energy and Manufacturing	2,890	31	5,068	27	75
Construction	642	7	1,077	6	68
Market services	3,736	39	8,205	43	120
Non market services	2,168	23	4,552	24	110
Total	9,459	100	18,934	100	100

Values are expressed in £m at 1995 values. The change in their value over the period is also shown.
Source: Cambridge Econometrics.

Employment

Although the population of the Glasgow Region continued to decline between 1975 and 2001, the number of working age remained almost steady and was estimated to be 1,009,000 in 2001. The good news was that the number of people in work increased by almost a quarter – from 600,000 in 1975 to 746,000 26 years later so the proportion of the people of working age actually in work increased from 57% to 74% over the period, with the greatest increase coming after 1993. Even during the grim days of the 1980s the number of people in work remained steady because the contribution of part-time and female employment obscured the loss of full-time jobs for men.

The rise in employment, an extra 146,000 jobs or nearly 25%, was entirely due to the service sectors, both market and non-market; and, of these two, there was a proportionately greater increase in the Government sector. The energy and manufacturing sector lost jobs while employment in the construction sector remained stable. Agriculture contributed a tiny number of jobs but their productivity nearly doubled. Figure 4.3 shows the numbers employed in the four sectors over the period and Table 4.3 compares the breakdown of the workforce at the beginning and end of the period.

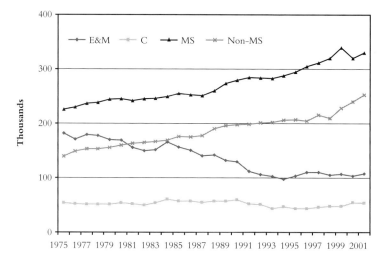

Figure 4.3   Employment (in thousands) in the four main sectors in the Glasgow Region between 1975 and 2001

Source: Cambridge Econometrics

The two service sectors created over 200,000 new jobs, compensating for the loss of about 75,000 jobs in manufacturing.

Table 4.3   Numbers (and %) employed in different sectors of the economy of the Glasgow Region in 1975 and 2001 and the percentage change in each sector during that time.

	Employed 1975 (x1000)	% 1975	Employed 2001 (x1000)	% 2001	% change
Agriculture	2	0.3	2	0.3	0
Energy and manufacturing	182	30	108	14	−41
Construction	54	9	54	7	0
Market services	226	37	330	44	46
Non market services	140	23	253	34	81
Total	604	100	747	100	24

Source: Cambridge Econometrics

Productivity

Manufacturing may be a declining source of employment and its contribution to the economy may be growing less quickly than services but it is getting progressively more efficient. Figure 4.4 shows the numbers employed between 1975 and 2001 in the sector and the value it added to the economy. The value added per worker increased from £15,879 in 1975 to £46,994 in 2001, not due to inflation since the currency has been standardised to 1995 values. Within the Region, there were some striking variations: in 2004, the GVA per employee in manufacturing was £125,000 in Inverclyde (albeit with only 2,000 workers), £116,500 in Renfrewshire but only £50,000 in Glasgow itself. The increase in productivity compares favourably with all other sectors. Within the manufacturing sector, the trend within electronics was just as marked. Somewhat surprisingly, the number employed in this sector peaked in 1975 and then declined, at first slowly and then more rapidly before making a modest recovery after1995. The value of electronic goods produced changed little until 1991 and thereafter rose, doubling in value in the next decade, once again showing a considerable rise in productivity.

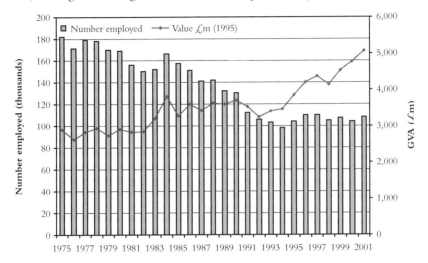

Figure 4.4   Manufacturing and energy in the Glasgow Region showing numbers employed (×1000) on left-hand scale and GVA (in £m 1995 value) on right-hand scale

Source: Cambridge Econometrics

The value added per worker in the market services sector increased during this period from £16,531 to £24,863 with the financial element being the most productive, output increasing from £22,929 per worker in 1975 to £39,326 in 2001.

The output per employee of the non-market sector increased only slightly from £15,509 to £18,017 per year, a real increase of about 0.6% per year over the period. Since most of the amount is made up of wages, Government was remarkably effective in restraining pay while it permitted a considerable growth in employment. The productivity of the construction sector also increased markedly since the value of its output rose by about 75% while the number of employees remained stable.

Therefore, the local economy doubled in value over the last quarter of the 20th century accelerating most quickly in the late 1990s. The manufacturing and energy sector continued to shed jobs at an alarming rate but the industries that survived increased the value of output thanks to huge gains in productivity. This may have been exaggerated by the tendency to contract services out: if, for example, a manufacturing industry provided its own canteen services, the workers would be classed in the manufacturing sector but if it contracted out their catering service, the workers who replaced them would be classed in the market service sector. This may account for some of the loss of jobs and apparent increase in productivity.

Despite these changes, welcome though they were, the loss of population continued in the late 1990s, although at a reduced rate. Since loss of population is a sign of failure, it may be interesting to compare the performance of the region with another in the same country.

Comparisons with Manchester

I have chosen the Manchester Region because it had a similar industrial history. Manchester did not have the boom associated with shipbuilding and its population did not suffer the same degree of overcrowding but it was presented with similar problems towards the end of the 20th century. Initially, it also suffered a loss of population and the rate of loss was similar in the two regions between 1975 and 1985; thereafter, the population in the Manchester Region stabilised whereas Glasgow's loss continued. As with the Glasgow Region, the working population remained more stable. The proportion of the population in work in Manchester in 1975 was 48% and remained unchanged in 2001. In the Glasgow Region, by contrast, the proportion increased from only 36% to 49%. Thus, if all else were equal, one would have expected the Mancunians to generate more wealth per head of the population in 1975 and the Glaswegians to have caught up by the end of the period. Figure 4.5 shows this was so. Not only did the people of the West of Scotland catch up with the Mancunians by 1997 but also over the next few years their growth was faster so by 2001 they were about 13% ahead.

Figure 4.5   The value added per head of the population in the Glasgow and Manchester Regions. The ratio is obtained by dividing the GVA of the region in £ (1995) by the total population.

Source: Cambridge Econometrics

The restructuring of the economies of the two city regions followed similar lines with an increase in service jobs and a reduction in manufacturing. The latter had a higher share of the workforce around Manchester in 1975, with 36% compared to 30% around Glasgow, but it fell to about 15% in both by the end of the period. This suggests that Glasgow started reconfiguring earlier. Employment by Government services was 2–4% higher in the West of Scotland than around Manchester throughout the period, reflecting higher Government spending in Scotland. Perhaps as a result, the market service sector's share of employment increased more quickly in the Manchester region and was higher than in the Glasgow area in 2001.

The value added in the two regions by the different sectors of the economy is interesting. There was a steady increase in the value of output per worker in the energy and manufacturing industries in both regions but, from 1993, it accelerated around Glasgow but slowed around Manchester so by 2001 the value added per worker was 32% higher in Glasgow (Figure 4.6).

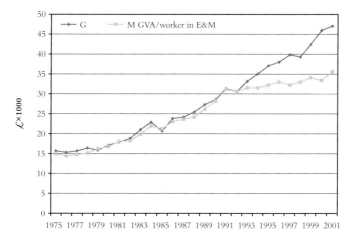

Figure 4.6   GVA per worker in Energy and Manufacturing sectors of Glasgow and Manchester Regions expressed in £ (1995) × 1000.

Source: Cambridge Econometrics

The value added per worker in the market services was almost identical in the two regions and slightly higher in the Glasgow Region's non-market and construction sectors.

In summary, the GVA per head of the population in 1975 was higher in the Manchester Region but thereafter grew more quickly in the Glasgow Region and overtook that of Manchester by 1996. Between 1990 and 1995 in Glasgow, the GVA grew at 2.1% per year, accelerating to 3.7% per year between 1995 and 2001. The equivalent figures for the Manchester region were 1.3% and 1.9%. In Manchester, the switch to service industries came a little later than in Glasgow and the two were equally productive. Manchester's loss of manufacturing and energy industries was swifter in the last quarter of the century but that was only because Glasgow's had already been blown away. However, the surviving industries in this sector are more productive than their equivalents in Manchester and this is the main reason for the higher GVA/head of Glasgow Region's economy.

Comparison with some European Regions

Every year, the City Council commissions an audit of the economy of the city and region. Different companies have been given the task. In 2003, the audit was undertaken by Experian Business Strategies, in 2004 by Oxford Economic Forecasting and SLIMS and in 2005 by BSK Basel Economics. The 2003 and 2005 reports gave detailed comparisons of the performance of the Glasgow Metropolitan Region (defined in Table 4.1) with other British and European regions and even some American city regions.

Experian, in their audit of 2003, chose ten European regions, each dominated by a large city, with which to compare the Glasgow Metropolitan Region. None were capital cities except Edinburgh (Lothian). Some of their details are shown in Table 4.4. Their populations varied between Lothian's 783,000 and Catalonia's (Barcelona) 6,077,100, with four having almost exactly the same population as the Glasgow Metropolitan Region. In terms of wealth generated per head of the population, Glasgow was about two-thirds of the way down the league. It had a reasonable employment rate but rather low productivity which was measured as regional GDP/the number in work. Almost all the regions with the exception of Catalonia and Western Sweden had a more productive workforce.

Table 4.4   City regions used in Experian's study

Key characteristics of the comparator regions, 2002					
City Region	Population (thousands)	% population of working age	GDP/ head of population (€)	% in employment	Productivity (€)
Metropolitan Glasgow	1747.7	65.5	22,715.0	63.3	54,810.2
Nord Pas-de-Calais	4028.2	70.7	17,373.1	44.3	55,462.2
Mid Pyrenees	2568.5	64.3	19,415.5	53.0	56,901.6
Western Sweden	1783.4	63.9	21,797.5	63.2	53,968.8
Catalonia	6077.1	68.3	22,285.5	65.0	50,163.5
Liguria	1605.5	64.6	24,162.5	62.3	60,088.1
Piedmont	4238.2	67.2	26,140.4	67.0	58,092.5
Lothian	783	66.9	27,135.8	72.2	56,165.2
Stuttgart	3981.3	67.0	28,207.7	65.6	64,188.0
Antwerp	1650.5	65.7	28,300.1	58.0	74,224.2
Hamburg	1741.4	69.2	39,175.7	75.1	75,381.8

Data collected for 1998. GDP per head of population is the GDP of the region/total population; result expressed in €/head. It was adjusted for commuting.
% in employment is the number in work as percentage of the number of working age
Productivity is the GDP of the region/working population measured in €/head.
Source: Glasgow Economic Audit Experian 2003

The contributions of different sectors to the economy of the different city regions are shown in Table 4.5. Employment in production (manufacturing and construction) varied between 17% in Edinburgh and 40% in Stuttgart, thanks to its domination of German car production. Glasgow's 22% was near the lower end of the range. Whether this reflected the more advanced development of the switch to service industries in the Central Belt of Scotland or whether the substitution of service industries is a short term expedient that cannot compensate for the loss of manufacturing will not be known for some time. It is a pity that comparisons were not made with Dusseldorf, a city with a similar industrial history and also trying to kindle some modern industries. Its region, Nordrhein-Westphalen, had a GDP per capita only just above the European average (EU15) of 101.5 in 2001 compared to 100.9 for Southwest Scotland (see Table 4.1 for definition) which suggests that German cities with a comparable history had comparable wealth. The two German cities chosen in Experian's study were exceptionally successful, Hamburg having a GDP per capita of 170.8, and Stuttgart with 125.7 compared to the EU15 average of 100.

Table 4.5   Proportion of the economy made up of different sectors

City Region	Agriculture	Production	Services
Metropolitan Glasgow	0.4	21.8	77.8
Lothian	1.1	17.1	81.8
Liguria	2.4	20.9	76.6
Antwerp	1.0	31.5	67.5
Hamburg	0.5	17.6	81.9
Western Sweden	2.2	26.2	71.5
Mid Pyrenees	6.1	23.7	70.2
Stuttgart	2.7	40.1	57.2
Nord Pas-de-Calais	2.3	27.4	70.3
Piedmont	2.9	34.7	62.4
Catalonia	3.3	35.1	61.6

Employment by sector in the 10 metropolitan regions. Source Glasgow Economic Audit Experian 2003

IBM set up a in Greenock in 1951 and was the first of the electronics companies in the Region

Experian estimated that the average annual growth in GDP between 1997 and 2002 was highest in those areas with the lowest GDP per head: it was 3.3% in Western Sweden and 2.5% in the two French regions as well as Metropolitan Glasgow. (As we have seen, Cambridge Econometrics rates for the Glasgow Region, a slightly different area, were higher at 3.7%.) Therefore, there is evidence of catch-up growth by the areas with lower GVA per head. The rate at which new jobs were created was high in and around Glasgow, being exceeded only in Catalonia and Western Sweden.

The conclusion of this comparative study was that the Glasgow Metropolitan Region was in the lower half of the wealth creation league of these European regions but was catching up. Hamburg, Stuttgart and Antwerp were appreciably more prosperous but the other city regions were not very different. Employment was relatively high and continued to increase at an above average rate but productivity remained poor. However, the difference in performance in 2000 compared to 1975 was immeasurably better and the rate of growth achieved and the rate of jobs created were grounds for continuing optimism

The audit for 2005 confirmed these findings. BAK Basel Economics compared the Glasgow Metropolitan Region with 20 other metropolitan regions of similar size in Europe and the United States. Its results were expressed as comparisons between Metropolitan Glasgow and the average of the other metropolitan regions. Growth in Metropolitan Glasgow's GDP was about the average for the other metropolitan regions in Europe but was above average when the GDP per head was analysed: this, of course, was due to the falling population. The actual GDP per capita in 2004 was about 73% of the average of the metropolitan regions, a rise of 9% in 25 years with most of the improvement occurring in the last decade.

What the authors found more worrying was that productivity was low by European standards, particularly when measured in output per hour. Thus although the number of jobs had increased impressively, the output per hour of each individual had not improved much relative to that of the other regions in the study. In 2004, a worker in the Glasgow Metropolitan Region produced about $28 worth of goods for each hour worked compared to $50 in Munich and $31 in Edinburgh. The reason, the authors thought, was the particular mix of the economy. They divided the economy into five sectors:

The New Economy Sector by which they mean IT and telecommunications, both hardware and software. This has grown dynamically in recent years and, therefore, is a good thing. Its share of Glasgow's economy was 7.1% compared to the metro average of 9.1%

The Old Economy Sector is the one that produces high technology goods such as chemicals and drugs, precision instruments as used in medicine and transport equipment. It is also a good thing because of the high value added per employee. It contributed 2.9% of Glasgow's economy compared to 4.3% elsewhere.

The Urban Sector provides the services within a city, town or even village and these range from financial services to restaurants and include estate agents, banks etc. It is usually associated with above average productivity and has grown significantly in the post-industrial age. No less than 44.4% of Glasgow's wealth was generated in this sector, still less than the average of 53.6% in the other metro regions.

The Traditional Sector is made up of low-tech manufacturing in which labour costs are a large part of their budgets and are particularly vulnerable to competition from the newly industrialising countries. The productivity of these firms is likely to be low. It was still relatively important in Glasgow, making up 17.3% of the economy compared to an average elsewhere of 12.1%.

The Political Sector comprises those industries and businesses that depend directly on political decisions. Health, education, police and other public utilities controlled by local or national Government make up this sector. It is associated with low productivity and contributed no less than 28.2% of Glasgow's GDP compared with 20.6% elsewhere.

Thus Glasgow's low productivity, argued the authors of this audit, resulted from its under-representation in the sectors with high productivity and its over-representation in the sectors with low productivity. The poor productivity in the Glasgow Metropolitan Region is not because workers don't work hard enough but because it does not have a big enough share of the élite industries with spectacular productivity.

Are there any signs of progress? There were until 2000, but thereafter growth stalled. Take the rate of growth of the New Economy Sector. It boomed in the region from 1995 to 2000 growing at about 14% per annum and contributed about 14% to GDP. From 2000 to 2004 it went into reverse and its contribution declined. The same is true of the Old Economy Sector although it had a much smaller share of the economy. So the two sectors likely to increase productivity failed to deliver after 2000. The Urban and Political Sectors both grew at about 2–3% per annum throughout the period and increased their share of the local economy. Glasgow is unusual in having one of the biggest public sectors in proportion to the total economy of any European metropolitan region – 28% compared to the average of 21%. And these jobs are not high value added jobs so, although welcome, they do little to improve the region's productivity.

Some of this is perhaps over-gloomy as Glasgow's poor showing is against some pretty remarkable city regions. Although Metropolitan Glasgow's GDP per head was low compared to the metro areas chosen, it is slightly higher than that of the EU of 15. The handful of city regions included in the study which grew faster than Glasgow in the 10 years to 2004 were pretty special; Oslo, London, Helsinki, Boston and, the star performer, Dublin.

If the City Council is serious in its ambition of closing the gap on the high flying regions like these, it will have to find a few aces to accelerate growth and productivity. The auditors did not think this likely. They defined three sorts of city-regions: high-tech cities nourishing highly innovative and specialised industries; business cities with flourishing service industries supplying the support for other businesses; or, thirdly, consumer cities geared to tourism, health and education services for an international clientele. Of the three options, the first was considered an unrealistic ambition because of the lack of world class companies in the region. The second was possible, particularly if an alliance were forged with Edinburgh to create a critical mass, big enough to compete for international customers for their services. But the third was the one they thought most likely. However, this distinction is largely arbitrary. There is no reason why policies designed to promote high-tech companies cannot exist alongside the expansion of services for business or for leisure.

Therefore, after 1975, the Glasgow Region turned its back on a century of contraction and misery. True it no longer boasted a world class economy as it had done in the 19th century but the rate of loss of population was abating and an impressive number of jobs had been created. Its share of high valued added industries or businesses was modest compared to many other European regions, but manufacturing was improving its productivity and the Glasgow region was in the middle ranks of European city regions. It was no longer a hopeless case.

CHAPTER 5

GLASGOW CITY

At the end of the 20th century, many still doubted Glasgow's future. The BBC News (November 1999) contrasted a successful Edinburgh with a failing Glasgow. Glasgow was losing population and jobs; it had a 33% lower GDP per head than Edinburgh; and higher unemployment. It was, in short, a city on the slide. Even more alarming was an article appearing in March 2003 entitled 'Glasgow economy sinks'. And the first sentence was: 'Glasgow, once Scotland's economic powerhouse, is dying economically according to an analysis of the latest data by leading business and financial adviser Grant Thornton'. The data on which this dire prediction was based included the poor start-up rate of new businesses, their high rate of failure with the worst three-year survival rate in the UK, a disproportionately high insolvency rate and a rapidly declining population. If this were true, why were retailers setting up in the city? How could a failing city earn the cash to justify such growth in the retail sector? Clearly, doomsters did not reflect all that was happening even if some of their allegations were true.

Glasgow was indeed losing population but the extent of the loss is unclear. The ONS (Office of National Statistics) recorded only 575,000 people living in the city in 2001, well below the expectations of the Council. The 2001 census figure published on SCROL (Scottish Census Results on Line) was 629,501 but even that is a loss of 35% of the population in just 50 years. Part of this loss is exaggerated by the emigration of its more successful workers to houses just beyond its borders. The functional population of Glasgow, by which I mean the number dependent on jobs in Glasgow, is much higher, perhaps 1.1 million, although it too has fallen by about 13% in the previous two decades. It is also true that the city's economy performed rather badly after 1960. It actually contracted by 0.6% between 1987 and 1992 during which time Scotland achieved a growth rate of 10% and the region also did quite well. But what the doomsters did not seem to realise was that in 1993 the economy turned round and the city was once again the economic motor of the region, growing faster than Scotland and the UK. After a decade of solid growth, its estimated GDP was £10.7 billion (at 1995 prices), about the same size as Glasgow Region – £10.1 billion. Indeed, for the eight years following 1993, the city's economy performed particularly well, vying with Bristol and Belfast for the title of Britain's most dynamic city (see Figure 5.1 for comparisons with three selected cities and Table 5.1).

Whereas Glasgow's GVA per head was 26% less than Edinburgh's in 1993, this had decreased to 16% by 2001. Between 1995 and 2001, Glasgow's contribution to the Scottish economy rose from 14.4% to 16% and Edinburgh's from 13.75% to 14.4%. This does not support the BBC's analysis of the two cities.

Not only did Glasgow's economy grow faster than other British cities, it also grew faster than that of any other county in south-west Scotland (Figure 5.2). The county with the next highest growth rate was North Lanarkshire followed by South Lanarkshire whereas East and North Ayrshire and Dumfries had the slowest. (This explains why Glasgow Region's growth rate is higher than Glasgow Metropolitan Region which in turn is higher than Southwest Scotland: see Table 4.1 for definitions.)

Figure 5.1   Changes in GVA per head of population in selected British cities. 1993 = 100%. Data of NUTS 3 areas except Manchester which is of Greater Manchester.

Source: ONS

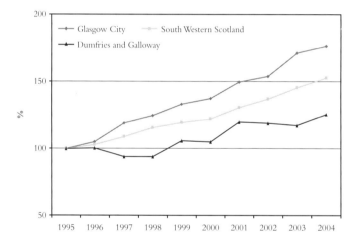

Figure 5.2   Economic growth of Glasgow city, the Southwest Region and Dumfries and Galloway: 1995 and 2004. Results expressed as a percentage with 1995 =100.

Source: ONS

Of course, a city's economy may grow well but start from a much lower base and, therefore, be flattered by data showing only the rate of change. To put the size of Glasgow's economy in scale: the profits of the big four British banks or the two major British oil companies were more than the whole contribution of Glasgow to the national wealth. So Glasgow's wealth creation, although welcome and increasing healthily, may be relatively modest. Yet, the GVA per head in Glasgow is quite good according to the Office of National Statistics lying sixth of the 11 cities shown in Table 5.1.

Table 5.1   GVA/head in selected British cities

City	GVA/head 1993 (£)	GVA/head 2001 (£)	Ranking in GVA/head league 1993 2001		% change of GVA 1993–2001	Ranking in growth league
Glasgow	11,467	19,110	6	6	67	2
Inner London	22,972	34,888	1	1	52	7
Edinburgh	14,484	22,168	3	2	53	6
Nottingham	14,633	20,782	2	3	42	11
Belfast	11,946	20,521	5	4	72	1
Bristol	12,345	19,450	4	5	58	4
Leeds	10,541	16,904	7	7	60	3
Cardiff	10,366	16,074	9	8	55	5
Birmingham	10,435	15,344	8	9	47	10
Manchester	9,359	13,920	10	10	49	9
Liverpool	8,848	13,317	11	11	51	8

GVA/head in different cities in 1993 and 2001 with their ranking in growth rate and wealth created in 1993 and 2001. Figures taken from ONS using NUTS3 data and are current values or not adjusted for inflation. Manchester refers to Greater Manchester and Cardiff to Cardiff plus the Vale of Glamorgan. Source ONS

It is interesting that four capitals, London, Edinburgh, Belfast and Cardiff are first, second, fourth and eighth in the GVA per head rankings of 2001. Clearly, it helps to be a capital (see Chapter 6). Nottingham, the highest ranking provincial city, was the slowest-growing city of all with only a 42% increase over the period.

A recent study commissioned by the John Prescott, Deputy Prime Minister at the time, on the economies of English cities highlighted their relatively poor performance compared to European cities. It was then updated for the Scottish Executive to include Scottish cities. The results are shown in Table 5.2. The three cities with the highest GVA per capita are all German whereas English cities are concentrated towards the foot of the table.

Table 5.2   A tale of 24 cities

Rank	City	GDP/head	Rank	City	GDP/head
1	Frankfurt	£51,159	13	Lyons	£19,889
2	Munich	£42,155	14	Dortmund	£18,230
3	Stuttgart	£36,801	15	Rotterdam	£18,003
4	Copenhagen	£34,881	16	Leeds	£17,592
5	Amsterdam	£26,245	17	Turin	£17,196
6	Stockholm	£24,544	18	Toulouse	£17,006
7	Helsinki	£24,261	19	Birmingham	£15,155
8	London	£24,090	20	Manchester	£14,489
9	Edinburgh	£24,052	21	Newcastle	£14,077
10	Milan	£22,063	22	Lille	£13,865
11	Glasgow	£21,905	23	Barcelona	£12,669
12	Bristol	£20,219	24	Liverpool	£11,307

*GDP per capita, source Barclays 2003 copied from the Scotsman

Glasgow does surprisingly well; at least it surprised me. But was Glasgow's GVA per head really that good? GDP per head is a measure of the wealth generated in a city in a given time divided by its resident population. It depends on many factors which include the percentage of the workforce in work, the number of hours they work and the value of their output and, crucially, the number that commute into the city. Commuters inflate the GDP per head because their output is attributed to their place of work but they themselves are not. The next sections analyse these contributing factors to see if Glasgow's GDP is indeed better than most English provincial cities.

Population, workforce, commuting and participation rates

In 1950 about 559,000 people worked in Glasgow in the post-war boom. Failing industries led to loss of jobs and many left the region altogether. By 1996, only 326,000 were working in the city. This was the nadir and was followed by a substantial recovery with the creation of 63,300 new jobs for employees and 500 jobs for the self-employed over the next five years. Encouragingly, 84% of these new jobs were taken by Glasgow residents which must have had a significant effect on social deprivation. Surprisingly, there were more women than men in work in 2002 and 69% of all employees were in full-time work. This prolonged period of job creation stemmed the loss of population: between 2001 and 2006, provisional figures show that the population remained stable but the population of working age increased by about 5% or 25,000 as more jobs were created.

The service sectors, market and non-market, were responsible for much of the economic growth and the surge in employment that occurred in the 1990s (see Table 5.3). The last column of Table 5.3 shows the number of Glasgow residents employed in each sector. Altogether, 166,000 workers commuted into Glasgow in 2001 making up 42.7% of the workforce. Public Sector workers and those working in the financial services were the most likely to live outside the city boundaries.

Table 5.3   Changes in employment by sector in Glasgow city (in thousands)

Sector	1991	1995	1996	1997	1998	1999	2000	2001	2001*
Agriculture	0.4	0.2	0.2	0.2	0.2	0.2	0.2	0.2	0.2
Energy/water	3.8	3.0	5.8	3.4	6.1	3.6	2.9	4.5	2.3
Manufacturing	43.7	34.6	31.1	31.7	31.4	31.1	30.0	31.3	24.0
Construction	34.4	17.7	15.6	17.4	18.7	16.3	19.8	17.5	16.7
Distribution/Catering	68.8	69.8	70.3	74.1	71.1	71.6	73.9	80.3	12.0
Transport/Communications	22.9	22.9	20.3	18.8	20.9	22.6	21.9	23.6	17.2
Financial/Business services	63.9	70.9	67.9	75.7	76.7	86.2	87.1	92.5	41.1
Public services	92.4	95.9	98.6	102.1	102.3	103.7	109.3	115.8	64.2
Other services	18.9	17.1	16.6	17.7	19.8	18.9	18.8	24.0	13.6
Total employees	349.2	332.1	326.4	341.1	347.2	354.2	363.9	389.7	223.0

Numbers × 1000 of workers in each sector whether commuters or resident in Glasgow. Source: Glasgow Economic Monitor Summer 2003 and derived from ONS.
2001* is the number of residents in Glasgow employed in the different sectors in Glasgow in 2001 – derived from census returns: SCROL.

The service jobs that arrived in Glasgow were not the result of local companies starting up or expanding but of outside companies setting up or expanding services in Glasgow. For example, Glasgow acquired many call centres employing a substantial number of workers between 1999 and 2001; Thompson Lunn Poly, a travel company, employed 1,000 people, Percepta of Fords, 400, E-sure, an insurance company, 400 and NFU Mutual Direct, 220. Call centre companies clearly valued the quality of workers available in the city but the work was demanding and led to an enormous turnover in staff, as much as 100% per year in one or two companies. In the early years of the 21st century, this type of service was sometimes transferred to India where workers were available and significantly cheaper. IT and software jobs were also attracted to the city, but the numbers were smaller. Services still creating jobs at the turn of the century were retailing, banking and other financial services, hotel and catering. Manufacturing employment fell by 28% during the 1990s but most of this loss occurred in the first half of the decade. By 2001, only 9% of the 389,700 employed in the city worked in the manufacturing and energy sectors. The profile of employment in the remaining manufacturing businesses is shown in Table 5.4 for 2001 and 2005.

The ONS does not give a value for the goods produced by the manufacturing sector in NUTS 3 areas such as Glasgow city but it does give a figure for all productive industries which include manufacturing, energy and construction. Their contribution to the city's economy and that of all services are shown in Figure 5.3. In contrast to the service industries, the productive industries have not grown at all; output remained stable between 1995 and 2002 while the service sector grew vigorously.

Table 5.4   Employment in the manufacturing sector in Glasgow in 2001 and 2005

Employment in Manufacturing (x1000)	2001	2005
Food, Drink and Tobacco	7.61	4.8
Transport Equipment	5.01	3.8
Paper, Printing and publishing	5.01	5.0
Machinery and Equipment	2.94	2.4
Metals	2.71	2.1
Electrical and Optical Equipment	2.51	1.8
Other Manufacturing	1.56	NG
Textiles and Clothing	1.46	0.57
Chemicals	0.70	0.58
Wood and wood products	0.64	1.9
Others	1.19	NG
Non metallic	NG	0.53
Total	31.34	23.48

Source: ONS/Experian and Glasgow Economic monitor August 2007. NG=Not given

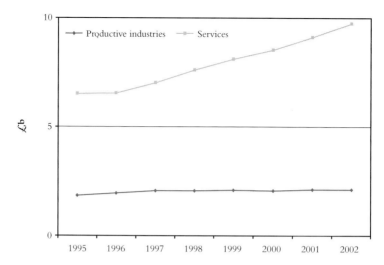

Figure 5.3   Contributions of productive industries and services to Glasgow's output between 1995 and 2002.

Source ONS: Results expressed in £b at current values.

Productivity

Productivity is the output of each worker in a given time. If the unit of time is long, such as a week or year, productivity can be improved by working longer hours. If the output is measured per hour, then the number of hours worked has no effect. The choice of unit can, therefore, radically alter results. For example, France and Britain have different patterns of work. The British tend to work longer hours and have lower unemployment than the French who have a shorter working week but are much more productive for any hour worked. There are two explanations for the difference. First, the French may work harder because they know they don't have to be at it for so long, whereas the British worker knows that a long day lies ahead and realises that 'he tires betimes that spurs too fast betimes'. Second, the labour laws in France make it difficult to sack workers whereas the French think it is notoriously easy to do so in Britain. Therefore, a French manager is likely to take on as few workers as he can and, instead, invest as much as possible in each one so that his or her output is maximised. That is one major reason why the French unemployment rate was about 22% in the under–25 year olds in the early years of the new century and why so many of them came to the UK to work. It may also have been a major contributor to the riots in Paris in 2005. On the other hand, the French see the British system of flexibility as contributing to low wages, job insecurity, frequent changes of job causing family disruption, unequal distribution of wealth and even public poverty such as in our transport and health systems.

In terms of productivity measured as output per worker per year, Glaswegians performed a bit below the average for Britain in 2003. As we have seen in the previous chapter, workers in the manufacturing sector produced most, followed by those in market services and Government-run services. Unusually, productivity was higher in the region than the city partly because manufacturing is much stronger in the region and this outweighed the city effect in the service sectors. Overall, it was £37,300 per worker per year in the region compared to £27,000 per worker per year for Glasgow city. Even the productivity in the manufacturing sector was lower in the city (£50,000 per capita) than in Glasgow Region (£69,000 per capita) probably because investment was less.

The productivity in different sections of the economy is shown in Table 5.5. The 4,000 work-ers in the energy and water sector produced goods valued at five times that of public service workers, although the latter's productivity is very difficult to assess accurately. All service sector categories were less productive than all types of manufacturing. However, in fairness to the fi-nancial sector, workers in financial firms were included with the less productive business service workers of whom those working in call centres form a majority. Nevertheless, manufacturing created more wealth per head but the service sector produced more than ten times the value of manufacturing products because of the much larger workforce.

Table 5.5   Number of workers and their productivity (GVA per employee in £) in different sectors of the economy in Glasgow and comparison with Scotland's

	Number employed	Productivity Glasgow	Productivity Scotland
Agriculture, Forestry & Fishing	101	28,901	34,784
Energy, Water Supply	4,219	115,813	72,257
Metals, Minerals & Chemicals	3,742	47,069	51,462
Engineering	10,575	37,288	46,610
Other Manufacturing	16,973	34,253	31,186
Construction	19,678	25,970	24,695
Distribution, Hotels & Catering	86,115	17,410	16,835
Transport & Communication	25,566	48,240	39,750
Financial & Business Services	93,517	31,396	28,879
Public Services & Other Services	147,795	21,352	19,665
Manufacturing	31,290	36,811	40,138
Non-manufacturing	376,989	26,070	23,692
Total	408,279	26,212	25,953

Source: Experian Business Studies 2003. Note that the definition of manufacturing is looser than the ONS figures quoted above. Productivity refers to value of output in £ per worker.

Although the productivity of Glasgow's manufacturing sector improved by 13% during the nineties, it remained well below the Scottish average. This may be attributed to less investment per employee than elsewhere in the country where large scale foreign investment in the electronic in-dustries during the nineties markedly increased productivity. Only 9% of investment into the man-ufacturing sector within Glasgow came from abroad and only 13% of manufacturing workers were employed by foreign companies compared to 53% in West Lothian and 45% in Renfrewshire.

Glasgow's output per head of population compares poorly with other European cities and not just the French ones. In the audit of 2005, the GDP per capita was more or less the same as for the metropolitan average of European and American cities chosen as comparators, but output per head of population was only about two-thirds of the metro average and had not improved relatively over the last 25 years. The increases in output have been gained by more jobs and longer hours. This productivity deficit is probably the result of the type of jobs available and, to a lesser extent, lack of investment.

Therefore superior productivity is not the cause of the high GDP per head of the city quoted by ONS and Barclays.

Earnings

If Glaswegians' GDP were high, this should be reflected in their earnings. They were indeed paid above the Scottish average but marginally below the British level in 2000. The average gross annual wage for full time workers was £24,355 in Glasgow, £22,711 in Scotland and £24,635 in the UK. The UK average was raised considerably by wages in the south-east and London which were higher than in all other regions. Table 5.6 compares the annual salaries of different groups of workers in Glasgow with other selected cities and with Kensington & Chelsea, one of the wealthier London districts. It shows that the average salaries in Glasgow were much lower than in the wealthy parts of London, and 5% lower than in Bristol and Manchester but marginally higher than in Leeds. Of the nine sectors detailed, the Personal Services Occupations (e.g. hairdressers and domestic cleaners) were better paid in Glasgow than elsewhere and members of the administrative and secretarial services were the worst paid. It is clear that Glaswegians' wages offered only a slight competitive advantage for businesses setting up in Glasgow. Earnings provide no evidence that the GDP per head of Glasgow is really greater than that of provincial English cities, and confirm that it is likely to be markedly less than London's.

An annual average salary of £24,335 compared with the average GVA per worker of £27,705 means that nearly 80% of the wealth generated was spent directly on wages.

Table 5.6 Gross annual earnings in 2000

Sector	Glasgow	K & C	Manchester	Leeds	Bristol
Managers and Senior Officials	35,652	35,652	35,652	35,652	33,322
Professional Occupations	34,559	39,577	33,231	32,767	34,443
Associate Professional and Technical Occupations	25,362	31,220	28,238	24,530	27,143
Administrative and Secretarial Occupations	16,587	20,659	17,365	17,104	17,189
Skilled Trades Occupations	21,808	25,719	21,858	20,916	22,468
Personal Service Occupations	16,278	14,990	16,034	13,890	14,617
Sales and Customer Service occupations	14,081	17,382	14,567	15,239	13,601
Process, Plant and Machine Operatives	19,017	19,414	19,456	19,338	20,427
Elementary Occupations	14,423	16,373	15,222	15,834	16,304
Average	24,335	34,670	26,152	24,131	25,544

Earnings of employees in different occupations in different British cities expressed in £ per employee per year. K & C is Kensington and Chelsea. Source NOMIS, 2003

Unemployment

Unemployment inevitably reduces GDP per head and Glasgow has suffered more than its share of unemployment throughout much of the 20th century. In 1983, there were nearly 73,000 citizens claiming benefit – not as bad as in the 1930s but still dismal. By 2004, this had fallen dramatically to 17,500. The changes were similar in other cities but less marked (see Figure 5.4). There were two reasons for this: Glasgow created more jobs than did other cities and, more ominously, it continued to lose population faster than most cities. Even in 2004, the claimant count, as a percentage of the working population, remained a fifth higher than the national average; although marginally below that of Liverpool and Manchester, it was nearly twice the rate of Edinburgh, Leeds and Bristol (see Figure 5.5). This is either an opportunity in that the GDP of the city could be increased considerably if the extra workers could be returned to work, or a curse in that those who remained unemployed, despite such a long period of job creation, may have lost the skills required to contribute. Be that as it may, the fall in the claimant count to a low of 4.8% in January 2004 was clearly a huge advance on the record of the previous century.

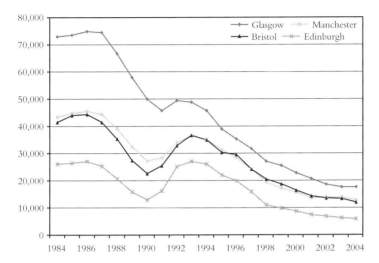

Figure 5.4   The claimant-count in Glasgow, Manchester, Leeds and Bristol between 1984 and 2004

Source: NOMIS

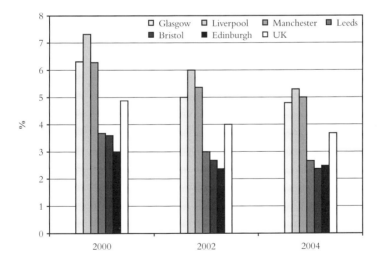

Figure 5.5   Claimant count as a percentage of the population of working age in the early 21st century

Source: NOMIS

Unemployment is unevenly spread in Glasgow, the highest concentrations being in the north and east. In 1998, Royston had a rate of 23.2% and Hutchesontown of 20.6% whereas in the South and West, Garrowhill's rate was 2.5% and Kelvindale's 3%. The figures are likely to have fallen subsequently but the proportion between the wards will have been maintained.

Apart from the unemployed claiming benefit, Glasgow also contains a high proportion of economically inactive citizens. A comparison with some of the major British cities is shown in Table 5.7. There appear to be two types of cities: Glasgow, Manchester and Liverpool on the one hand and Edinburgh, Leeds and Bristol on the other. The former have about 17% fewer of their citizens in employment although their claimant counts were only about 2–3% higher. People may not be working for a variety of reasons; perhaps because they were looking after children or a sick relative or were studying full-time but one of the commoner reasons was that they were unfit and claiming Invalidity Benefit. In the 1980s, the Conservative Administration encouraged workers made redundant by its reforms to claim Invalidity Benefit in order to massage the unemployment figures downwards during a time when it was under intense pressure about unemployment. The unemployed liked this because it increased their income so it has proved difficult to reverse, perhaps because receiving incapacity benefit with the approval of Government and medics fundamentally changes individuals' perception of themselves. Not surprisingly, invalidity benefit was claimed most frequently in areas of high unemployment, particularly where the coal and steel industries were lost.

Table 5.7 Some characteristics of the employment profiles of certain British cities

City	Population	Employment rate %	Unemployment rate %	Economically inactive %	% of inactive who want a job
Glasgow	557,350	60.1	11.3	32.2	46.1
Bristol	381,618	78.0	3.3	19.3	28.0
Edinburgh	448,080	77.3	3.8	19.6	25.7
Leeds	716,513	77.3	5.1	19.7	29.8
Manchester	422,302	60.2	9.1	33.8	20.9
Liverpool	441,477	59.5	10.8	33.3	22.6

Employment rate is that percentage of the population of working age in employment.
Unemployment rate is that percentage of the population of working age who were out of work at the time of the survey but available for work.
Economically inactive rate is that percentage of the population of working age who are neither working nor actively looking for a job. They may have retired early, be looking after their family or studying full-time. The proportion of this group who would actually like a job is shown in the last column.
Source: NOMIS Labour Force Survey 2001–2

In Glasgow, the scale of the problem of economically inactive citizens was huge in 2001 when an estimated 146,000 out of a population of 577,350 were either unemployed or economically inactive. One in four citizens was not contributing to the economy. In Leeds, by contrast, only one in ten was economically inactive, 74,000 out of a larger population of 716,513. Therefore, it seems unlikely that Glasgow's GDP per head would be higher than that of Leeds in the absence of higher productivity.

The reason why the effect of economic inactivity was so poisonous was that it was heavily concentrated in some areas where work seemed to be the exception rather than the rule. The areas blighted in this way suffered multiple handicaps which were often linked – unemployment, poor performance at school, teenage pregnancies and drug abuse leading to concentrations of the 'socially excluded' (see Chapter 9). However, there was a trend that suggested that the problem was lessening. Whereas in 1996 only 55% of the population of working age were in work, this figure had risen to 60% in 2000, 66% in 2003 and 69% in 2005, confirming that most of the new jobs were being taken by Glasgow residents so that the proportion of commuters in the workforce fell by about 3% between the censuses of 1991 and 2001. This suggests that the problem of social exclusion was being eroded as the pace of economic activity quickened.

Companies

Over the last decade of the 20th century, Glasgow created jobs as fast as any city in the UK and the increase in wealth creation was as good as most. What changed compared with the dismal performance over the rest of the post-war years?

Unfortunately this was not because dynamic new companies were being set up by enterprising citizens as happened in the 18th and 19th centuries. Government has collected statistics on the number of companies paying VAT since 1994. Not only has the stock of companies remained steady between 1994 and 2002, but, of all the cities, only Liverpool has a lower number of companies per head of the population. Indeed, Bristol, Leeds and Edinburgh all did better than Liverpool, Manchester and Glasgow, also suggesting that Britain has two types of cities.

The number of manufacturing companies decreased in all cities and those with the highest number at the start of the period decreased most, confirming that manufacturing was retreating throughout Britain during this period. Even so, Nottingham and Birmingham had twice as many companies of this type proportionate to population as Glasgow.

Companies dealing with public administration increased most: Edinburgh topped the league throughout but the number in Glasgow increased more than in any other city, rising by 41%. Surprisingly, the number of companies in the financial sector fell from 180 to 150 per 100,000 of the population over the period and the number of companies in the hotel and restaurant trades increased modestly from 1,220 to 1,260 per 100,000 of the population. Only Edinburgh had more of this type of company proportionate to population than Glasgow. The number of construction companies fell by nearly a quarter, from 1,210 to 920 per 100,000 of the population, despite the rebuilding programme.

Therefore, as expected, the company profile of the city continued the switch from manufacturing to services, particularly those dealing with the public sector and tourism. The rest of the service sector did not so much increase the number of companies as increase the number that the companies employed. The fact that Glasgow became attractive as a site for this type of investment reflects credit on the Council's campaign to change the city's image and the quality of the employees but does not signify a rebirth of entrepreneurial Glasgow.

The largest companies in and around Glasgow in 2004 are shown in Table 5.8. Two were concerned with supply of energy, the biggest by a huge margin; two were in the financial sector; two specialised in hiring industrial equipment; one was the company that runs Scottish Independent Television services; and only one specialised in manufacturing.

Table 5.8   Glasgow's largest companies

Name	Type	Value added £m	Name	Type	Value added £m
Scottish Power	Energy	2,195	Aggreko	Hires lighting and heating equipment	184
British Energy*	Energy	1,157	Hewden Stuart	Hires industrial equipment	169
Weir	Manufacturing	293	SMG	Media	123
Clydesdale Bank	Finance	234	William Grant*	Whisky	119
Arnold Clark Automobiles	Car Dealer	187	Abbey National Financial	Finance	114

*indicates company in Glasgow Region outside city limits.
Source: Glasgow Economic Audit 2004

Therefore, productivity, employment rates, earnings and company formation provide no explanation of why Glasgow's GDP per head is higher than most English cities as shown in Tables 5.2 and 5.3. Indeed, since productivity is lower in the city than the Metropolitan Region, why should GDP per head be £6,000 higher in the city? The only satisfactory explanation is the very high commuter contribution to the workforce.

This was confirmed by recent data from the ONS analysing factors contributing to the GDP per head of the ten richest NUTS 3 areas in the UK (see definitions page 91). Glasgow came tenth out of 133 with a GDP per capita about 30% above the UK average. The factors considered were commuting, activity rate, employment rate and productivity and the definitions and results are shown in Figure 5.6. The study concluded that commuting artificially enhanced Glasgow's GDP per head by more than 30%, since both activity rate and productivity were a little below the national average. Commuting artificially increases the GDP per head of cities at the expense of the commuting belts which explains why Dunbartonshire, where so many prosperous people working in Glasgow live, had the third lowest GDP per head among all NUTS 3 areas of the UK.

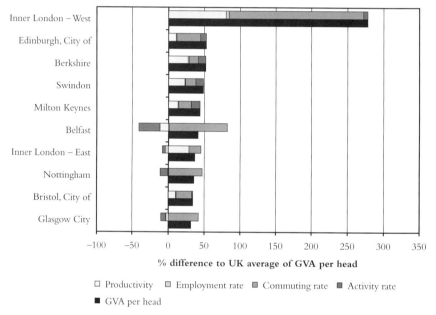

Figure 5.6   Analysis of differences in GVA per head from the UK average in the top ten performing NUTS3 areas, 2004 Productivity is output per worker, employment rate is defined here as workplace based employment as a proportion of the workforce, the activity rate was the proportion of the population in work and commuting was the workplace-based labour force as a proportion of the residence based labour force.

Source: Economic & Labour Market Review Vol 1, No 8, August 2007.

Glasgow is not unique in having GDP per capita boosted by commuters. Table 5.9 shows the values for some British cities and their regions. Most of the cities with the highest GDP per head had the biggest difference with their respective regions, suggesting that their GDP per capita was also overstated and none more so than Belfast. Edinburgh, on the other hand, benefited from commuting to a lesser extent and had an activity rate and productivity above the national average. Thus their GDP per head was only reduced from 150% of the national average to about 120% or about 25% higher than Glasgow's, closer to the BBC's estimate quoted at the beginning of this chapter.

Table 5.9   Comparison of GVA/head in selected cities and their regions

City (NUTS 3)	GVA/head 2001 (£)	Region (NUTS2)	GVA/head 2001 (£)	Difference %	Rank	
					City	Region
Inner London	34,888	London	22,236	56.9	1	1
Edinburgh	22,168	Eastern Scotland	13,866	59.9	2	6
Nottingham	20,782	Derbyshire and Nottinghamshire	13,066	59.1	3	8
Belfast	20,521	Northern Ireland	11,331	81.1	4	10
Bristol	19,450	Gloucestershire, Wiltshire and N Somerset	15,416	26.2	5	2
Glasgow	19,110	Southwest Scotland	12,831	48.9	6	9
Leeds	16,904	West Yorkshire	13,581	24.5	7	7
Cardiff and Vale of Glamorgan	16,074	East Wales	14,319	12.3	8	3
Birmingham	15,344	West Midlands	14,095	8.9	9	4
Greater Manchester	13,920	Greater Manchester	13,920	NA	10	5
Liverpool	13,317	Merseyside	10,414	27.9	11	11

The rank of the city or region refers to their ranking by GVA/head. Source: NUTS2 and NUTS3 data from ONS. (Note this data is from 2001 whereas data in Table 2 is from 2003)
Difference % shows the difference of GDP/head of city and region as a percentage of the region's
NA = not available

Therefore, the much vaunted resurgence of Glasgow's economy is true as far as the rate of change is concerned but the GDP per head has been overestimated by more than 30%. If the position of Glasgow in Table 5.2 is re-examined, its ranking may be not 11th but 19th or about the same level of Birmingham.

Nevertheless, Glasgow's economy grew more quickly than the UK average over the period, more than that of most other UK cities and more than that of the other counties in the region, and its prosperity increased quite dramatically between 1993 and 2004. It just has not been quite as successful in absolute terms as official figures have indicated.

Glasgow's image; opinion surveys

How do businessmen, responsible for decisions about where to invest, perceive the city? The most quoted survey is that of Cushman & Wakefield, Healy & Baker which ranks thirty European cities by various criteria in a survey of 500 European businessmen. The respondents were asked which qualities were most important in making a decision of where to invest. The most important four were availability of well qualified staff, ease of access to markets, the quality of telecommunications and how easy it was to travel to other cities. Only London, Manchester and Glasgow were included from Britain (until 2006 when Birmingham and Leeds were added). London, as usual, topped the poll by a huge margin but the other British cities came well down. Between 1990 and 2007, Manchester had slipped from 13th to 18th and Glasgow even more precipitously from 10th to 25th. Birmingham was 21st and Leeds 30th in 2007. The results are not particularly encouraging and Glasgow was ranked poorly in the four criteria that the businessmen thought most important. Only in cost of staff did the city do well, being ranked seventh. It is possible that the fall in the ratings may have been a product of success, with skilled labour and suitable office space becoming scarcer and more expensive as a result of the surge in the number of jobs created at the turn of the century. Or it may simply have been that the high rating in 1990 was while Glasgow was receiving favourable publicity during its year as European

City of Culture. The respondents admitted that less than half the cities were known well by at least half of them. Cities ranked lower than Glasgow included Rome, Helsinki and Moscow giving the strong impression that businessmen do not like operating in the periphery of Europe. Altogether, it is difficult to understand why so much importance is given to this survey but all councils including Glasgow's take notice of it.

In 2006, the same company produced a UK Cities monitor which reported the results of a survey of 14 UK cities conducted among 201 senior executives of UK companies. They ranked Glasgow seventh, behind London, Birmingham, Manchester, Leeds, Bristol and Sheffield. They thought it the best city to locate new backroom activities or a call centre but the eighth best for a new headquarters. Only four cities were thought to have better qualified workers available. Therefore, according to Cushman and Wakefield, Glasgow is little known on a European scale and lies in mid-table on a UK one.

There are other surveys: one by Matt Thomas reported in *Growing Business* March 2005 used data rather than opinions and came to the gratifying conclusion that Glasgow was the most business friendly out of 20 of the biggest cities in the UK. Seven criteria were used:

- Location (population; region)
- Workforce (availability; quality; skills; labour costs; universities)
- Premises (office stock; local authority business rates)
- Quality of life (house prices; schools; crime)
- Grants and funding (available grants; business angel networks; regional venture capital)
- Transport (average road speeds; motorways and airports)
- Business activity (business population; growth rate; corporate insolvencies)

The results were interesting in several ways. The top five cities in different categories were:

- The sexiest cities – London, Manchester, Leeds, Birmingham and Glasgow
- The worst for crime – Nottingham, Manchester, Edinburgh, Hull and Aberdeen
- For ease of help with funding – Sheffield, Glasgow, Liverpool, Edinburgh and London
- For availability and cost of premises – Liverpool, Birmingham, Manchester, Newcastle and Glasgow
- For quality, availability and expense of labour – Bristol, Edinburgh, Leicester, Cardiff and Belfast.

The sexiness of a city depended on the range of theatres, museums and other attractions available and, not surprisingly, London scored heavily. The speed of traffic was surprisingly high in Glasgow averaging 30.3mph compared to 11mph in London and house prices were about a third of those in the capital. Labour was cheaper but less skilled in Glasgow than London or Edinburgh but better and more expensive than in Leeds, Manchester and Liverpool. The overall top six were (with their scores):

1	Glasgow	69%
2	Birmingham	68%
3	London	68%
4	Edinburgh	67%
5	Coventry	66%
6	Liverpool	65%

The bottom five cities were:

16	Aberdeen	55%
17	Sunderland	54%
18	Belfast	53%
19	Southampton	53%
20	Hull	49%

The authors said of Glasgow:

> Glasgow is traditionally known for industry and football. While Rangers and Celtic are still locked in a fierce Old Firm rivalry, Glasgow in recent years has changed as a place to live and do business. A decade of aggressive regeneration is starting to pay dividends. Key prospering industries include financial and business services, communications, bioscience, software and tourism. The financial and business services now account for 24% of employment in Glasgow, while jobs in the knowledge industry have increased by 22% between 1998 and 2001.

Glasgow now boasts:

- higher employment gains than anywhere outside London
- 168,000 students (second only to London)
- 3.1 million tourists a year – the fastest rate of growth of all British destinations
- Europe's fastest growing conference destination – doubling market share since 1997
- More businesses than any other Scottish city
- Outward trade of more than £1b
- 62 university or research spin-out companies in the last five years.

The survey report then lists some of the plans of the City Council which I will come to later. In concluding, the authors comment:

> We found a city that ticked every box of what you need to successfully grow your company. Performing consistently well across all our criteria, Glasgow proved that, of all the cities facing a similar challenge, it's adjusted best to post-industrial life and recreated itself as a modern centre of entrepreneurial activity.

So if European businessmen do not know much about Glasgow, the city scores better among British businessmen. This may be the explanation for the surge in employment powered by companies with head offices elsewhere. What is needed next is some favourable publicity to bring these improvements to the attention of overseas businessmen. Cities like Barcelona, Madrid and Dublin were thought to be best at self-promotion and have benefited accordingly. Will the Commonwealth Games do the trick for Glasgow in 2014?

Surveys about the cost and quality of life within cities have been performed. Mercer Human Resource Consulting found that Glasgow was the second most expensive city in Britain and the 36th in the world in 2007 with an index of 88 compared to 100 for New York. London, naturally, was the most expensive city in the UK with an index of 126. What was more alarming was the speed of Glasgow's rise. In 2006, it ranked 60th with an index of 81. Birmingham was the third British city with a ranking of 41st and an index of 87. The same company produce a Quality of Living Survey which is really designed for businessmen to give a guide to the sort of life their employees may expect if working in the city. It is based on 39 criteria such as the quality and availability of housing, the quality of the social, political, and economic environments including shops and the availability and quality of recreational facilities. Glasgow came 55th out of 215 cities in 2007. London was the only British city in the world's top 50 but was ranked only 39th compared to Paris at 33rd and New York at 48th: so three of the sexiest cities were heavily out-scored by Zurich, Geneva and Vancouver which topped the poll.

When the residents of Scotland were asked what they thought about the place where they lived, 35% of Glaswegians thought Glasgow a very good place to live and 50% thought it fairly good. This compares with 48% and 45% respectively for Edinburgh, 53% and 41% for Aberdeen, 49% and 42% for Dundee and 52% and 41% for Scotland as a whole. Therefore, Glasgow's own inhabitants do not rate their city as enthusiastically as Scots do elsewhere. The figures would look better if East Dunbartonshire and East Renfrewshire were included. In these suburban counties populated by Glasgow commuters, all but 3% of their citizens rated their neighbourhood as a very good (67%) or fairly good (30%) place to live. The EU carried out an Urban Audit which examined residents' opinions about their city. When asked whether they liked living in their city, Glaswegians approval ratings were 12th out of 31 major European cities (Dr E Helander). More encouraging was the fact that most thought that Glasgow would improve over the next five years.

Audit

Progress has been audited by outside experienced consultants both for the region, as already de-scribed, and the city. The Glasgow Economic Audit of 2003, conducted by Experian, concluded that progress was mixed. Of the five headline indicators or targets which were set for 2005, three were met as early as 2003: the number of new jobs created, the rate of growth of the economy and the reduction in unemployment. However, social exclusion was still high and, lastly, attempts to reduce the area of derelict land had failed, indeed it actually increased, but the area of vacant land was reduced according to target. This progress shows both the strength and weakness of the recovery. Of the supporting indicators, the negative points were that growth in the sunrise industries such as chemicals, pharmaceuticals and opto-electronics was disappointing with only 2,960 jobs compared to a target of 4,500. The rate of new firm formation had not accelerated at all. These observations confirm the impression that the recovery in the city is due to jobs created by outside firms rather than any resurgence of enterprise in Glasgow.

CHAPTER 6

THE WIDER CONTEXT

The economy of every city has a national and international context heavily influenced by the actions of governments, local or national. Most agree that inappropriate governmental actions can easily ruin an economy but there is less agreement about whether governments can make one. Many, for whom Mrs Thatcher was such an effective spokesman, believe that Government usually acts incompetently and is more likely to hinder than help. They believe that its role is limited to removing unnecessary regulations and reducing taxes. Thereafter, it is the markets' job to do the rest. Adam Smith, whom Mrs Thatcher admired, was particularly scathing:

> It is the highest impertinence and presumption in politicians to pretend to watch over the economy of private people, and to restrain their expense. They are themselves always, and without any exception, the greatest spendthrifts in the society.
> Adam Smith, An Inquiry into the Nature and Causes of the Wealth of Nations

Ivor Tiefenbrun, a distinguished Glaswegian entrepreneur, who built up a company that made high quality record players, backs Adam Smith's judgement.

> economic growth and prosperity in Scotland have been thwarted, battered, dragged down and even 'hijacked' by more than 100 oppressive years of socialism … . Socialists are by nature and ideology intent on taxing businesses to the point of almost non-existence and too many want to rebuild the former Soviet Union in Western Europe.
> *The Herald* Dec 2004

He believes that entrepreneurs should be helped by grants from families or rich citizens prepared to invest in individuals. He was given his start by a grant from his father who, in turn, was helped by his employer to set up his first business. He thinks this is the best way to encourage entrepreneurs and, practising what he preaches, now helps the next generation. Families are indeed a major source of capital for those wishing to set up in business and the rich do support entrepreneurs. Sir Tom Hunter, who made his first fortune out of a sports equipment business, both endowed the Hunter Centre for Entrepreneurship at Strathclyde University and set up West Coast Capital for supporting new enterprises.

But the story is not that simple: there have been occasions when Government actions boosted the economy, for examples: the linen trade in Scotland in the 18th century; different Governments bailed out Rolls-Royce and Weir's both of which recovered to become jewels of manufacturing in the region; regional planning helped bring new jobs to the West of Scotland just before and after the Second World War; even more recently and at a European level, the rise and rise of Airbus serves as an example of effective central planning which created thousands of jobs in Europe and it became the biggest supplier of passenger aircraft in the world in 2004. The Scottish landscape is being filled with wind turbines, most of which were made in Germany or Denmark. The manufacturers consider that early help by their Governments was crucial in their success. Scottish companies received no help and, although early into the field, made little impact. Therefore, 'political' input is not without its successes. What the critics find difficult to accept are their failures, and of failures there have been plenty. However, the same is true in the private sector but the difference is that private failures lose private money whereas government failures lose ours.

Should the Government, local, national (Scottish or British) or super-national (EU) decide to inter-vene, it has various options. It can arrange a net transfer of funds to an under-performing region. Scot-land in general and the West of Scotland in particular have received and still receive a generous share of overt Government spending, partly due to the Barnett formula. (I have called it overt to distinguish it from covert spending from which London benefits – see below.) Government funded services are an important source of employment providing 115,000 jobs directly in the city and securing many more indirectly. A major hospital, for example, employs about 5,000 staff, making it one of the biggest employers in the city. However, although welcome, regular subsidy is not capable of transforming the economy to the standard of the premier European cities which is the council's ambition. The experi-ences of Eastern Germany or Southern Italy attest to that; Italy, in particular, is extraordinary because the North's GDP per capita is nearly twice that of the South despite all the cash transfers.

Secondly, Government can try to set up businesses by direct investment or by 'bribes' as did Harold Wilson when he persuaded Rootes to build cars at Linwood. The main policy of Scottish Enterprise in the 1990s was a variant of this approach, making inward investment attractive through direct grants. The boom in foreign-owned electronic factories followed and boosted Scotland's manufacturing sector and foreign earnings. However, it proved a temporary success, lasting not even as long as car making at Linwood. This form of governmental action is usually ineffective unless there are other advantages of investing in the area, in which case it may not be necessary.

Thirdly, it can encourage its own entrepreneurs to set up businesses with potential for growth. This is necessarily a long-term solution and would have little impact on the economy for a dec-ade or more. To foster an entrepreneur-friendly environment, Government can adjust taxes and regulations and teach the population the value of business to society. The Executive has started by ensuring that schoolchildren visit a business as part of their curriculum but trying to change Glaswegians' opinion about the value of business is a major undertaking. Remember the reaction of the press and public to the founding of a private hospital in Clydebank in the 1980s. Here was a town, scourged by unemployment following the near extinction of its two main industries, suddenly offered a new opportunity – a large private hospital that might provide numerous jobs and create opportunities for small local companies. The welcome was vitriolic perhaps because private medicine was considered parasitic on the NHS. One of the consultants recruited had been born in East Germany and then moved to the United States where he worked in the world-renowned Mayo Clinic. He thought the local response to the hospital was more like that of so-cialist East Germany than capitalist America. Not only has the entrepreneurial spirit of the 19th century vanished but it has been replaced by an antagonism to business rooted in folk memories of the exploitation that their forefathers suffered during Glasgow's period of economic pomp. For the re-emergence of entrepreneurship in the region, this has to be reversed.

Government can do its best to make the city an attractive and easy place in which to live and do business. It can ensure that there are suitable premises to house businesses, provide good trans-port links and educate the citizens to provide well qualified workers. This may also be achieved by encouraging suitable immigration. Lastly, it can lead a campaign to promote the city. Glasgow's profile in Europe is low and despite some successful attempts, most foreign businessmen surveyed did not know much about the city.

The record of Government (both local and central) in Scotland is mixed. Glasgow, like Scot-land, is a net recipient of Government spending and this has been a major source of new jobs which have helped to drive the local economy, as we have seen. Local Government has also vastly improved the local infrastructure.

But Government can also discourage enterprise. Firstly, they may spend too much. About 50% of Scotland's GDP was spent by the state in 2003 and even Jack McConnell thought this too high. It is a truism that the larger the share of national income spent by the state, the less sympathetic is the environment to business. There is one glaring exception to this apparent rule; the Scandinavian model. They have high levels of taxation – about 50% of GDP in Sweden and Denmark and a little lower in oil rich Norway. Consequently, their public services are excellent but they also have a very good record of setting up new businesses resulting in resilient economies. This may be because their culture is a peculiar mix of neighbourliness and business. *The Economist* even coined the word 'flexcurity' to describe Denmark's labour market. Often the Scandinavians seem to get the best of both worlds whereas other countries have to choose between them. It may be because their societies are more homogeneous so that the prosperous are prepared to help the less well off with whom they sympathise readily. This interpretation is supported by their surprisingly strong reaction to the recent burst of immigration, with the natives resenting paying for social services for people who have not contributed. Scotland is far from homogeneous and is famous for some of its prejudices. It does, however, enjoy a unique advantage in that it is taxed at the UK rate of 37% but spends at the Scandinavian rate of 50% – unless oil revenue is included. This may seem a wonderful outcome, and indeed it does have distinct advantages, but it stifles private initiatives if only by taking an unfair share of local talent which is then denied to the entrepreneurial and business sectors. This is the second way in which Government can stifle business. Many of the brightest students become civil servants, doctors, vets, lawyers and providers of other routine services: bright students apparently prefer jobs providing status and security with minimum risk. This has long been a problem in Britain, aptly illustrated by the lowly esteem accorded to engineers. It may be an even greater problem in the West of Scotland. Policies aimed at directing talent into business would help the local economy enormously.

Lastly, Governments can make it very laborious to run a business if they develop complicated rules on health and safety, taxation and pensions. The Burden of Regulation is measured and international tables prepared. The British economy remains relatively lightly regulated by international standards and this is considered a major attraction for inward investment. However, regulation has risen under the Labour Government and this colours the way that businessmen perceive it. One of the most persistent demands of businessmen in Scotland is for reductions in red tape.

Therefore, a Government wishing to encourage business is likely to choose policies that encourage and reward entrepreneurs, that build up suitable infrastructure and that educate the young in the value of business to society. Whether it takes the next step and arranges conditions so that they can flourish even at the expense of Government run services depends on the priority it attaches to this part of their programme. But there is a balance: business flourishes in a low tax environment but it also needs an educated workforce and decent infrastructure both of which depend on Government spending. This paradox can be solved during a virtuous cycle because tax receipts increase when business flourishes. However, the reverse cycle can also operate: a depressed economy leads to reduced Government income and increased expenditure on unemployment and social security. The reverse cycle operated for much of the 20th century, with the exception of the 20 years from 1955 to 1975, and Glasgow floundered. Its renaissance came as the cycle turned benign again in the last decade of the century.

Manufacturing or services?

Should Government decide to try to shape the economy, what should its priorities be and, in particular, does the current loss of manufacturing matter? Robert Walpole wrote in 1721 that 'nothing so contributes to promote the public wellbeing as the exportation of manufactured goods'. That was the time of the South Sea Bubble, one of the great speculative frenzies of British history. Has this truism become outdated? 'Don't weep for our lost factories' wrote Will Hutton (*Observer* December 2004). He thought it inevitable that manufacturing would move to where labour costs were cheaper: Chinese wages were a twentieth of British ones at that time, so why would anyone make anything in Britain unless the process required skills unobtainable in China? Even within the European Union, wages are significantly lower in the countries to the east and 'routine' manufacturing investment is likely to be concentrated there for some time to come. Nor should we attempt to run factories on low wages: we tried that in the 19th century and it led to the social blight that still afflicted whole suburbs of Glasgow 100 years later. What is needed, says Hutton, are high value jobs that design the products that are then produced in the East. Dyson, for example, moved their factories to Malaysia, made bigger profits as a result which allowed more investment in research in Britain. Since a significant proportion of manufacturing in the East is actually owned by companies from the West, profits can be spent on services in the owner's own country. It sounds logical but is it true?

How are the other countries of the developed world making the transition? Figure 6.1 shows that the proportion of the economy contributed by manufacturing between 1970 and 2003 declined in all the G7 countries and that the US had the smallest manufacturing sector as a proportion of their economy. Since the US is the leading economy, this process appears to support the Hutton hypothesis.

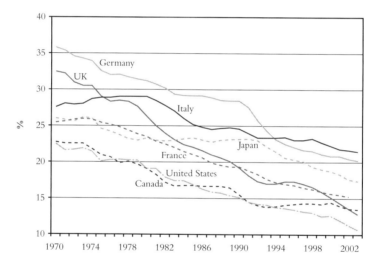

Figure 6.1   Percentage contribution of manufacturing to total GDP in the G7 economies from 1970 to 2003

Source: *OECD The changing nature of manufacturing in OECD economies* Pilat D, Cimper A, Olsen K and Webb C. 2006

But measuring manufacturing as a percentage of GDP may be misleading. Faster growth in the service sector automatically reduces manufacturing's share even if it continues to grow, albeit more slowly. The explanation could be that the British economy grew faster than those of France and Germany, for example, in the last few years, largely due to the expansion of the service sector and therefore the proportion of GDP generated by manufacturing decreased more. Another reason for the decline in manufacturing's share of GDP may be that inflation is higher in the service industries because the greater gains in productivity in manufacturing keep prices more stable. Therefore, developed countries may be growing by creating more and more services on the base of existing and successful manufacturing. Figure 6.2 confirms that the value of manufacturing output did indeed grow during the period between 1970 and 2002 in all G7 countries but that the growth was least in Britain, where it was only 20% greater in 2002 than 1974. Clearly, manufacturers in the other G7 countries, particularly the non-European members, coped with the new conditions better than the British.

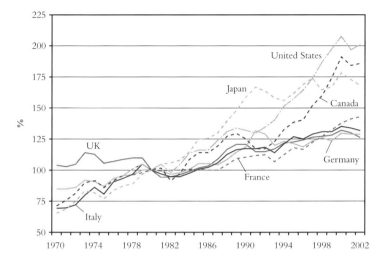

Figure 6.2   Index of manufacturing output in G7 countries between 1970 and 2002. 1980 = 100

Source: *OECD The changing nature of manufacturing in OECD economies* Pilat D, Cimper A, Olsen K and Webb C. 2006

Figure 6.3 shows the actual value of manufacturing output in the G7 countries expressed in dollars per head for 2002. The UK produced about the same as Italy or France but significantly less than the other four countries. The comparison with Italy is instructive because manufacturing accounted for a higher proportion of its GDP than in the economies of the other six countries and yet its absolute value per inhabitant was the lowest. This suggests that the Italians have a greater problem with their service sector than the UK has with its manufacturing sector.

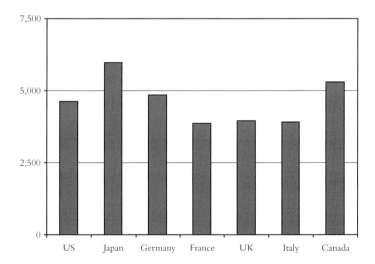

Figure 6.3   The value of manufacturing products produced in the G7 countries in 2002 expressed in $/head

Source: OECD, STAN database and UN Statistics Division.

GDP per head was highest in the US ($36,000 in 2002) but was much the same in the other six countries, varying between $30,000 in Canada and $27,000 in Italy. The US appears to be powering ahead in both services and manufacturing, but is it sustainable? The US and the UK had huge balance of payments deficits (Table 6.1) and the lowest savings ratios in the early years of the 21st century. In effect their economies are built on debt both to other countries and to their banks. On the other hand, Germany and Japan, where manufacturing counted for a bigger proportion of their economies, had massive balance of payments surpluses. The conclusion may be that once manufacturing falls below a certain share of the economy, a balance of payments deficit results because services suck in goods made elsewhere. All the countries of G7 with a positive balance of trade in goods had a surplus (Canada, Germany, Japan and Italy – just) whereas those with a positive balance on services all had an overall deficit (US, UK and France). Even in the UK with its vaunted service sector, the value of exports of services was less than half the value of exports of goods in 2005.

Table 6.1   Balance of trade in goods and services in the G7 countries in 2005

Country	Goods			Services			Combined
	Exports	Imports	Balance	Exports	Imports	Balance	Overall balance
Canada	11,265	9,682	1,583	1,670	1,973	−303	1280
France	7,217	7,686	−469	1,952	1,735	217	−252
Germany	11,920	9,546	2,374	1,980	2,552	−572	1801
Italy	6,401	6,389	12	1,537	1,548	−11	1
Japan	4,463	3,718	745	833	1,051	−219	526
UK	6,347	7,397	−1,050	3,455	2,716	738	−312
US	2,961	5,567	−2,606	1,286	1,045	241	−2365
Euro	4,721	4,549	172	1,563	1,422	140	312

Values are $ per capita for each of the G7 countries. Source OECD modified for population.

The results of the balance of trade in goods and services shown in Table 6.1, which is standardised by showing the values per capita. The value of goods exported by each American is about a quarter that of each Canadian. There is little wrong with the UK's exporting prowess in goods except that its appetite for imported goods is so much bigger.

Is this imbalance widespread within the UK? If the economies of the regions of the UK are analysed, it is clear that those with a low proportion of manufacturing had a balance of payments deficit: London, the Southeast and the East of England, the only regions in which manufacturing accounted for less than 20% of their economy (Figure 6.4), were responsible for most of the country's balance of payments deficit (Figure 6.5).

The British balance of payments deteriorated in the 2000s. The ONS commented on the figures for 2004:

> for the year as a whole, the UK's deficit on goods and services rose to a record £39.3 billion. A record surplus on trade in services of £18.3 billion partly offset a record deficit of £57.6 billion on trade in goods. Excluding oil and erratic items, the volume of exports were up by two per cent while imports rose by five and a half per cent to reach a record annual level.

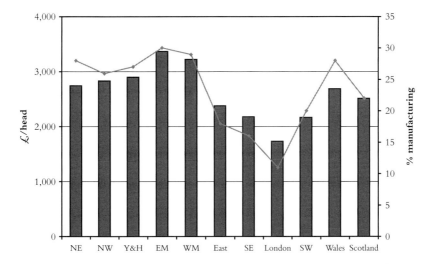

Figure 6.4   Size of manufacturing sector in different regions and countries of Britain (expressed in £/head) (columns) and the contribution of manufacturing to regional GDP (line) in 1998. NE=Northeast, NW=Northwest, Y&H=Yorkshire and Humberside, EM=East Midlands, WM=West Midlands, East=East of England, SE=Southeast and SW=Southwest. Oil and gas not included.

Source: ONS

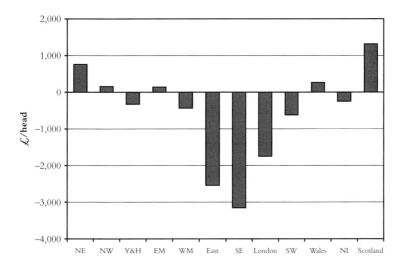

Figure 6.5   Contributions to the balance of trade by the different regions of the UK in 2001 expressed as £/head. NI=Northern Ireland,.

Source: ONS

Thus, even the vaunted service industry with its huge foreign earnings was incapable of meeting the bills the British ran up with foreign manufactures. And this was at a time when Britain was still producing oil and gas. The conclusion from these data is that the manufacturing sector is of vital importance: once it falls below a certain level, the country is unable to earn enough foreign currency to pay for its imports. Increasing personal debts (Figure 6.6), fuelled by the easy availability of credit, leads to deficits in the balance of trade. The huge success of London as a financial centre seems to have blinded many to its influence on the imbalance in the country's books.

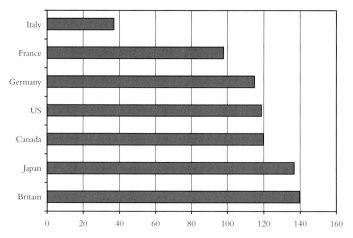

Figure 6.6   Household debt as % of disposable income in 2003 (Japan and Italy 2002).

Source: *Economist* Feb 2005

Although manufacturing is seen as dispensable in Britain, it is considered vital in Europe. In the EU 15, manufacturing contributed 22% of GDP in 2003 compared to 16% in the UK. High-level committees discuss what needs to be done to keep it alive. This summary appeared in December 2004:

> Today, Europe's manufacturing industry directly contributes around 22 per cent of EU GDP. However, it is estimated that each job in manufacturing is linked to two jobs in manufacturing related services, ensuring that an estimated 75 per cent of EU GDP and 70 per cent of jobs depend on the manufacturing sector.
>
> As a result, many analysts believe that if Europe is to become the world's most competitive knowledge-based economy by 2010, the presence of a strong and competitive manufacturing sector is indispensable. In this context, the Commission invited a high level group of executives from research organisations and industry to develop a shared vision of the way ahead for EU manufacturing, and on 6 December they published the report MANUFUTURE – a vision for 2020.

No such discussions seem to occur in Britain despite the key observation that manufacturing underwrites most other jobs. The Chancellor frequently argues that the British economy is more successful than those of other big European countries and that they should follow our model. After all, in 2004, Britain had lower unemployment, a higher GDP per capita and faster growth than Italy, France or Germany. But Britain has a chronic trade deficit, even when invisibles are taken into account, amounting to about 2% of GDP (compared to a surplus of 3% in Germany) while benefiting from the temporary advantages of North Sea oil and gas. Is it sustainable? Once individuals start to reduce their debts, the high personal spending that spurred on the economy in the Labour years will bring growth to a halt.

The centre of Britain's service industry is the fabulously successful City of London. Ever since it was set free by the Big Bang of the Thatcher era, it has grown prodigiously and made London one of the great world cities. Could the failure of Britain's manufacturing sector to grow at the same pace as that of other G7 countries be due to the precedence given to the financial sector based in London?

The London effect and the advantages of being a capital city

The sheer size and success of London's economy affects the rest of the country. It is massive by European standards. It produces almost a fifth of the UK's total GDP with an eighth of the population; next in size is Paris with an economy a little over half the size of London's. As always, definitions can be difficult: the economy of the Ile de France, which may be described as greater Paris, is 28% of the French total and is bigger than London's. Paris and London have a lot in common. They are by far the largest and richest cities in their respective countries whereas the provincial cities of both countries do poorly, particularly when compared to the very successful western German and even northern Italian provincial cities. Do French and English cities do badly because of the dominance of their capitals? Do German and Italian provincial cities do well because they operate in 'young' countries where the capitals do not have the same historical advantages? Table 6.2 shows the relative wealth of the richest regions of the four countries in 2005. The London and Paris regions were the richest by far in their respective countries – only the Southeast of England was above the national average in the UK and all French regions were below their average. Is it possible that these older countries, more centrist in their organisation, still make decisions to bolster the role of their capital cities at the expense of the provinces?

Table 6.2   Relative wealth of different countries contrasting their capitals' regions with the next five wealthiest regions

UK	119.3	France	111.9	Germany	115.2	Italy	104.8
London	185.2	Ile de France	172.6	Berlin	98.5	Centro	118.1
Southeast	130.0	Centre Est	109.5	Hamburg	202.1	Nord Ovest	127.3
East	113.6	Sud Ouest	99.9	Bremen	157.1	Nord Est	125.2
Scotland	113.3	Ouest	99.6	Hessen	139.5	Sud	69.6
Southwest	111.7	Méditerranée	99.6	Bayern	128.8	Isole	70.6
East Midlands	109.1	Est	97.9	Baden-Wurttemburg	128.8		

GDP per capita expressed as PPS (purchasing power standard) with EU 27=100 for 2005. The value for the countries is given in the top row and for the five richest NUTS1 regions in the rows below. Italy is divided into only five NUTS 1 regions, fewer than half the other countries. Rome is in the Centro region and Paris in the Ile de France. Source Eurostat.

In Britain, during most of the 20th century, there was a migration to the south where the opportunities were. This resulted in a huge loss of population in many northern regions, especially the West of Scotland. At first, London and Birmingham were the prime destinations, but the decline of the British motor industry left the Southeast with no rivals. New industries, based on new technologies, spread along the M4 and M11 corridors. London became by far the richest region of the country by 2005 with a per capita GDP of €46,524 compared to €28,468 per Scot. Only London, the Southeast and the Southwest improved their share of national GDP in the preceding five years; all the Northern Regions as well as Scotland and Wales lost ground.

The reason for the dominance of London and the Southeast is not that their population is somehow more dynamic and able than in the rest of the UK, but that it has advantages given to it by Government: it is the centre of administration so a high proportion of the country's highest paid civil servants work in London (attempts to send them to the provinces have never been successful); it is the location for all foreign embassies and a large number of headquarters of businesses, unions and charities; many of the major galleries, museums and other artistic establishments are there. The salaries of the top people working in these institutions are high and often have to be boosted by London weighting so that they can afford to pay prices raised by overcrowding. These salaries are spent in London making the local economy even more dynamic. Successive Governments have also taken care to endow the capital with the first of everything and if the second was too expensive then other cities have gone without. For these, the rest of the country pays a hefty subsidy to maintain the capital. London is a city choking on the goodies tossed its way by Governments, past and present. Wealth attracts services and the cycle is reinforced.

London dominates almost all aspects of national life. Take transport as an example. Look at a map of the nation's motorways – about 80% head straight for London. The first East–West motorway north of London is the M62 connecting Liverpool, Manchester and Leeds. The only one further north is the M8 connecting Glasgow and Edinburgh, surely the poorest motorway in Western Europe connecting two comparable cities. No motorway from anywhere runs to Felixstowe, Britain's main commercial port, and the rail link is a single track branch line. That is truly remarkable and cannot help exports of manufacturing. A journey from Glasgow to the continent by road is painful. Going south from Glasgow (or Manchester or Liverpool), after the congestion of Birmingham, you have to head for the overcrowded M25, a motorway ring road around London built to ease congestion but resulting in more commuting thus adding to the potential population of the city and congestion for all its users.

Other forms of transport present their own problems. Going directly by air only became possible with the advent of budget airlines. It has taken their entrepreneurs to 'beat' Government planners whose favoured option remains a dominant airport hub in the southeast. Planners feared that if Heathrow did not offer whatever the major airlines demanded, they would transfer to a continental airport and London would suffer. Traffic using Heathrow regularly threatens its capacity and the solution has always been to expand at Heathrow or another south-eastern airport. The three BAA airports in the Southeast of England are all bigger than any other British airport. Manchester came closest with 20 million passengers in 2003 compared to 20.5million at Stansted, 30 million at Gatwick and 63 million for Heathrow. Just 8.1 million went through Glasgow and 7.8 million through Edinburgh that year. To fly to any British provincial city from abroad, a businessman would have to go through a southern airport. That is not hugely attractive and is something that the Scottish Executive has tried to improve with limited success.

A rail journey to France presents similar problems. The extension of the TGV north of the channel was planned to connect to the northern cities but the cost was too high and only the section to London, costing over £6b, was completed even though it only saved 20 minutes. Were you to start in any of the great northern cities of the UK, you would find your journey slow, crowded and often late because of failure to invest over the years. You would also find it impossible to avoid London where you must change not only trains but stations too. The West Coast mainline is being upgraded at a cost of about £8b, only marginally more than getting the TGV to London: this is a powerful signal that communications for Londoners with the continent are more important than British internal communications.

All this infrastructural favouritism has led to London being the businessman's favourite European city in which to do business. This in turn has attracted ambitious young people south to advance their careers. The resulting overcrowding has made London an increasingly unpleasant place to live and Government is under intense pressure to solve the bottlenecks so that more people can be accommodated. London's dominance of the economy and transport cuts the Northern cities off from their European markets leading to the relative isolation of other UK cities. This results in the absurdity of plans to build more houses in the Southeast and to demolish unwanted houses in the North.

Many Londoners would disagree with this analysis. They seriously think that the rest of the country holds London back! They argue that anyone with ambition moves to London because the Northern cities are not dynamic enough to offer similar opportunities. Success must be reinforced and this justifies further infrastructural investment. They sometimes dream of independence for the Southeast of England which would become one of the wealthiest European states and all the more prosperous for shedding the burden of the North. The following extract is from the website of Business Europe;

> The gap between Government revenue raised in London and the level of public spending within the capital amounts to what is commonly termed the 'London deficit'. The current balance of revenue against expenditure means that the capital pays more in tax than it receives in public spending.
>
> Estimates as to the full extent of the London deficit vary according to whether measurement is based on a residency or employment basis, but it is generally accepted to fall between £15 and £20 billion. If employment is used as the basis for measurement, the reality is almost certainly the higher figure. Latest figures from the London School of Economics (LSE) estimate London's contribution to be up to £17.45 billion. Between 2001 and 2002, London paid between 16.5% and 17.4% of total taxation in the UK, while receiving 14% of public expenditure (LSE, *London's Place in the UK Economy 2003*, Corporation of London October 2003). It is true that London does receive more Government expenditure than any other English region, amounting to £42.2 billion or £5,874 per head of the (residency) population, 17% above the English average (LSE, *London's Place in the UK Economy 2003*, Corporation of London October 2003). Nonetheless as the latest figures reveal, London still contributes more than it receives in Government expenditure. The 'City' alone is estimated to contribute as much as £8 billion (net) to the UK economy. Moreover, and significantly, this does not tell the whole story. For example this expenditure includes the provision of services such as the Civil Service, based in London yet benefiting the UK as a whole. (LCCI London Economy Research Programme, *London's contribution to the UK economy*, December 2002). Additionally, regional funding is determined according to population size, which fails to account for the large number of people who live outside London but commute into it on a daily basis. London's idiosyncratic work patterns are being overlooked in the funding formulae.

There is one argument in the passage which is completely specious. Senior civil servants do indeed work for the whole country and everyone contributes to their salaries but they spend them in London and the home counties. So money is raised in Yorkshire, for example, but spent around London thus enriching all the services providers in that area to the detriment of those in Yorkshire. Even the balance of taxation described may be inaccurate. The following extract appeared in the *New Statesman* in November 1999:

> all the candidates (in the London mayoral campaign) seem convinced that the rest of Britain – and particularly Scotland – owes its living to London … were it not for the huge dynamism, efficiency, enterprise and all-round economic virtue of London and Londoners, the rest of Britain would be in a terrible pickle. This, they suggest is especially true of Scotland, a society that only exists thanks to all those London generated tax pounds that are diverted up the M6 and A1.

Greater London and the South-east of England are by far the most heavily subsidised, tax-cosseted, feather-bedded regions of Britain, bar none. The array of public spending programmes and tax favouritism that is available around the Great Wen would, if known about, turn the rest of this green and pleasant land even greener with envy. But the rest of Britain does not know.

Take for example, public spending. There are two definitions of public spending: what the Treasury warlocks call 'identifiable' public spending and what they refer to as 'total' public spending. The gap between the two is enormous. At a recent count it was in the region of £30 billion. It may be more. Which raises the questions: what are the billions spent on? And where is the spending done?

The answers are that most of the money goes on defending the realm and funding the panoply of Her Majesty's Government. And most of that is done in the South-east of England and, particularly, London. Almost all the huge apparatus of the British state is concentrated in London and the South-east: the Government offices, the Government research centres, the Government test centres and the Government funded research councils.

George Rosie, the author, points out that almost all the 42 defence agencies were in the South and only two in Scotland. Most of the BBC's budget of £2.1 billion (this was in 1999) was spent in London, only 16% going to the provinces. Remember too that the £30 billion he estimated as part of the unofficial subsidy of the Southeast was more than the budget of the Scottish Executive. To this has to be added the boost to London's economy given by the high salaries of headquarter staff so the average salary of Londoners was about a third higher than the average British salary. Ah, say the Londoners, but it costs so much more to live in London. This is true but even so the disposable income is also higher in the south (Figure 6.7). Thus London and the Southeast have the highest GDP per head, the highest salaries and the highest disposable income. Londoners have more than compensated for the higher cost of living.

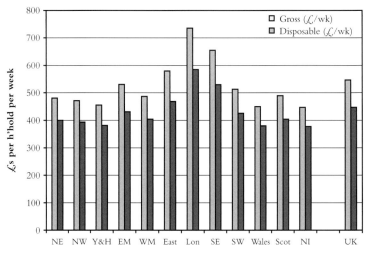

Figure 6.7   Regional per capita household income, 2001–3 From *Income Wealth and Inequality*,

Source: House of Commons 2004.

Interestingly, London and the Southeast share one other characteristic: they are almost entirely responsible for the country's balance of trade problems (see Figure 6.5). The frustrated

Northerner might complain that not only does he subsidise the Londoner's way of life but also that he or she uses that wealth to make matters worse by spending too much on foreign products.

The Scots are not the ones with the biggest cause to complain. The large Northern English cities have suffered more. The deputy prime minister suddenly discovered in the second term of the Labour administration that they were under-performing economically in comparison with equivalent European, particularly German, cities. To quote from an Independent report in January 2004 of the resulting study commissioned by Mr Prescott,

> Many (English cities) lag behind their competitors (in Europe) in terms of GDP, innovation, education, connectivity, social cohesion, quality of life, political capacity and connections with their wider territories. Crucially, they lag behind in the eyes of international investors.

It sounds like a list caused by under-investment. What was not highlighted was that the performances of French provincial cities were nearly as bad. So both Britain and France have huge and successful capitals and poorly performing provincial cities. The obvious explanation is that both capitals have been the recipients of unparalleled Government largesse over the years. They act as magnets for businesses and talented, well-qualified workers, sucking the vitality out of provincial towns. Scotland, being further away and having its own national institutions, is not so deeply in the shadow of the London upas tree, a tree that is said to suppress all life around it. And that may be one reason why Edinburgh and perhaps Glasgow have higher GDP per head than Manchester, Liverpool and Birmingham.

Apart from attracting more than its share of investment and talented youngsters, the sheer scale of the success of London's service sector has two other consequences which damage the manufacturing sector. It leads to higher interest rates than suits manufacturing which in turn causes a higher valuation of the currency. One makes it more expensive to invest and the other makes it more difficult to sell goods abroad. After all, interest rates have never been raised because the economy in the North was overheating. The fact that interest rates are perpetually higher than needed in the provinces inevitably diminishes the contribution of their manufacturing businesses to the economy and led to widespread closures in the Thatcher years. In January 2005 (as I write), the European Central Bank has set interest rates 2.75% below the rate set by the Bank of England even though at that time inflation was higher in Euroland. No wonder that investment in British factories is among the lowest in Europe. The higher interest rates are required to reduce spending partly stimulated by increases in the value of houses. This started in London where the housing pressure is greatest. Services, particularly those in London, thrive because the interest rates set by the Bank of England are low for London but high for the North. Therefore, London's success increases its role partly by diminishing the contribution of other regions. To this extent, Londoners' opinion that the rest of the country depends on them is becoming more justified.

Without high interest rates, the value of the currency would fall until the country's manufacturing products became more competitive and investment in them would become a more attractive proposition. Northern cities would then contribute more. As it is, all of them are moving from manufacturing into services and an unbalanced economy. The UK Government has regarded London as the pearl in the oyster; it must be protected or the whole country will suffer – particularly as most British economists, planners and commentators (usually London based) consider that manufacturing is not viable in advanced economies. In their judgement, Britain is ahead of the game because it has embraced the transition to services earlier than its rivals. They had better be right or we are in deep trouble. An interim judgement is that London, successful though it is, is not big enough to be the only motor in the British economy and yet policy decisions in its favour curtail the development of other motors.

Mitigating the London effect

Would a reduction in London's dominance help or would the whole country be diminished? I suspect that it would help significantly. Most British provincial cities have great difficulty in becoming known to the outside world. Foreigners usually only think positively of London; for them Manchester is still the hell described by Engels and Glasgow still retains the aura described in *No Mean City*. When Manchester and Birmingham applied for the Olympic Games, they got nowhere. The considered verdict was that, if Britain were to host the Olympics, it would have to be in London because it was the only 'acceptable' British city. Yet Manchester's hosting of the Commonwealth Games was a huge success. Of course, now that London has been awarded the Olympic Games, substantial investment will be necessary so there will be less for other cities. Similarly, the table of European cities in which businessmen want to do business has London top by a huge margin (with Paris second). Glasgow got as high as 10th shortly after being in the public eye as European City of Culture but slid down the league thereafter with most business-men professing to know little about the city.

A city may increase its profile by a propaganda coup such as putting on the Olympics or be-coming European City of Culture but it must also invest in suitable infrastructure to back up the propaganda coup. How do Manchester, Liverpool and Glasgow get a decent rail service except by major public investment? How can northern airports be developed when the Southeast has priority? How realistic is it that any Government would reverse its policies and, for example, provide a TGV to the north, decant all future gains in air traffic to a northern hub airport such as Manchester and build a road to the south coast that is sufficiently far from London to avoid commuter traffic? It is difficult to imagine, which shows how widely the present priorities have been accepted. If London had to get by with its present infrastructure, it would become an even more unpleasant place to live and thus encourage dispersal of firms, charities and others to save money by moving north where affordable housing is available. Unthinkable, so build the fabu-lously expensive Crossrail which will cost about double the amount spent on upgrading the West Coast main line.

On the other hand, London is the motor that drives the British economy at a time when all other motors are broken. Without London sending service jobs north, would the relative renaissance of provincial cities have happened? The problem with this model is that if London's economy stalls, the rest of the country will too; there is simply no second string and without encouragement of the peripheral economies none will be forthcoming.

There are at least three positive ways in which Government could reduce the pressure on London. First, it could be divested of some of its functions. The most radical solution would be to move Government north taking ministries and foreign embassies with it. This would lessen the pressure on London's housing and routine services such as health, education and transport and, more importantly, spur the development of better links between northern cities and Europe. The periodic bouts of house price inflation would be less likely and interest rates lower as a result. It would also move the centre of attention northwards. The plan is far too radical even to be considered but the Government could decide to reduce the heavy subsidies that are given to London, for example in R&D grants, encourage head offices of quangos, charities, professional bodies and others to leave by bribing them heavily. (Incidentally, how do charities justify having head offices in London?)

A second option would be to join the euro. Euroland would then become our 'economic country' and, because of its size, the currency's value would not be so heavily weighted by the performance of London. Investment would benefit from lower interest rates and exporting companies would enjoy the advantages of negotiating contracts with our main customers without having to worry about exchange rate fluctuations. The downside would be that London's economy would overheat and its present problems be accentuated, at least in the short term. This is the main reason why we have not joined as yet. On the other hand, many consider that London's future as the premier European financial centre is not secure in the medium term if the UK remains outside the euro. Therefore, a bit of pain for London may be worth its long-term gain. Even the short-term pain could be mitigated if London were to shed some of its present functions.

The third possibility, at least for Scottish cities, is an independent Scotland using either an independent currency or the euro. This is in some ways a more practical solution. If it joined the euro at the right rate, industry would be encouraged by lower interest rates and trade with Euroland, already our major export market for manufactured goods, would increase. A parliament responsible for all aspects of Scotland's prosperity would be able to enact measures to take full advantage of the opportunities. There would, of course, be a considerable price to pay in the short term as public spending would be reduced but this would free manpower for new businesses and could encourage another wave of inward investment (see Chapter 10).

Even so, the dominance of London has helped the recent welcome expansion in the economies of British provincial cities as it sites back offices and branch offices further north but the difference between them and prosperous German cities remains huge. It also makes northern cities dependent on the health of London's financial sector.

Conclusions

London is a big success but is it big enough? It has spearheaded the recent surge in economic growth around the country but at the cost of vast borrowing. The economy is too dependent on services and has an inadequate production base. As a result, the UK has perennial balance of payment deficits. Add in the recent milestone of personal debt which exceeded £1 trillion in 2004 and it is clear that, like the US, much of Britain's recent good record on growth has been achieved by borrowing. When the borrowing stops, a major slowdown is inevitable.

CHAPTER 7

PLANNERS' SCHEMES FOR GLASGOW

Introduction

If the Council's ambition to take Glasgow into the top tier of European cities were to be realised, the economy will have to change up another gear. But what sort of economy should be encouraged? If you were to rank the different sectors in order of their importance, manufacturing jobs may be worth more than service ones since they create more wealth per employee and because services thrive in areas with wealth to spend and will therefore follow automatically. That is not to underestimate the value of service industries especially those that earn foreign currency, such as the Scottish Exhibition and Conference Centre (SECC).

Home-grown manufacturing jobs may be worth more than imported ones if only because their head offices will be located in the city and they are less likely to pull out when times are difficult, as happened when the electronic bubble burst late in the 1990s. However, it takes time for indigenous industries to develop whereas foreign companies can set up large factories employing significant numbers of workers quickly. Therefore, Government should encourage manufacturing rather than services; home grown rather than imported; many small companies rather than one big one; high value added rather than assembly lines; these should be the priorities for development.

There is one big problem with manufacturing, as Will Hutton pointed out: it can usually be done more cheaply elsewhere. Only processes that require high levels of skills and lead to high productivity are likely to survive in high cost areas of the developed world. Furthermore, processes that require unusual skills one year may be automated or become routine enough for the process to be exported the following year. There is more chance of success if numerous small-scale projects are encouraged. This usually leads to another problem: small companies are good at innovation but poor at marketing and evolution of their products which is usually done better by large companies. There is, therefore, a strong likelihood that a promising start-up company will be bought up by a larger company in order to acquire the patent and expertise. Since there are few companies of this size in the region, it is probable that many promising small companies will be swallowed up and be lost to the local economy unless used for product development and design. Even then, the headquarters are likely to be elsewhere. Therefore, the odds against such a policy transforming the regional economy are long especially as encouraging entrepreneurs is difficult in the West of Scotland where antipathy to business is ingrained in the culture.

Assuming that such a plan is adopted, who should be responsible for its implementation? There are only two candidates – free enterprise and Government. Since there are no remaining industrial giants

left in the West of Scotland, Government or its agencies have to take the lead. Individuals with expertise and cash could help, as suggested by Ivor Tiefenbrun, but it is doubtful whether the funds available
would be sufficient for the task even if the budding entrepreneur could find a willing backer. Business
angels and venture capitalists do contribute significantly but do not deal with the earliest stages of
company development. That means that it falls to Government to fulfil the roll, directly or indirectly.

If this policy were successful, a series of companies starting up, expanding or failing, but succeeded by the next wave, would follow. The expected life of enterprises set up in Scotland is not
long with less than 40% surviving eight years. If one in fifty becomes a big fish lasting 20 or 30
years, it may well repay much of the cost of the whole programme for those years. The big prize
would be to gain and keep a company big enough to acquire some of the start-up companies and
to invest in developing and marketing their products. This would be the beginning of a cluster
which is crucial to moving up a gear.

In essence, this is the approach adopted by Government.

Plans for Glasgow

Whatever Glasgow lacked at the beginning of the 21st century, it was not short of plans. Over the
previous 20 years, the City Council had generated 43 plans. The last of that generation to enter the
portfolio was the Greater Easterhouse Local Plan of March 1998. This multiplicity led to confusion
and lack of focus so, sensibly, all were scrapped and an overall plan for the city drawn up. This was called
the Joint Economic Strategy and was launched in 1999. In March 2001, the Glasgow Economic Forum was formed to edit and modify the plan. Many organisations contributed to this Forum including the City Council, Scottish Enterprise, Glasgow (the successor of GDA), the Glasgow Chamber of
Commerce, the institutes of further education and the Scottish Trade Union Congress.

There were several objectives:

1   To halt and reverse the decline in population. Single people tended to be attracted into Glas-
    gow only to leave when they got married and had children. The plan called for appropriate
    housing to try to stem the loss of families. New estates on brown-field land in Garthamloch,
    Ruchill, Drumchapel and Oatlands were planned as well as on some smaller green-field sites
    resulting in a possible 1,950 new houses.
2   To continue to generate jobs and to do so in such a way that deprived areas receive some of the
    benefit. The method chosen to fulfil this ambition was to build high quality business premises in ar-
    eas of need in order to encourage development. The Council undertook to ensure a supply of land
    suitable for development by industry or business. It proposed four Core Economic Development
    areas in Govan, North Clyde, the East End and North Glasgow. Seven sites were identified where
    amenities for business and industry would be built or expanded at Cambuslang Investment Park,
    Robroyston Business Park, Cardonald Park, West of Scotland Science Park, Pacific Quay, Glasgow
    and College Business Parks. The plan noted that earlier development of some of these parks had
    helped to transform the city's reputation as a place to do business.
3   To develop a transport system with as little dependence on private cars as possible. Car owner-
    ship in Glasgow is among the lowest in the UK which undoubtedly helps congestion. How-
    ever, a large proportion of commuters use their cars. This will be discouraged by progressively
    reducing available car parking space. Plans for housing and businesses will be constructed so
    that workers can live near their employment. Cycle paths will be developed to encourage
    bicycle use. Business' transport problems will be eased by the completion of the M74 link-
    ing the present M8 south of the Kingston Bridge with the M74 heading south. This should
    reduce the congestion on the Kingston Bridge. A separate road, the East End regeneration

route, will connect the M74 completion at Polmadie through the East End of Glasgow to the M80/M8 junction at Provan Road. This is expected to encourage businesses to locate along its route. The suburban rail network is one of the largest in Britain and its capacity will be increased by the Cross Clyde Link. Buses are the most commonly used form of transport in the city. Express bus routes will be allocated to encourage their use and discourage cars. The underground is at near capacity despite a significant upgrade in the last decade. A planned rail link to the airport should improve speed of access to the city centre making the airport more attractive and Glasgow more accessible to visitors.

4 To nurture the environment by which was meant looking after the buildings, particularly old ones, and transforming some 800 hectares of derelict land that blight the city.

5 To maintain the city centre as the second ranked key retail area in the UK and to develop it as the entertainment and tourist centre for the Clyde Valley. It was hoped that as many of the service companies as possible would use the city centre although it was recognised that the old buildings were not always suitable for modern office accommodation. Alternative uses for these premises would be considered provided they added to the vibrancy of the area.

6 To improve the banks of the Clyde so that the river becomes reconnected with the city.

7 To concentrate development in areas of deprivation covered by the Social Inclusive Partnership (SIP) programmes of which there were eight, each responsible for development in a defined deprived area. Plans will be constructed in consultation with all interested groups of these areas.

8 To improve the skills of the unemployed or economically inactive by training projects in, for example, the construction industry and by the Glasgow Literacy and Action Plan.

9 To harness the expertise available in the city's universities by developing City Science in the Merchant City. £56m will be invested with the expectation of creating 3,000 new jobs, a cost of under £19,000 per job (and therefore unrealistic unless private companies invest much more). The College Business District will be developed nearby for the purpose of nurturing businesses spun off by City Science.

How have they got on? It is too early to judge definitively but there are early indications. The decline in the population has been slowed or halted. Censuses are only performed every ten years, but more informal assessments showed that the population was stable in the first five years of the new century.

There has been steady progress in the building of business parks. The first serious step along this path was taken well before the Joint Economic Strategy was written. In 1993, a report prepared by the City Council's planning department identified the lack of good quality, well-equipped buildings as a drag on growth. Companies often had to move elsewhere to expand. The same failing discouraged inward investment. The report recommended that sites should be developed with easy access to the motorway system. Suggested options were: Cambuslang Investment Park, Robroyston, West of Scotland Science Park, Darnley Mains and Springhill (since renamed Glasgow Business Park). This approach was almost precisely the same as had been adopted in the late 1930s with the construction of the Industrial Parks at Hillington, Shieldhall and elsewhere to mitigate the effects of the slump of that time.

In 1994, the Glasgow Regeneration Alliance Industrial Strategy Group was formed, comprising officials of the City Council, Strathclyde Regional Council and Glasgow Development Agency. This group drew up a plan called the Strategic Industrial Sites Programme which aimed to build premises attractive to businesses wishing to expand or to set up in Glasgow. Over 200 hectares has been converted for industrial use. Figure 7.1 shows the geographical location of the three phases of the project. Ease of access to motorways has proved a key ingredient in the success of the different areas.

As a result of this building programme, the city increased its share of business development in the Metropolitan Region from 5.4% in 1995/96 to 27.9% in 1998/99 and the sites accounted

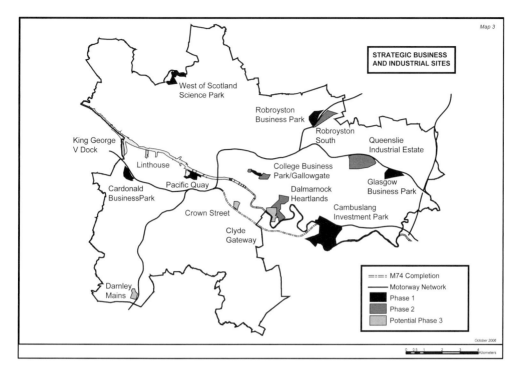

Figure 7.1   Plan of business parks in Glasgow. Motorways, including the southern connection between the
M74 and M8, are shown.

Source: Report by Director of Development and Regeneration Services 2006.

for over 33% of industrial/business development in the City in 1998/99. However, the director
of this programme's opinion in 2006 still maintained that lack of developed industrial or commercial premises was a constraint on growth. Unfortunately, older premises continue to deterio-
rate and the director's report continued:

> Over 50% of the City's industrial property is over 20 years old and around 10% of floorspace
> is vacant, although vacancy rates as high as 30% are experienced in some areas. Higher vacancy
> rates may emerge as structural changes in the City's economy continue. The condition of
> many of the areas presents a barrier to new industrial and business investment and creates an
> environment which encourages existing occupiers to relocate, often outwith the city.

Much done, much needing to be done.

The Clyde Waterway Regeneration Project

Perhaps the most spectacular and important of these developments is on the banks of the Clyde.
When completed, this will alter the profile of Glasgow radically, adding a large area of new buildings to the real estate of the city, both for business and for housing. It is designed to attract foreign
companies, expand local ones and improve the city's architectural profile.

Glasgow and eight other local authorities are implementing the Clyde Valley Joint Structure
Plan. The City Plan is that part which affects only Glasgow, some 300 hectares, and lays out
objectives for five years starting in 2001. These are under way and the changes are widespread,
eye-catching and welcome. Thirty-two major projects attracted about £1.6b in 2003–4 of which

the council contributed about £155m. The expected expenditure in 2004–5 was £2.6b. What have we got for this investment? There have been 1,900 new homes built with another 3,300 in the pipeline to encourage people to move towards the city centre thus reducing either the need to commute or the distance commuted and help to stabilise the population of the city. Transport will be improved in various ways including new routes dedicated to buses. New crossings over the Clyde will be built, one of which, the Glasgow Arc or Squinty Bridge, has already opened at Finneston.

There are three particularly ambitious programmes within the overall plan. A media centre at Pacific Quay, a financial centre in Bromielaw and a conference centre at Finneston which is already functional.

Pacific Quay consisted of 27 hectares of derelict land once at the heart of maritime Glasgow. The first development on the site was the construction of the Science Centre, Glasgow tower and IMAX cinema which cost about £74m to which European Funds contributed £18m. It was completed in June 2001. The plans had presumed that 3,500 jobs would be created but this proved woefully optimistic and only 300 new jobs were in place by the end of 2002. The explanations included the technical failure of the Tower and the lack of a bridge between the site and the north side of the river at Finneston which was delayed by planning procedures. These factors severely limited the expected private investment. In 2003, Scottish Enterprise downgraded the forecast to 1,800 new jobs. BBC Scotland moved into a new and slightly disappointing building, at least from an aesthetic point of view, in 2006 and was followed by SMG, the parent company of Scottish Television. A digital media centre will be built on the campus and its development will be able to draw on funding from the ITI concerned with these activities (see later). Nearby, Govan Town Hall is to be converted to a centre for film production and the base for Filmcity, modelled on a Danish institution which has proved successful.

Scottish Exhibition and Conference Centre The SECC was one of the first initiatives of the City Council to re-equip Glasgow. It opened in 1985 on the north bank of the Clyde. It was an ambitious project aiming to tap a market for large international conferences and trade fairs which, in the UK, only Birmingham was equipped to service. There are not many in the whole of Europe. The complex opened in 1985 and was expanded in 1997 when the Armadillo, a large conference hall capable of seating 3,000 delegates, was added. The complex is run by a company called The Scottish Exhibition Centre Limited of which the Council is the major shareholder, with over 90% of the shares.

The city benefits from the money that the visitors spend in hotels, restaurants and other places during their stay and from the publicity resulting from visitors who may learn a bit about the attractions of the city. SECC has also created or maintained about 3,500 jobs, itself quite a boost to the local economy. It has been a major cause for a large expansion in hotel rooms. In 2006, there were over 8,000 of these and the occupancy rate was about 73%. Even that may be insufficient. A conference of the European Respiratory Society in 2004 attracted 14,000 delegates of whom more than 3,000 had to commute into the city from as far away as Edinburgh. This problem is common to all Conference Centres since it is uneconomical to build hotels which would remain empty except when very large conferences are held.

The SECC met its financial targets four years earlier than planned. In 2001/2, it had a turnover of £11.59m and made a profit of £0.55m. It hosted 237 events and attracted 1.5m visitors of whom about 11% came from outside Scotland and 45% from Scotland but outside the Greater Glasgow area (see Table 7.1). Conferences attracted most foreigners. Indeed, it accounts for nearly a quarter of overseas visitors to Glasgow.

Table 7.1   Visitor numbers and origins of visitors to SECC in 2001/2

	VISITOR ORIGIN		
	Greater Glasgow	Rest of Scotland	Outside Scotland
Exhibitions	201,200	285,945	42,362
Conferences	14,984	13,622	84,910
Concerts/Events	459,141	388,503	35,319

Source: SECC website

The economic benefits to the city in 2001–2 were calculated by an independent auditor, System 3 Scotland, to be £83.6m, up from £44.6m ten years earlier.

Future plans remain ambitious:

- the City Council has decided to add an arena capable of hosting major concerts and sporting events and seating an audience of 12,500. Since most of the audience would be local, this project would not be restricted by the number of hotel beds. Foster and Partners have been appointed to design it and construction is expected to cost about £50m.
- a casino is planned and Kerzner International Limited has been appointed to mastermind the project. This, however, depends on Westminster's approval.
- an urban village is to be built. You may think that living next door to a complex that can attract more than 10,000 people during the day and another 10,000 in the evening may make for frequent disturbances. However, life there may well have compensations in terms of vitality, easy access to public transport and the central location. Elphinstone has been appointed preferred developer.

The International Financial Services District was launched in 2003 with the expectation that it would create or attract 20,000 jobs for Glasgow – in addition to the 28,000 already employed in the financial sector in 2002. Public bodies' contribution of £80 million towards the IFDS was dwarfed by the £600 million of the private sector producing well equipped offices with advanced electronic communication facilities. Recruitment of firms started slowly; by January 2005 only 4,000 jobs had been promised as a result of redeployment from elsewhere in Glasgow and new arrivals. JP Morgan, Esure, Morgan Stanley and Goldfish were among those that moved in. By January 2007, nearly halfway through the ten-year project, £750m had been invested, 13,100 jobs created and one million square feet of grade A space built. In addition, retail outlets (65,000 sq ft), leisure accommodation (36,000 sq ft) and 500 residential units were built. More firms, ACE Insurance, First Data and Barclays Wealth moved in.

Despite the very ambitious targets set, the first half of the project has yielded encouraging results. A distinct locality for financial services seems to be attractive to companies when considering where to invest. Therefore, the council's plans for the Clyde waterfront to date have been remarkably ambitious, imaginative and successful. Not since the 19th century has a council provided infrastructure so successful in creating jobs and reviving the economy.

But this is a success in the service sector. It consolidates the gains in the economy but renders the city's economy vulnerable to a downturn in the financial sector. To engage that extra gear and develop alternatives, locals, not outsiders, will have to step up and create productive companies that have the potential for growth. An early initiative was the creation of Business Parks, one of which was the West of Scotland Science Park so it is reasonable to examine its record.

The West of Scotland Science Park was built within a couple of miles of the main campus of Glasgow University and opened in September 1983 towards the beginning of a rash of such parks that swept the UK. There were only two in 1982 and about a hundred by 2003. Nowhere was that rash as dense as in Scotland which had the most science parks and the biggest floor area of all the regions in the UK in 2003, but the number of jobs per area of floor space was among the lowest.

The idea behind Science Parks is that they should provide a ready made and sympathetic site for the conversion of academic research into high tech industries. Although the projects should be based on new technology and provide high value output, they would not necessarily create a large number of jobs. The record of these Parks has been mixed; some, like Cambridge, are very successful and others have not been able to attract enough high tech projects and have reduced their entry criteria.

The stakeholders in the West of Scotland Science Park were Glasgow City Council, the universities in Glasgow, Scottish Enterprise (Glasgow) and private investors. These institutions do not necessarily share the same ambitions. All want to encourage start-up companies but the main objective of the Universities and private investors is to generate as much cash as quickly as possible for other uses or to return to shareholders; they may therefore hope to sell successful businesses on to the highest bidder even if that means the headquarters, and perhaps the whole business, moving outside the city. The City Council and Scottish Enterprise, on the other hand, want to encourage the growth of as many businesses as possible within the city boundaries thus increasing employment and value produced locally.

The bald statistics of the development of the Science Park are these. It expanded enormously and covered 24.9 hectares of land by the end of 2001 when the floor area completed was 14,961 sq m and a further 3,000 sq m was under construction. Total investment in the project was £35m of which £4m was invested in 2001 alone. The universities contributed £1.5m and Scottish Enterprise £20.8m with the private sector providing rather less at £12.8m. Therefore, the public sector was the major contributor but its role may decrease once construction is complete and re-use becomes more common. There were 26 companies on the site at the end of 2001. Four employed between 50 and 300 people but 9 employed between 1 and 5. The total number was 749. Eleven of the 26 companies were in the biomedical sector, 5 were concerned with computer or telecom projects and another 5 were 'materials related'. All 26 companies were undertaking research and development and designing new products or processes. Eight of the companies sprang from the Universities but 17 moved onto the Science Park from elsewhere within a thirty-mile radius of the city; they could be considered transfers. Eighteen of the companies were independent single site companies and six were subsidiaries of larger companies. During 2001, ten companies increased in size, ten remained stable and six contracted. Four companies introduced a new product during that year.

By April 2004, the number of employees had increased to nearly 900, a rise of 7.5% on the previous year and 20% on 2001. The premises had been extended by the completion of two new buildings on the Kelvin Campus, one of which won an award for the quality of its environmental and technical design.

At first sight, the cost of creating these jobs appears excessive. Each one resulted from an investment of £47,000 of which the public sector contributed nearly £30,000. But the jobs were in the new economy sector and likely to be highly productive which is exactly what the city needs. It would, therefore, be nice to know the collective value of the companies in the Science Park to the Glasgow economy, but, as far as I know, the figure is not computed. However, Scottish Enterprise must be satisfied because it has helped organise others in the West of Scotland.

Innovation Centre (Scotland) is another child of Scottish Enterprise which set up and runs a well equipped business park at Hillington, just outside the city boundaries, with Caledonian Land/MEPC and Strathclyde European Partnership. Its aim:

… is to create the premier incubation and company building mechanism in Scotland. Its mission is to support the development and growth of the next generation of knowledge base, high growth technology businesses in Scotland by providing critical support and connections.

In the first four years of its existence, 87 businesses moved in and 31 were successful enough to expand elsewhere. The failure rate of companies it incubates has been comparatively low. It did well in a competition run by the Centre for Strategy and Evaluation Services which assessed 25 incubators in 15 countries. A more important accolade is that others are seeking to imitate it. This park seems to have been much more dynamic than the West of Scotland Science Park, but its history is much shorter.

A plan for a third science park was approved by the Council in June 2002, when it allocated £55m for the development of the City Science Park near the city centre and Strathclyde University, which was expected to create 18 new businesses and up to 3,000 high-tech jobs.

Nova Technology is the fourth location built to try and foster more high technology companies. The first tenant was the Wood Group based in Aberdeen which opened an office in this park to take advantage of the pool of engineering talent in Glasgow. It employs about 250 skilled workers.

These Science Parks may be the incubators of companies which could take Glasgow's new economy sector into a higher division, but the results from the first Science Park do not encourage optimism. Somehow innovation has to be linked more effectively to business if the Council is to fulfil its laudable ambition to propel the city into the top quartile of European cities. This requires finding and nurturing home grown inventors and entrepreneurs, and ensuring that their talents are translated into growing businesses. Planners everywhere have turned to universities as the source of innovation. The universities, at first, were reluctant to direct research into areas suitable for commercial exploitation because they considered their function to be primary research regardless of its immediate economic relevance. But Governments control the purse strings and enthusiasm for the new direction increased when the universities realised they may actually make money from intellectual property which would bring additional income to their cash-strapped institutions. Changes in funding had put all but the top graded research departments in danger of being closed whatever their teaching skills and the quality of their graduates. Another source of funds could ease the pressure. Therefore, universities began to encourage their staff to seek a commercial outlet for their ideas. The Government, in turn, saw the universities as geese to lay the golden eggs of future industries.

There have been a few historical examples of success from this approach: in Glasgow, Lord Kelvin's work led to many patents and some industrial production. In the middle of the 19th century, Professors Barr and Stroud won a competition to build a range finder for the Ministry of Defence and set up a company which still produces optical instruments. But, perhaps the best European example is Gottingen which benefited hugely from the insistence of Prof Felix Klein that academia, particularly the sciences, must retain links with the practical world.

(He) initiated the foundation or further extension of many astronomical, physical, technical and mechanical institutes in Gottingen. There gradually grew up around them, in consequence, a whole private industry for the production of scientific measuring apparatus and optical precision instruments. The old-fashioned town became a cradle of the most modern technology.

Robert Jungk in *Brighter than a Thousand Suns* 1956

High tech clusters emerging from a city's universities are the golden eggs. The initiative of a dean in Stamford University is thought to have made possible the emergence of the Stanford

University Network: Microsoft was one of its offspring. Thus the consequences of his action were literally fabulous. Contrast that with the internet, the invention of an Englishman working for CERN, given free to the world. Governments want more of the former and less of the latter. Scottish and British Governments are no exception. The model encouraged in Britain is for a university to identify a discovery of commercial interest, to claim the rights to the intellectual property and then either form a spin-off company or license its use to an existing company or use it for consultancy practices, whichever is appropriate. The most successful British university in this regard is Cambridge, which also happens to be the second ranked university in the world according to the Shanghai-Jiao Index.

For academic success to be convertible into industrial innovation, several conditions have to be met: the quality of research has to be good enough to produce a number of marketable ideas; those ideas have to be converted into a plan attractive to investors; a company has to be set up and run which requires very different skills from those available in universities; development has to be managed; and a market identified and informed. This route is the only one available to politicians wishing to enhance manufacturing, however long a shot it may be. The only alternative is hands off and let the market work by itself.

Scotland's universities' economic potential

A *Herald* headline (January 2005) asked: 'So just where is the greatest science being done?' And the answer was, of course, Scotland. And whose opinion was that? A Scot, but a Scot with a difference. Dr Jim Brown's career had included jobs in the bioscience industry of the UK and USA and his opinion was delivered after a tour of Scotland's research institutions. He was quoted as saying:

> I can tell you that what I saw in terms of Scottish science was the best I have seen … Singapore is fantastic, Australia is quite good and the Taiwanese have a lot of good stuff, but looking at what is coming out of Scotland is the best I have seen.

Allowing for fondness for his native country and for politeness, it is still possible to believe that Scottish universities can deliver. There are more formal assessments of the quality of British Universities' research which suggest that it is indeed excellent. For people like me who like league tables, Britain had eight of the world's top 50 universities in 2004 according to the Shanghai-Jiao Index, among them Oxford, Cambridge and four London institutions but none in Scotland. Of the top 200 universities, the US had most with 62, followed by Britain with 30, Germany 17 and Australia 14. In European terms, British universities were dominant with 18 of Europe's top 50 universities. Glasgow University was ranked 30th in Britain, 44th in Europe and 127th in the world and Strathclyde University about 50th in Britain. The UK produced the second most published papers (5% of the world's output) after the US, and British papers were cited (12% of all citations of scientific papers) more commonly than those of any other country except the US in 1997 (frequency of citation is a guide to quality). In terms of value for money, British universities produced more papers per £m invested in science than any other country, with Denmark second. But the transfer of this performance into industrial output has been a traditional British weakness. This can be assessed by the number of patents issued. European countries, with rare exceptions, have taken out fewer than the US or Japan. Brigitte Hasewend examined the reasons for this in a study for the European Commission in 2004. The league table she produced showed that the UK did not perform well in world terms, registering fewer patents per head of the population than the average of the EU15, let alone the US or Japan. The causes of the poor performance of Europe relative to the US or Japan, despite comparable expenditure on research, were thought to be a stronger emphasis on basic research in Europe, looser ties between business and universities and the concentration of manufacturing in mature sectors, such as chemicals, motor vehicles and aerospace. And it shows: EU high technology products were responsible for a lower proportion of exports than from either Japan or from the US (see Figure 7.2).

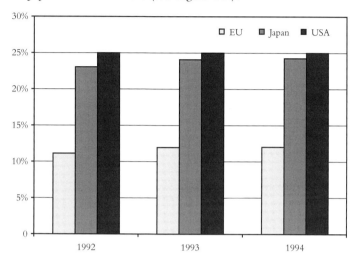

Figure 7.2   Proportion of exports made up of products derived from advanced technology in EU, Japan and US.

Source: RTD Info 20

Therefore, the conversion of research into viable businesses is a European and British weakness. No wonder politicians believe that forging a more effective link between universities and business may deliver. No Government has acted with quite as much single minded determination in pursuit of this goal as the Scottish Executive. After the relative failure of Science parks, it came up with the idea of 'proof of concept' awards on the advice of the Knowledge Economy Task Force in 1999. These awards were designed to finance the first steps on the road from an idea to a level at which it may attract venture capital. The categories selected for investment were life sciences, microelectronics, food and drink, opto-electronics, digital media and creative industries, communications technologies, forest industries, tourism and energy.

It is too early to judge its effectiveness but the uptake was sufficiently encouraging to increase the total funds available. In the first seven rounds nearly 200 projects were accepted from all Scottish Universities with an overall rejection rate of 75%. Altogether, about 500 new jobs have been created, 33 new companies formed and 31 licensing deals negotiated. Price Waterhouse Cooper (an accountancy firm) was asked to audit the first six rounds and they concluded that the funding offered by this scheme was critical to the development of 80% of the projects taken up and that they had added about £125m to the economy for an investment of £28m. They thought it offered value for money and expected that the returns to the Scottish economy would increase with time. It works out at about £56,000 per job and each produces about £250,000 benefit for the community – not the same measure as productivity but quite impressive if PWC's sums are correct. The fact that the concept has been copied around the world suggests that they may be.

The projects supported cover a wide range and include: a lightweight electrical generator to harness energy derived from wind, wave and tide; the development of a new flood management tool; a slow-release dental insert to prevent gum disease; and video fingerprinting for the prevention of piracy in digital assets management.

Therefore, it looks as though the Proof of Concept Project has indeed stimulated the conversion of academic research into economically advantageous forms. But no crack-a-jack has yet been delivered.

Glasgow's universities are reasonably successful in the competition for Proof of Concept awards and are holding their own in Scotland in terms of commercialisation of ideas, but how does Scotland compare with the rest of the UK and beyond? The British were careful to collect their data so that they could be compared with American universities. The Higher Education Business Interaction Survey (HEBIS) has published the results for 2002. American universities received almost six times the level of funding both from industry and Government. Industry provided only 7–8% on both sides of the Atlantic although it was worth much more in America. Many more licences were taken out by American universities and the income generated as a result was much higher even when calculated as a fraction of the research expenditure: 4.3% in US and a dismal 0.6% in the UK. American universities created about a third more companies although the British ones were considerably cheaper.

The financial reward from spin-off companies (both with and without HEI ownership) was not spectacular at £358 million and nearly 13,000 full-time equivalent jobs created in the whole of the UK yielding about £27,500 per employee – not a fantastic return.

The same survey found that Scottish universities performed relatively well in 2001–2. They were strong in the fields of biotechnology and information technology. They produced 14% of the UK total of invention disclosures (302), filed 11% of new patents (104), 15% of new licences (107) and spun out 31 companies representing 14% of the total for the UK. Edinburgh University has had the biggest income among UK universities in recent years (about £3m in 2001), almost entirely due to sales of their Hepatitis B vaccine. In the same year, Strathclyde took out more patents than any other British university. British Universities appear to be warming to this task. The second Annual Survey on University Technology Transfer Activities, published in November 2003, concluded that UK universities are more active in attempting to commercialise their research ideas but that, although the number of patents and licences are rising to the levels of Canada and the US, the income generated from them is still much less than in the other countries.

Dr Smailes, of Edinburgh University, has compared Scottish universities to American equivalents and found that:

> in 2002/03, the performance of Scottish universities was as good if not better than the average in the US across all metrics. This is not a recent phenomenon but continues an annual performance at least back to 1995/96. This is a strong achievement and is difficult to reconcile with criticisms the university sector has received in terms of failure to exploit its research base. Indeed the universities of Harvard and Penn State jointly with twice the research activity of the Scottish sector in 2002/03 evaluated 275 disclosures, filed 165 patents, licensed 89 technologies, generated $19.4m in royalties ($17.8m from Harvard) and created 6 spin-outs. In the same year the Scottish universities evaluated 261 disclosures, filed 197 patents, licensed 85 technologies, generated $12.7m in royalties and created 13 companies from half the combined research income.

This encouraging analysis suggests that Scottish universities are rising to the task but there is little evidence that it has made much difference to the economy as yet.

Sources of capital

Once the project has been defined and licked into shape by the proof of concept funds, the next stage in forming a new company is to attract venture capital. The amount available is a matter of controversy. The British Venture Capital Association estimated that £119m was invested in new business ventures in Scotland in the four years to the end of 2003 but a recent study by Professor Richard Harrison, from the Centre for Entrepreneurship Research at Edinburgh University (reported in the *Herald* of 30 November 2004) reckoned that the total was about £673m. The difference (£554m) was invested by venture capitalists not linked to the BVCA, business angels, family members and private investors. The Hunter Centre for Entrepreneurship conducted a survey of entrepreneurial activity in 2004 and found that 78% of Scottish informal investors provided the funds for a member of their family to set up a business. This informal investment was thought to amount to between £500m and £1b each year making families the most important investors in new firms in Scotland. Interestingly, most family investors do not expect any return on their contribution. The family is a key unit in the business life of Scotland. About 900,000, some 50% of the private sector workforce, work for family firms which make up about two-thirds of all businesses.

Is there enough to fund likely projects? Opinion within the Venture Capital business appears to be divided. Callum Paterson, managing director of Scottish Equity Partners, certainly thinks that the main problem is not finance but a shortage of good projects. On the other hand, Geoffrey Thomson, CEO of Braveheart Ventures, thought that 'several promising Scottish companies have fallen by the wayside as a result of being unable to access private sector cash in the past'. In 2005, his company announced that it would make £10m available to projects which had passed the Proof of Concept stage from Glasgow and Edinburgh Universities. One study commissioned by UBS Wealth Management, examined the number of firms backed by venture capital in the UK in 2006. London had 53 companies per million of the population but Scotland topped that with 54 making it 'the most entrepreneurial region in Britain'. The authors attributed this success to serial entrepreneurs passing on their experience. 'The study showed Edinburgh and Glasgow ranking alongside Oxford, London, and Cambridge as the country's leading centres of business innovation'. This sounds encouraging but there is little other statistical evidence to suggest a renaissance of Scottish entrepreneurship. Therefore, there is controversy about the availability of venture capital, but Scotland does at least as well as the rest of the UK.

Management of new companies

The next step is perhaps the most important: finding capable management for the fledgling company. This is the one that the British traditionally fail. Jim Brown, he who said that Scottish science was world class, implied that the main problem was cultural since he had often met good Scottish managers working abroad implying that they had left Scotland because of the lack of opportunity or support. American venture capital companies investing in Scotland often insert their own chosen manager which is hardly a ringing endorsement of local managerial talent.

Any process is only as good as its rate limiting step. In Britain, this appears to be the supply of entrepreneurs that can convert an idea into a business. The main emphasis in the last decade has been on getting the universities to commercialise their ideas and little effort has made in identifying, training and encouraging managers to convert ideas into a flourishing businesses. Is this still happening? The Lambert review commissioned by Gordon Brown claimed that there was a plethora of spin-out companies from universities yet the universities' technical transfer offices rarely made money. Studies in Britain have shown that wealth generation depends more on the actions of entrepreneurs than the exploitation of intellectual property which led Stephen Allott, in an article in *Prospect* (April 2005), to argue that universities' main effort should be the attraction and training of people with entrepreneurial flair. British society has been somewhat reluctant to endorse business and wealth creation as an honourable way of earning a living, reserving its approval for administrators, doctors, lawyers and even journalists. This is reflected in the universities that have courses for entrepreneurship which are not given much kudos and which are often taught by part-time staff with few formal academic qualifications. Some teach a course about entrepreneurship and others a course for entrepreneurs.

Strathclyde University, with its Hunter Centre for Entrepreneurship, is a pioneer:

> In Scotland, the only business school to achieve a 5 star rating in the Research Assessment Exercise, Strathclyde Business School, houses the Strathclyde Entrepreneurship Initiative, which provided 450 places in seven different entrepreneurship electives for undergraduate students of all faculties of the university in 1998/99. Sixty percent of these students were from science and engineering. This was a much wider provision than other Scottish universities, or indeed any university in England.
>
> *Entrepreneurship Education in Higher Education in England: A Survey*
> Jonathan Levie, London Business School, 1999

Once the business culture is seen to be innovative, dynamic and admired, local entrepreneurs may be more inclined to emerge. Recently, the press has given much more coverage to entrepreneurial activity and this may bode well for the future.

Conclusions

The attempt by Government to use the universities as a resource to provide the country with innovative companies has been serious and shows signs of success, although limited to date. The incubation of these high tech firms is also something that the Government has tried to encourage and is the subject of the next chapter.

CHAPTER 8

THE MIDWIFE – SCOTTISH ENTERPRISE

Scottish Enterprise is the Government designed catalyst to convert innovative ideas from any source into wealth creating businesses. If Glasgow is to move up a league, this is the organisation which should deliver the push. It started life in 1976 as the Scottish Development Agency, a product of the then Labour Government and was headed by Gavin McCrone, an economist and civil servant with little direct experience of business so it was not surprising that he set up the Agency on civil service lines. Since the world economy at that time was in turmoil following the oil shocks of 1970 and 1974, the new Agency was designed to save as much of the manufacturing sector as possible. The advent of Mrs Thatcher's Conservative Government in 1979, strangely, did not lead to its sudden death. First George Younger kept it going aimlessly and then Malcolm Rifkind, his successor as Secretary of State for Scotland, used it to pioneer urban regeneration in Glasgow, Dundee and Leith. George Mathieson was appointed chief executive and had some success in improving the quality of the housing and infrastructure in these areas without transforming their economies. He also started a service to help start-up companies.

Then Bill Hughes, treasurer of the Scottish Conservative Party, became enchanted by a model of regeneration that he had seen in America. Important businessmen had taken on the challenge of improving hopeless districts of some American towns by seconding staff to projects in the rundown areas, teaching skills and using their contacts to introduce new businesses. The local businesses levied taxes on themselves to fund these developments. He thought the same might work in Scotland and, more importantly, he had Mrs Thatcher's ear. He advocated a series of private consortia which would bid for government grants to transform the local economy. Success would be rewarded by more cash and failure by oblivion. Eventually, the successful groups would be self-financing. However, Malcolm Rifkind decided to keep political control of the organisation, which he merged with the Scottish division of the Manpower Services Commission responsible for training. The new organisation was called Scottish Enterprise and it started work in 1991. Highlands and Islands Enterprise was set up at the same time to perform a similar role for the North. The budget awarded to Scottish Enterprise was massive, nearly £500m or just short of one percent of the country's GDP. Crawford Beveridge, who had experience of high-tech business on the American west coast, was appointed to run it. His chosen policy was to attract a number of manufacturers of semi-conductors to the central belt of Scotland creating a cluster which would acquire sufficient mass to lead to the formation of new companies and a solid base for future growth. Silicon Glen became the marvel of British manufacturing with a gain of 40,000 direct jobs and perhaps 30,000 secondary ones. Production grew by about 20% per year during the 1990s and Scotland's manufactured exports rose steeply.

The strategy was obviously a huge success but a hollow one: it all depended on foreign firms, and few of the jobs they provided required much skill. Furthermore, there was no indigenous large company with deep roots in the region. When the electronic bubble burst at the turn of the century, all collapsed together and exports fell back to the 1996 level leaving Scottish Enterprise to start again.

Robert Crawford was brought in to supervise the next stage in January 2000. He came from Ernst and Young where he had specialised in foreign investment. The Executive's number one priority at the turn of the century was the development of the Scottish economy. Crawford's task was to implement the Government's Smart, Successful Scotland programme. The remit was very wide:

> … helping business start-ups and helping existing companies to grow; promoting and encouraging exporting; attracting inward investment; highlighting the importance of developing skills and providing the means to do so; breaking down barriers to employment and ensuring disadvantaged groups and areas are not left out; and making Scotland a more competitive location through the provision of business sites and premises and improving the environment.

> SEn assists companies in all parts of the Scottish economy, focusing in particular on areas in which Scotland has a recognised world-class standing. These include oil and gas, semiconductors, opto-electronics, software including multimedia, food, biotechnology and tourism. Other areas of priority include the Business Birthrate Strategy, commercialisation of academic research, and the globalisation of Scottish companies.

Generous funding was provided: its budget peaked at £584.9m in 2000/1 and fell to £521.5m in 2003/4. Of this, £426.1m came from government and £75.4m from its own assets or from European funds. It spent most, £149m, on developing skills and encouraging learning, £124m on global connections and £107m on 'growing businesses'. It had £22.4m to spend on research and development. Scottish Enterprise directly employed 1,600 people in 2003/4, 400 in the head office in Glasgow.

It is a hydra-headed organism with chameleon qualities. The number of its offshoots is legion and almost impossible for an outsider to understand, particularly as they proliferate, change titles and share functions. Scottish Enterprise has spawned a network of subordinate companies responsible for a given area, one of which is Scottish Enterprise, Glasgow. These offshoots have a degree of autonomy which enables them to set up organisations whose remit is confined to one area only. This can cause confusion as Scottish Enterprise seems to provide different services in different parts of one small country.

There are three organisations responsible for helping with the formation and development of spin-off companies: SDI, ITI and SCF.

Scottish Development International (SDI) was set up in October 2001 to replace Locate in Scotland and the former export promotion group, Scottish Trade International. It is a joint venture between Scottish Enterprise and the Scottish Executive and its task is to raise the profile of Scottish businesses and ideas internationally. It has 21 strategically placed offices around the world, three of which were opened in 2005, in Singapore, Shanghai and Boston. It helps Scottish companies to 'internationalise' or export and attempts to attract inward investment. Another of its tasks is to arrange finance for start-up companies by liaising with venture capital companies abroad. A member of an American company, Vision Capital, wrote a fulsome testimonial of this aspect of SDI after a successful investment in Atlantech.

> A lot of the difficulty experienced in identifying and raising venture capital is timing. One of the things that we rely on SDI for is to be a bit of a matchmaker in this respect. They give us visibility into the market in Scotland and also spend time with the Companies to make sure that they understand what our expectations are and what we're looking for. I communicate on

a regular basis with their folks in San Jose, as well as Glasgow, about not only specific deals but also about the larger aspects of VC financing in Scotland including the legal environment, the management talent pool, the state of technology transfer out of Universities and into start-ups, the state of 'syndication opportunities' with Scottish VCs, etc. On all of these issues and many others, SDI provides us with an unbiased, continuously updated source of information, which helps us focus on the particular company opportunities more closely.

I would also say that SDI is somewhat unique in their ability and willingness to pro-actively assist in these things. Certainly there are SDI-like groups in most countries or regions of Europe, but my experience has been that SDI is the most progressive and most forward thinking of the lot. I have no doubt that this serves and will continue to serve Scotland's entrepreneurial community extremely well into the future. There is enormous potential in Scotland and SDI really helps me get a handle on that opportunity.

What you have to realise is that there's some really fundamentally deep technology coming out of Scotland. Lots of the innovation we take for granted has its roots there, telephony, television, the works. What really excites you is the coming together of a modern day version of that intellect, which is driven by a superb education system, particularly at University level, alongside existing skills and experience in areas like Opto and software development. We attempt to tap into all that and integrate management with a flexibility and velocity of mindset that can really make the business fly on a global scale.

True, this tribute was found on SDI's website but it does at least show that someone thought it competent. Essentially, its role in company formation is to help find financial assistance from overseas capital. Its other roles are more important; see below.

Not content with Scottish Development International, Scottish Enterprise, in partnership with Highlands and Islands Enterprise, set up **Intermediary Technology Institutes** (ITIs) in 2002. Three subdivisions were created, ITI Life Sciences in Dundee, ITI Techmedia, comprising communication technology and digital media, in Glasgow and ITI Energy in Aberdeen. Each operates as an autonomous division and has a third of the budget of £450m to be invested over the first ten years. The purpose of these institutes is to foster start-up companies in their specialties so that they develop into 'world-beating' companies. Scottish Enterprise's research predicted that the initiative would lead to the formation of at least 75 successful spin-out and start-up companies after ten years rising to 170 after 20 years. Each institute will create a bank of the best ideas relevant to their area of interest produced by local expertise, particularly from Scottish universities, and then find a quality company to help commercialise the ideas. By 2007, ITI Life Sciences had invested £51.65m in five R&D programmes involving 12 Scottish and International organisations. ITI energy had initiated eight R&D programmes and invested £27.8m and ITI Techmedia had invested £37.5m in seven R&D programmes and collaborated with 37 organisations. Altogether, 87 patents had been taken out, six licensing agreements with commercial partners sealed but the main harvest of their efforts was anticipated to be another four or five years off when their income should start to be significant if their ambitions were realised. It is obviously too early to judge their effectiveness.

One ITI has already impressed Peter Stadler, president of the German Association of Biotechnology Industries. He had known the chief executive of CXR Biosciences, a Dundee firm, for years but they had never linked up until ITI Life Sciences injected the funds that made co-operation possible. He was reported in the *Herald* of March 2005 as saying:

I think this ITI concept could be a prototype that other countries or regions will imitate. I have explained (to the German Ministry of Research) the high degree of innovation of this concept … They were very interested.

In 2006, ITI Life Sciences announced that

> it had reached its first commercial milestone with the signing of commercialisation licences with CXR Biosciences (Dundee, Scotland) and Artemis Pharmaceuticals (Cologne, Germany). The licences will allow both companies to commercialise new technology and services aimed at improving the discovery and development of new drugs.

Perhaps as important is that it took a major German player to Dundee where he was reported to be impressed with various activities there and was anxious to co-operate with other companies. This sort of networking may multiply the benefits and help to create clusters. Another example; the ITI in life sciences recently attracted Inverness Medical Innovation with a grant of £30m to set up in Stirling. This company is a subsidiary of Johnson & Johnson and already has a large presence in Inverness. The company will invest £67.5m of its own money and set up a large research and development programme employing 500 skilled workers. Staff would be recruited from Scottish universities and from around the world. Any foreign scientists recruited would, of course, live and work in Scotland and their children may become Scottish, an important consideration in a country with a falling population. The company's products would be manufactured in Stirling. Adding together the royalties for products sold, the contracts for subcontracted tasks and services supplied locally, the potential benefits are considerable particularly if other companies follow IMI's lead. In 2007, the new company introduced Smartcheck, a device for monitoring people on anticoagulants so that checks can be made without the need of a hospital visit. However, the ITI in life sciences spent its budget for two years on one goose which may or may not lay a golden egg. Meanwhile, local start-up companies will have to wait for support. The justification for the decision will become clear with time.

The third arrow in Scottish Enterprise's quiver is the **Scottish Co-Investment Fund**. This body was set up in 2002 with £45m capital, part provided by the European Regional Development Fund, in response to the difficulty new companies experience in obtaining early finance. Officers of the fund identify companies with a potential for growth, and help with grants of between £100,000 and £500,000 supplemented by private partners. In 2003, the first year of operation, it invested £2.3m in 21 companies but helped to attract a further £8.4m from private sources. It is hoped that this will encourage company formation.

In conclusion, Scottish Enterprise is designed to be the midwife of the rebirth of entrepreneurial Scotland. It helps with networking and by arranging finance. It also offers advice on how to set up and run a company and with the training of individuals. It is the government's key enforcer of the Smart Successful Scotland policy. You can argue about its structure and its expertise but you cannot deny it is a serious attempt by Government to change the business climate of Scotland.

Has anything changed?

With all this emphasis on new company formation over the last decade or so, one would expect a surge in activity. There is no sign that this has happened as yet but it may be too early to judge. One real risk is that all of this infrastructure, although logically designed and adequately financed, may simply not be up to the job. A recent report accentuated this possibility:

> The chief executive of an agency (the Kelvin Institute) financed by the taxpayer to commercialise university technology is understood to have been edged out after it produced 'next to nothing' during his three years in charge.

Bill Nisen, a former Silicon Valley high-flyer, was reputed to be earning over £100,000 per year as chief executive of the Kelvin Institute when he came into conflict with SE, which provides most of its funding.

Scotland on Sunday April 2005.

The Kelvin Institute was set up in 2003 as a joint venture between the Universities of Glasgow and Strathclyde with support from Scottish Enterprise. Clearly it has not succeeded in any of its aims so far. It could be that the quality of staff recruited as midwives was simply not up to the job.

Scottish Enterprise produces an annual report which analyses performance against a number of designated targets. In 2004, one target was to assist in 35 start-up companies from universities or other research institutions. In fact, only 27 were helped; but this represented an improvement since only 62 had been helped over the previous five years. High-growth start-up companies were also identified and 192 got help as opposed to a target of 140 in 2004. Altogether, the knowledge industries were thought to employ 70,000 people in Scotland, a growth of 22 per cent between 1998 and 2001. The increase was even higher in Glasgow: SLIMS (a consultative company specialising in economic and labour market analysis) estimated that employment in this sector increased by 48% in the seven years to 2002 and that the increase was greater than in any other British city (see Figure 8.1).

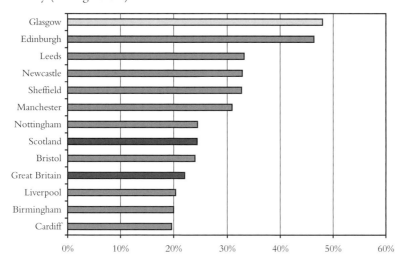

Figure 8.1   % increase in jobs in knowledge economy 1995–2002.

Source: SLIMS and Oxford Economic Forecasting

Unfortunately, this surge has not been maintained, according to the audit of 2005 conducted by BAK Basel Economics (see Chapter 4). Between 1995 and 2000, the new economy sector grew by a massive 14% per annum but screeched to a halt so that between 2000 and 2004, it actually contracted. The old economy sector followed the same pattern but with gentler swings – a growth of 1.5% in the earlier period and slight contraction in the later period.

The official inquiry into the performance of universities in commercialising their intellectual property, the Lambert Review, concluded that:

> the available evidence suggests the economic and social returns from public funding of university research are attractive, and certainly justify increasing investment in this area. More money will be needed for the university system to reach its full potential.

It certainly seems that Scottish Enterprise is pursuing policies which could help form high tech businesses leading to a restructuring of the economy but to assess its impact more usefully it would be better if the audit were to report not only the number of companies helped but also their turnover. Clearly, one company with a turnover of £1b is worth more than several companies with a turnover over of millions. At present, the audit merely notes the numbers.

Scottish Enterprise also hopes to attract the right sort of foreign investment.

Foreign Direct Investment, new style

Direct inward investment, welcome in the 1990s, became somewhat discredited when so many companies withdrew after the electronic sector bubble burst at the turn of the new millennium. However, the right sort of inward investment remains a powerful accelerator in the economy, as Ireland has shown. Scottish Enterprise has set both Scottish Development International (SDI) and ITI Scotland Ltd the task of attracting companies which provide skilled jobs and encourage research. The role of the ITIs has already been described and is confined to the three areas in which they specialise.

SDI also has a more old-fashioned role which involves facilitating and encouraging companies that express an interest in setting up in Scotland providing they are the right sort of company – i.e., ones that offer high value added employment of skilled workers. SDI is apparently quite good at this task and was adjudged to be among the best of 187 agencies serving regional or national inward investment by GDP Global, a London company. This nicely complemented another survey conducted by *The Financial Times* on the most attractive country or region for inward investment. In its submission for this competition, Scottish Development International reported that 74 foreign investment projects had been undertaken in Scotland in 2002/3 and that the SDI had been involved in 57 of them. Scotland won the competition and was named the European Region of the Future, 2004/5. Judges admired the large-scale investment in infrastructure such as mass broadband connection, science parks, urban regeneration and research institutions. They recognised that Scotland had transformed its reputation with foreign investors. As an example of this, Glasgow was judged to have the best developed electronic communications in the world in another competition, this time based in New York.

Old-style inward investment still happens. In 2005, Dell was encouraged to set up a call centre in the recently upgraded City Park which used to be the Wills tobacco factory in the East End of Glasgow. For a grant of £7.48m, 800 jobs will be created relatively cheaply at £9,350 per job and a major user found for the premises.

So, with all this effort, one might expect to see results for all the investment made. The ONS has published changes in regional economic indicators for the period 1999 to 2005 and, sadly, they show little sign of a Scottish resurgence. In particular, the amount spent on Research and Development in Scotland is well below the UK average and shows little sign of increasing. This is starkly different to the East of England which is partly driven by spin-off companies from Cambridge University. And remember that the British expenditure on R&D is low by international standards, perhaps because company bosses think that it is easier to grow by acquisition than by developing new products.

VAT registrations and de-registrations, which reflect entrepreneurial activity, show a similar story. In 2005, only 5.6% of new companies in the UK were Scottish compared to its 8.2% share of the population. There was some encouragement in that the balance in company formation and demise was over 500 in 1999, fell to virtually zero in 2001 and then rose progressively to 1,400 in 2005. Does this indicate that a corner has been turned?

Investment as measured by net capital expenditure should provide evidence of future gains in productivity. The amount invested in Scottish industries was high both in absolute terms at

£9.2b and as a percentage of GVA, just under 12%. This was the highest of any region in 2007 and may herald productivity gains.

These last two chapters have supposed that the main way forward is for businesses to arise out of research undertaken in universities. The reverse direction may also be fruitful; that is, businesses use universities to undertake their research. This was identified in the Lambert Review:

> The main challenge for the UK is not about how to increase the supply of commercial ideas from the universities into business. Instead, the question is about how to raise the overall level of demand by business for research from all sources. Measured against other developed countries, the research intensity of British business is relatively low – and the position has been deteriorating in recent decades. This has had an adverse impact on the overall productivity of the UK economy.
>
> The UK's R&D intensity is much higher than the international average in two broad areas – pharmaceuticals/biotechnology and aerospace/defence. It is below average in all other important sectors. The UK's business research base is both narrow and fragile, and is heavily dependent on the investment decisions of a dozen large companies mainly involved in pharmaceuticals and defence.
>
> Lambert Review 2003

And, of course, defence and pharmaceuticals are about the only two manufacturing sectors in which UK firms have an international reputation. This may be changing slowly because the Review describes how most new industrial clusters are linked to their local universities. Companies co-operating with universities were almost twice as likely to improve their range of goods, reduce costs and win new markets. This may be because companies with more potential were more likely to seek university advice but the advantages seem so manifest that this approach deserves encouragement.

Conclusions

Government, which includes the City Council and the Scottish Executive together with all their creations such as Scottish Enterprise, has been extremely active in building infrastructure capable of enhancing the recovery of the city. But if the city is to join the top league of European cities, it requires significant growth in industries capable of delivering highly productive jobs. The universities seem capable of providing the ideas; there are numerous business parks with excellent facilities; money is available for investment; the politicians are making the right noises – but very little progress is evident as yet.

CHAPTER 9

THE OTHER GLASGOW: THE LEGACY OF PAST GLORIES

Glasgow's economic prowess in the 18th and 19th centuries came at a considerable cost to the society it created. The sheer speed in the increase in population during the industrial revolution led to the creation of some of the most sordid slums in Europe. The Liberal-dominated Council made few attempts to improve housing but the Labour Councils of the 20th century spent huge sums on trying to better the living conditions in these slums. Some of these attempts were misguided but, by the end of the century, the quality of housing had improved substantially: but this did little to eradicate deprivation. Deprivation was not simply a matter of poverty and bad housing, it was cultural. It gave rise to a series of problems: alcohol dominating the minds of social improvers in the 19th century, crime at the beginning of the 20th century and drugs at the end of that century. These problems are often seen as the cause of deprivation but are really the result, even though their effect is to make social deprivation even more intractable. Has the recent recovery changed the blight of intense social deprivation that has scarred the city for so long?

The size of the problem

In 2005, about 110,000 people of working age were economically inactive in the city. This was 30% of the total and compared with a UK average of 22%. Thus there were about 20,700 'extra' inactive people in Glasgow. Although poor by UK standards, Liverpool, Nottingham and Manchester are worse and the rate at which Glaswegians have been drawn into work since the 1990s is faster than any other large British city. Table 9.1 shows the employment rates in Scottish cities in 1996 and 2003. Over 9% more were in work in 2003 than seven years earlier. This is not only the best rate in Scotland but also in the whole UK with Bristol second. There is, therefore, some evidence that the recent recovery is dragging many into work. Can further expansion be relied on to solve the problem? The answer to this question depends on whether the extra 20,000 are different in some way which makes them unemployable even in good times.

Table 9.1   Employment rates in Scottish cities in 1996 and 2003 and the percentage increase

	1996	*2003*	*Change in percentage points*
Aberdeen	78.1%	79.5%	1.4
Edinburgh	71.9%	74.8%	2.9
Stirling (LA)	73.1%	74.5%	1.4
Dundee	64.0%	69.4%	5.4
Glasgow	55.1%	64.3%	9.2
Scotland	70.2%	73.4%	3.2

Source: *Competitive Scottish Cities?* by Mary Hutchins and John Parkinson, published by Scottish Executive 2005

Education and qualifications

Some 85,000 citizens of working age had no qualifications at all in 2004, i.e. 23% compared to the UK average of 15% (see Table 9.2). The difference between the two gave Glasgow an 'extra' 20,700 people without qualifications.

Table 9.2   Different levels of qualifications in Glasgow, Scotland and GB

	Glasgow City (numbers)	Glasgow City (%)	Scotland (%)	GB (%)
NVQ4 and above	96,000	26.0	28.4	25.2
NVQ3 and above	165,000	44.6	47.6	43.1
NVQ2 and above	217,000	58.6	64.7	61.5
NVQ1 and above	256,000	69.2	76.1	76.0
Other Qualifications	29,000	7.8	7.3	8.8
No Qualifications	85,000	22.9	16.6	15.1

NVQs (National Vocational Qualifications) are work-related, competence-based qualifications
Source: local area labour force survey (Mar 2003–Feb 2004) see NOMIS 2005

The performance of Glasgow's schools is sometimes blamed. League tables have been published which show that the results in Glasgow's schools were the worst of all Scottish cities at the end of S4, S5 and S6 in 2003/4, although Dundee is only marginally better.

Nor was there evidence of any catch-up. The results in all cities improved slowly in the eight years after 1996 but there was no evidence that Glasgow's children were closing the gap.

This picture may be needlessly grim because of the artificial nature of Glasgow City's boundary. East Renfrewshire and East Dunbartonshire are almost entirely populated by Glasgow commuters and therefore it is reasonable to factor them into the equation. As it happens, they have the best exam results of all the districts in Scotland (see Table 9.3)

Table 9.3   Percentage of children from different districts entering S4 who passed three or more highers in 2004

Area	No of children	% of S4 roll that pass 3 or more highers
Scotland	31,5768	30
Glasgow	29,387	18
Edinburgh	20,940	32
Aberdeen	10,845	31
Dundee	8,657	22
E Dunbartonshire	8,859	56
E Renfrewshire	7,346	52

If the results from the schools of these councils is added to those of the Glasgow schools, 28% for the S4 roll achieved passes in three or more highers, more in line with other cities but still below the Scottish average. This should not obscure the truly awful performance of some of Glasgow's schools which are at best average and at worst awful. The awful schools tend to be smaller and to have lower pupil/teacher ratios than the average suggesting that investment is not lacking. A more likely explanation is the 'disinterest' of the pupils and their families. This is partly due to the migration of ambitious parents to the suburbs just outside the city boundary. Moreover, 13% of Glasgow secondary school children crossed the council border to attend schools in neighbouring councils, particularly East Dunbarton-shire and East Renfrewshire in 2004. A further 15% attended private schools. The absence of these children, nearly a third of the total, whose parents are likely to be more motivated and demanding, may have a severely detrimental effect on the city schools because there are insufficient motivated children remaining to cope with disruptive behaviour from the minority with little interest in learning. The schools with the very worst results tend to be in the poorer parts of the city where all problems are accentuated. The results of poor edu-cational achievements are predictable. The 2004 report on Poverty in Scotland by the Joseph Rowntree Foundation found that:

> One of the most telling indicators compares the risks of unemployment and low pay and how they vary according to the level of education that a person has received. In each case, the lower the educational qualifications the higher the risk – but even more importantly, the risk of low pay is much greater than risk of unemployment. Indeed, for people aged 25 to 50, half of all those who are in work but lack a Higher grade or above are in low paid work, rising to two-thirds for those with no qualifications.

> For those with no qualifications, their chances of further training once in a job are limited: although there has been some improvement over the last decade, people with no qualifica-tions are still three times less likely to have received job-related training than those with some qualifications – and the more qualifications you have, the more training you are likely to get.

This sets the scene: poor school results, no qualifications, either no work or at best low paid work: no escape and another generation beaten.

Paradoxically, Glasgow was relatively well endowed with well qualified workers because it hosted more students in tertiary education than all UK cities except London in 2004. There were about 42,000 full-time students attending the three universities and several thousand part-timers attending the colleges of further education. This is an enormous strength and helps recruitment for skilled jobs. About 35% of graduates from the universities go on to work in Glasgow and a further 17% in the Glasgow region. Graduates from other universities rarely choose Glasgow as a place to work and, since the universities recruit their undergraduates from Southwest Scotland, the workforce has a very strong West of Scotland representation – completely unlike London, for example. The drain of well qualified workers to better jobs in the south was a diminishing problem, but still a considerable one.

However, university is not always a relevant target for more than a minority of pupils attending some of the city's worst schools.

Health

Lack of qualifications is one cause of economic inactivity and poor health is another. Health problems blight the lives of a much higher proportion of Glaswegians than other Scots who themselves are not particularly healthy. The differences can be startling. A boy born in Calton can expect to live only 54 years – a Third World statistic; by contrast, a boy born in Bearsden or

Clarkston, only seven miles away, can expect to live to 80. By most criteria, the health of Glaswegians is bad: in 2004, about 275,000 were claiming benefit because of poor health. This was a much higher proportion than anywhere else in Scotland; in Edinburgh, the proportion claiming benefit was only 14%. Poor health may be an important reason why 20,000 extra Glaswegians are economically inactive.

Identifying the cause appears relatively simple. Admissions to hospital show that Glaswegians were far more likely to seek help for life-style diseases than people in Edinburgh. Once again, this adverse statistic is exacerbated by the artificial separation of the city's prosperous suburbs from Glasgow itself. Its northern suburb, East Dunbartonshire, has an intermediate rate of coronary heart disease but has appreciably lower rates of drug or alcohol abuse than either city.

Table 9.4   Admission rates to hospital for different causes in different places between 1992 and 2002

Cause of admission	Glasgow	Edinburgh	East Dunbartonshire
Coronary Heart Disease	466	264	274
Drugs	315	131	45
Alcohol	1272	737	432

Expressed in hospital admissions per 100,000 of population. Source Scottish Neighbourhood Statistics. Coronary Heart Disease is partly a result of life-style choices and can therefore be included among the self inflicted diseases.

You may think it self-evident that individuals must shoulder the blame for their own problems. After all, they did not have to fail at school, take up cigarettes or drugs, exercise too little and eat too much of the wrong foods. We have spent enough educating them and letting them know how to live a decent life. It is up to them. The pronouns in this sentence are important: is it 'them' that fail 'us' – or are 'we' part of the problem?

A wealth of evidence from many countries has accumulated showing a strong link between status and health. The basic rule is that the higher one's status in a society, the longer one lives compared to others in the same society. The difference cannot be entirely explained by bad habits such as smoking; it may be safer for someone from Bearsden to smoke cigarettes than someone from Dalmarnock. Both educational achievements and income are good guides to status. So if your parents are poor and you fail at school, your chances of dying young are much enhanced. If, however, you live in a more egalitarian society, such as Sweden, the poverty of your parents and your lack of educational achievements appear to be less damaging to your health. Therefore, the self destructive behaviour of many of the deprived may be exaggerated in a less egalitarian society and mitigated in a more egalitarian one. The Thatcher reforms may have improved Britain's economic performance but they also made inequality worse. Figure 9.1 plots the Gini coefficient in the UK over the last 25 years: the higher the value, the more inequality there is in society. There was a sharp increase during the Thatcher years followed by a plateau until 2001 when it started to fall slightly. Britain's Gini co-efficient of 34% is low compared to the USA's 40% but is at the top end of European countries – Sweden, 25%, Germany 28%, France 33% and Italy 36%. The reason for the increased mortality among the poor of countries with more inequality is thought to arise from chronic stress caused by living in neighbourhoods with low levels of trust and poor social cohesion. Individuals feel that they have little control over their destinies so tobacco, alcohol and other drugs may seem more attractive or less threatening; indeed they may appear to offer solace.

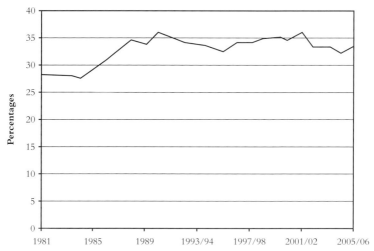

Figure 9.1   Income inequality in the UK over the last 25 years as measured by the Gini co-efficient. The higher its value the more inequality exists.

Source: ONS 2007

In his book, *The Impact of Inequality*, Wilkinson shows a graph correlating the age-adjusted death rates with inequality of income within cities of the UK, Australia, Canada, US and Sweden. There was a clear correlation with mortality rising as income inequality increased. Egalitarian Swedes in their cities had a lower mortality than unequal Americans in theirs. Income inequality in Glasgow was about the average for the cities included in the study but its death rate was one of the worst. Therefore, there may be an extra toxic 'Glasgow' factor; exactly what it is remains a mystery. Perhaps it is one of the most stressful cities in which to live if you are poor.

Therefore, poor health contributed significantly to the high rate of economic inactivity in the city with 32% of working-aged Glaswegians claiming benefits, compared to 23% in Dundee and 14% in Edinburgh in 2004. Poor health may be a result of dysfunctional communities rather than the cause. The evidence also points to a link between poor educational attainments and poor health which is why the 20,000 extra Glaswegians with no educational qualifications may be the same as those living off disability living allowance.

Drugs

Alcohol and drug abuse are very good ways of breaking down social cohesion. Perhaps a third of men and a fifth of women in the Glasgow metropolitan area over the age of 16 drank more than the recommended amount. But 13,500 or 3.4% of adults between the ages of 15 and 64, with four times as many men as women, had a major alcohol problem in 2003. Hospital admissions caused by the effects of alcohol and death from cirrhosis both increased steadily between 1991 and 2003.

Alcohol, which is legal, is a traditional disrupter of societies even if in small doses it helps con-viviality. Drugs have no plus sides for society and are illegal which may compound the problems they cause. Once again, Glaswegians seem particularly prone to the temptation. In 2003, 11,325 drug addicts were thought to be living in Glasgow and 14,111 in the counties around. Of the population between the ages of 15 and 54, 3.3% in Glasgow and 2.6% in Greater Glasgow were addicts. In Dennistoun, the rate was 11.2%. There were more hard-drug addicts than elsewhere in Scotland. It is difficult to overstate the size of the drug problem in Glasgow.

Drugs and crime

It is unlikely that many of the 25,000 addicts in Greater Glasgow were working. Eighty percent of those starting a drug rehabilitation programme were unemployed and 15% had never worked. Each addict had to find about £18,000 per year to pay for his or her habit and therefore necessarily turned to crime – mainly theft, but women also resorted to prostitution. It has been estimated that each addict commits an average of 300 crimes a year. That works out at about 330,000 each year in Glasgow. If this is true, then the number of crimes reported by the police in 2003, which was only 77,210, suggests gross under-reporting.

The threat of crime affects everyone. The following was posted on the web in 2005:

> The St Enoch centre. You know, I've actually heard this place described as 'a beautiful building'. I'm serious, I read that somewhere. Anyway, the centre itself isn't so bad but for some reason it does seem to attract many hundreds of common neds. They hang around at the front end of the centre and sit on the steps leading to the main door (there seems to be a lot of young girls with prams on those steps too). This side of the center is reasonably ok and the neds don't cause too much trouble, just the odd bit of shop lifting but then how is a ned meant to get by these days on just a giro, disability benefit, child support, housing benefit, free holiday … . When you stray to the other side of the St Enoch centre you will be astonished at the change in atmosphere from quite threatening to very threatening. I don't recommend going to the back end of the St Enoch centre. There's only a car park and the odd mugger anyway and maybe a prostitute or two. Oh, and a big Argos.

The police offer more hope. Their website reports:

> Glasgow City Centre has recently been voted the best shopping environment in the United Kingdom and officers in Glasgow Central and West Division work hard to ensure that your trip to the city is a safe and enjoyable one. During daytime hours, however, one of the main problems identified in a predominantly retail environment is that of shoplifting and associated crime. Over the last three years, the 'Hard Target' Initiative has been working with retailers to reduce shoplifting, fraud and petty theft within Glasgow City Centre.

> In Glasgow, the various shopping malls, large department stores and smaller outlets are all hoping for good trading throughout the year. However, in common with all major shopping centres, retail crime in the form of fraud and shoplifting does exist in Glasgow and accounts for 55% of all reported crime, with shoplifting accounting for 30% of the total.

> Reducing retail crime is all about partnership working across the retail community, sharing responsibilities and best practice. Retailers play their part in reducing the risks to their premises by adopting crime prevention measures and, to this end, numerous businesses have already been supplied with practical advice on how to prevent thieves from entering their premises, and more than 7,000 members of staff have received training.

> The initiative continues to be successful and retail crime in all its forms has been dramatically reduced. Since 'Hard Target' started in November 2000, reports of theft by shoplifting have reduced by 44%, fraud reduced by 55% and petty thefts reduced by 26%. Those crime reductions are set against a backdrop of a 20% increase in retail space within the city over the last three years. Such massive reductions in crime figures in Glasgow City Centre speak for themselves as Glasgow continues to be a robust, thriving business community (and the safest city in the United Kingdom).

This rosier picture may be based on poor information. Jennifer Johnston reckoned that shoplifting cost the Scottish economy about £166m in Scotland in 2003 (*Sunday Herald*). She wrote:

Glasgow is the worst affected city in Scotland – losing £28m a year to shoplifters, a 7% rise since 2000. Edinburgh came second in the stakes for losses due to shoplifting, losing £22.2m worth of goods and Aberdeen third with £12.8m.

Across the UK, police only attend about one-third of the cases of shoplifting they are called to. In certain big department stores staff actually limit their calls to the police for the most serious or costly incidents that they encounter.

In the UK every year 650,000 shoplifters are arrested – the problem is that the retailer ends up with a shoplifter sitting in their security room and if the police choose not to attend, then the retailer is risking an assault charge by detaining them or forcibly taking them to a police station.

Glasgow is, of course, not the only city with the problem. London is the worst. Gerald Eve, a company specialising in property advice, published their assessment in 2004:

Retailers in London's prime locations of Oxford Street, Bond Street and Regent Street have bemoaned the 'ugly' trading environment and the highest rate of shoplifting in the country. Gerald Eve's survey suggests shoplifting loses 5.8% of trade in London's West End – considerably more than other UK cities such as Sheffield (1.3%), Bristol (1.7%), Cardiff (1.7%) and Glasgow (2.0%).

Assessing the amount stolen from a shop is notoriously difficult. The estimate of £28m stolen from Glasgow's shops is likely to be a huge underestimate since 11,000 addicts require an estimated £200m a year to buy drugs. The total damage to the city's economy may be £500m each year since thieves only realise a fraction of the value of the goods that they steal whereas replacements are charged at the full price. Shoplifting is not the only source of income but is likely to represent a major one. Even if it only accounts for a third of the income of drug addicts, the value of stolen goods is likely to exceed £150m each year.

Studies have attempted to quantify losses from individual shops. One by David Farrington and co-workers of the Institute of Criminology in Cambridge University used a method of counting daily what was in the shop. In January 1990, his team studied various Dixons and Curry's stores in different cities and picked out ones which had high rates of shoplifting for study. One chosen was a Curry's shop somewhere in Glasgow where they recorded a loss through theft of 35% of items leaving the premises. It sold goods to a value of £406 daily compared to a loss of £209 in items stolen. The study then looked at the effect of redesign, electronic tagging and uniformed guards on the shoplifting rate and found that electronic tagging of goods was the most effective and although redesign also had an effect, it may have been temporary. Uniformed guards were no deterrent at all.

Five hundred million pounds is quite a large economy in its own right – some 4% of the city's legitimate GDP of about £12b. The money acquired by this trade has to be laundered and this, in turn, gives rise to a large number of small businesses which are, in effect, subsidised by crime and prevent the development of other legitimate competitors. Mini-cab companies, entertainment businesses and security firms are thought to be the main vehicles for money laundering. The size of the criminal and black market sectors attracts workers away from legitimate businesses and may be another reason why there are more people of working age who are economically inactive than in other cities. One taxi driver volunteered as he drove me through a district in the East End that everyone living in that neighbourhood earned their livelihood through crime. I do not know if he was right but it is possible given the size of this economy.

Therefore, a large proportion of the extra 20,000 non-contributors that live in Glasgow may be either drug addicts or living off the trade in drugs. Solve addiction and you solve deprivation. Unfortunately this is unlikely to be true since addiction is a symptom of deprivation.

There have been many initiatives to try and help addicts. The Greater Glasgow Health Board set up a Glasgow Drug Problem Service, which is the largest of its kind in the UK, in 1994. It established a needle exchange programme and organised pharmacists in the city to administer a methadone substitution programme. It works with the Glasgow Drug Court, established in 2001, the police and the social work department to try and break the cycle of addiction and crime. The court imposes Drug Treatment and Testing Orders which were piloted in the city and in Fife. Instead of sending offenders to prison, they are given a programme supervised by the Drug Problem Service and are regularly tested to ensure compliance. Assessment of the project showed that an offender, after six months on the programme, reduced his/her drug consumption by about 90% with an equivalent reduction in crime. The programme cost about £8,000 per person per year compared to £28,000 for a year spent in prison. Since crime was also reduced, the project was judged a success and was implemented. The promise was confirmed in the early days of its formal introduction.

These measures appeared to be having some effect because Glasgow University's Centre for Drug Misuse Research found that there had been a 15% drop in the number abusing drugs compared to a 6% fall in the rest of Scotland in the early 2000s. It also found that the number using the services had risen by 10%. There was also some encouragement from the Rowntree Report of 2004 which found that drug abuse among adults younger than 25 was less in Glasgow than in Aberdeen, Dundee or Inverclyde, adjusted for population. Whether this represented a reduction in addiction among the younger generation of Glaswegians or an increase in the other cities was not made clear, but the other evidence suggests the former explanation.

Another possible solution is legalising all drugs and providing them at a reasonable cost in licensed premises. This is not as crazy as it sounds; many chief constables have come out in favour. If there is no profit to be made, there would be no pushers. If no pushers, the pressure to try drugs would be reduced. The medical consequences would probably be less severe than those of alcohol and the dangers caused by the illegality of drug use would be reduced. These include infections caused by injecting contaminated material, leading to abscesses and venous thrombosis, transmission of viral diseases such as AIDS and Hepatitis C through shared needles and accidental overdose caused by variation in the potency of the drugs supplied, to which addicts coming out of prison are especially vulnerable. If addicts received their drugs from a controlled supplier at little more than cost price, crime would be reduced dramatically. So, with less crime and fewer addicts with fewer side-effects, it is difficult to see the arguments against legalisation.

Meanwhile, the problem remains considerable. Between 1999 and 2002, there were three times as many admissions proportionately to hospital for drug misuse in Glasgow than in Scotland as a whole. Alcohol abuse caused four times as many admissions but was less than twice the Scottish average.

Single parents

One other major problem of the city's deprived areas is that of children living with one parent, usually a young mother. There is a growing dichotomy in society in the age of first pregnancies: the rich are having theirs later and the poor earlier. Some first-time mothers in affluent areas of Glasgow were older than some grandmothers in the city's poorest communities. Figure 9.2 shows how social deprivation affected the age of women bearing their first child in 2001/2. The commonest age for the most deprived mothers to have their first child was 18 compared to 31 for the least deprived women.

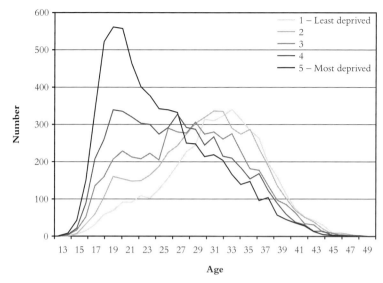

Figure 9.2   Age of mother when first child delivered in quintiles of differing deprivation

Source: Scottish Health Statistics ISD 2007

Many teenage mothers end up as single parents. Fully 40% of families in Glasgow in 2004 had only one parent, the highest in the UK according to a report by a children's charity, NCH Scotland. Why do young women from disadvantaged backgrounds become pregnant when young and unmarried? Many think financial poverty is a major factor. The implication is clear: no poverty – no problem.

But the reasoning is circular. Money alone is unlikely to break the cycle. The cause reflects the girls' upbringing.

> Teenage pregnancy rates, like violence among young men, are among the clearest statistical in-dicators of the social damage of inequality and low social status … .Girls are likely to become sexually active and become pregnant earlier if they are brought up without a father.
>
> Richard Wilkinson *The Impact of Inequality*

So girls bought up in deprived circumstances meet similar young men, have a child early but are unable to sustain their partnership and split up. It is another symptom of deprivation which leads to poverty. Poverty is the result, not the cause.

Childhood culture

Young children acquire their values primarily from their parents. Studies from 1950 onwards have shown that both boys and girls raised without fathers are more likely to have difficulties at school leading to poor exam results, to indulge in antisocial or delinquent behaviour and to have more difficulty in maintaining close relationships particularly with the opposite sex. These studies only used the criterion of whether the father was present or not; other studies, not surprisingly, showed that the better the relationship between father and child, the better the child's development. Both boys and girls benefited from the presence of a father in the home but boys benefited more. Therefore, on average, two parents are better than one. This is not to deny that many children bought up by a single parent do very well, it is that on average they are at a disadvantage compared to children of two-parent families.

The 'academic' level of deprived children starting school may be as much as two years behind their contemporaries. This has little to do with poverty *per se* but with input from parent(s), diet and perhaps nurseries. It doesn't cost much to read to children or to play games with them but parents are much less likely to do so if their own parents did not do so or if life is a struggle. The state started providing help with nursery schools in 2002 and this may narrow the gap that exists when poor children start school.

Boys brought up without a father and going to a primary school without male teachers lack a male role model. So that role is performed by elder brothers or school mates. While in primary schools, they are initiated into territorial gangs by their elders. These gangs offer company, adventure and an illusion of security. The following extract is Jimmy Wilson's account of the gang culture in Easterhouse which he was trying to eradicate:

> Until we started working with the young people there was a clearly defined progression, with an awareness of territorialism starting to build up around the ages of nine or ten. The kids would watch older brothers or other teenagers they know, seeing or hearing about incidents where rival gangs would taunt each other, and then they would become aware of the physical boundaries in terms of different areas belonging to different gangs. But it wouldn't really become a problem until secondary school, when they started to get involved rather than just watching.

> This means that at a young age boys in particular were likely to be making almost unconscious decisions about their future.

> Boys say that being involved in a gang offers protection. JT, aged 14, has been involved in territorial fights, but doesn't feel he had much of a choice … 'There's always been gangs here and you know where you belong to, so you know where you can go without fear of getting into trouble'.
>
> Source, article by Joan McFadden in *The Herald* Society, March 2005

The gangs may do more than just defend their territory: some progress to crime and some to drugs and crime. Both lead to brushes with the police. In 2004, the Scottish Prison Service found that the chances of a young man from the poorer areas of Glasgow being sent to prison before the age of 23 were one in nine. By definition, that means a lot of normal young men go to prison, since one in nine cannot all be freaks.

Children of parents with drug or alcohol problems have an even harder upbringing than most. Indeed, it is almost unimaginable. They are quite a large minority.

Social deprivation

The problems discussed above all lead to and result from social deprivation. Deprivation in areas of Glasgow has always been and remains among the worst in Scotland, the UK and beyond. Table 9.5 lists the twenty most deprived areas in 2003 compiled by the Scottish Executive using the Scottish Index of Multiple Deprivation criteria (see below). There was one district each from Edinburgh, Dundee, Highland and Renfrewshire. The other 16 came from Glasgow and most from the East End.

Table 9.5   List of the most deprived areas in Scotland

THE 20 MOST DEPRIVED AREAS IN SCOTLAND	
1 Keppochhill, Glasgow	11 St James, Renfrewshire
2 Drumry, Glasgow	12 Braidfauld, Glasgow
3 Parkhead, Glasgow	13 Ibrox, Glasgow
4 Craigmillar, Edinburgh	14 Barlanark, Glasgow
5 Hutchesontown, Glasgow	15 Ashfield, Glasgow
6 Bridgeton/Dalmarnock, Glasgow	16 Whitfield, Dundee
7 Queenslie, Glasgow	17 Milton, Glasgow
8 Merkinch, Highland	18 Wyndford, Glasgow
9 Royston, Glasgow	19 Easterhouse, Glasgow
10 Glenwood, Glasgow	20 Summerhill, Glasgow

Source: BBC News March 2003 quoting release from Scottish Executive

The 2004 report by the Joseph Rowntree Foundation found that three-quarters of British children living in poverty were in London, Manchester, Liverpool and Glasgow and, of these, Glasgow was the worst. It had 28 council wards where half the children lived in households receiving some sort of means tested benefit. Liverpool, the second worst performer, had only 12 such wards. The contrast with other Scottish councils was highlighted in the same report which ranked Scottish Local Authorities for 14 categories of deprivation. Glasgow occupied an unwelcome first place in eight of these categories which were:

> Number of small areas with high proportion on low income
> Number in receipt of out-of-work benefits
> Children in low income homes
> Limiting long term illness
> Overcrowding
> Drug misuse
> Premature death
> Low income pensioners

Why does Glasgow have this burden of deprivation? Poverty itself is unlikely to be the main cause. In 2004, 274,000 Glaswegians worked full-time and 110,000 part-time. Those in full-time work living in Glasgow had an average weekly wage of £408 compared to £480 in Edinburgh, £383 in Dundee and for £430 in Leeds (data from NOMIS 2005). Therefore, the jobs created in Glasgow are reasonably paid. The influx of new jobs has reduced the number of the economically inactive which fell by 18,000 to 111,000 between 2000 and 2004. The question for planners is whether those who remain without work are capable of it. If they are, creating more jobs should solve the problem; if not, other remedies will be required. The probability is that there is a sizeable minority who are at present unemployable because of their destructive lifestyles, lack of qualifications, crime both as victim and perpetrator, drug abuse and prison. Young girls who are teenage lone parents may also find work difficult. These people may simply be unfit for work. Many of them feel quite hopeless and powerless to change anything even though their lifestyle brings misery, leading to suicide four times more often than among those from more prosperous areas.

Deprivation is cultural

It is as though there are islands of deprivation resistant to the creation of new jobs because of an alternative lifestyle which exists in parts of the city based on different rules. People in these areas are normal individuals who are victims of the prevailing culture which is difficult to resist due to peer pressure. It takes an enormous effort to be born in to it and not to be swallowed up. A janitor of one of the blocks of flats which is used to house immigrants told me that he was fascinated to see how they differed from the Scottish tenants. Within a week or two many immigrants were leaving for work dressed in suits. A few weeks later they were driving away in cars. The Scots who lived in the same block were bitter that the immigrants had been given so much help apparently not realising that they themselves had had even more help over the years. Immigrants are not part of the prevailing culture even though they too lived in the same flats and were just as poor. Their culture was to solve their own problems and they did. The culture of the ones caught in the 'poverty trap' is one of helplessness.

The picture I have drawn is of about 20,000 extra people, disadvantaged for one or more reasons, living in Glasgow compared to similar cities elsewhere in the UK. By implication the remaining citizens are 'normal'. Is this true?

The Scottish Executive measures deprivation using six criteria compounded into a single index, the Scottish Index of Multiple Deprivation (SIMD). This has been applied to small geographical areas called data zones of which each has an average population of 775. There are 6505 data zones in Scotland and 693 in Glasgow. The results for 2004 were published in the Scottish Neighbourhood Statistics. Between 40 and 50% of Glasgow's data zones are in the worst 10% of Scotland's data zones on all parameters except access to services and telecommunications. Housing was particularly bad (Table 9.6).

Table 9.6   Aspects of deprivation in Glasgow's data zones in 2004

SIMD	46.69%
Current Income domain	41.35%
Housing domain	58.65%
Health domain	48.41%
Education, Skills and Training domain	43.08%
Employment domain	42.22%
Geographic Access and Telecommunications domain	0.00%

Numbers refer to the percentage of Glasgow data zones in the most deprived decile of all Scotland's data zones
SIMD = Scottish Index of Multiple Deprivation
Source: Scottish Executive's Scottish Neighbourhood Statistics 2005

Thus 47% of Glasgow's data zones were among the most deprived ten per cent in Scotland in 2004 according to this index – a truly extraordinarily high proportion. The criteria used to assess deprivation had six domains. The current income domain did not assess actual income but the proportion of inhabitants in each zone receiving one or other form of income support. The housing domain recorded data on two criteria – the presence of overcrowding and central heating. Health was measured on a comparative mortality factor, admissions to hospital for defined causes, low birth weight babies and the number taking drugs for depression or anxiety. Education was defined by some school results, the proportion with no qualifications, the proportion of 16-year-olds who had left school and 17-year-olds who had not attempted some form of higher education. The employment domain took into account the Unemployment Claimant Count, the number of working-age inhabitants who were receiving incapacity benefits and the number of New Deal participants. In all these domains, the results were appalling. Only in the domain of access to telecommunication services did Glasgow score well.

Using these data it is possible to see whether there are two Glasgows; the Glasgow of the deprived and the Glasgow of the prosperous, which I had expected to be the case. The data shown in Figure 9.3 prove otherwise. The data zones of Glasgow and Edinburgh have been plotted in ascending order of deprivation. The Edinburgh line is nearly horizontal to start with, indicating that many data zones have no deprivation (i.e. low SIMD scores) and then kicks up steeply as deprivation gets serious. Deprived areas are isolated and identifiable. By contrast, the blue line of Glasgow rises remorselessly from the outset so that each data zone is a little more deprived than its predecessor. There is no division between rich and poor or normal and deprived, there is only a spectrum of steadily increasing deprivation. In particular, there is hardly any upwards kick at the end which would have indicated ghettoes with a different order of deprivation. It could be argued that the rich commuter belt should be considered in this equation. But the addition of two of the most prosperous districts in Scotland does little to alter the picture except that the early part of the Glasgow curve has been flattened out a bit and is nearer to that of Edinburgh and the Lothians for the least deprived 200 data zones but thereafter the two curves diverge as before.

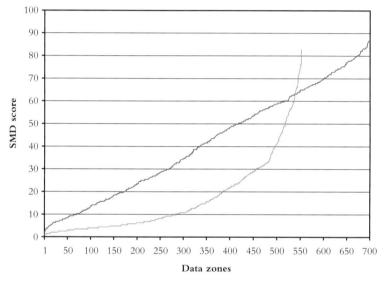

Figure 9.3   SIMD scores in the data zones of Glasgow and Edinburgh arranged in order of increasing deprivation

Source: Scottish Executive statistics 2005

If red represents normal and blue deprivation, Edinburgh is a red city with blue dots and Glasgow a blue city with red dots. Therefore, the idea that Glasgow is a normal city with a bit of extra deprivation may not be correct. It is a city of deprivation with a few islands of normality which, if one is optimistic, may be expanding as more find jobs. Who makes up the 47% of the population who were in the most deprived 10% in Scotland? It probably includes the 19% who are economically inactive and the 17% of the city's population who are pensioners. This generation of pensioners may be particularly unfortunate in that their working years were blighted by the high unemployment of the 1980s and therefore have little to live on but the old age pension and other grants. The remainder of those suffering deprivation are likely to be the children of the economically inactive.

The increasing numbers in work should have reduced deprivation and the next generation of pensioners may not be as poor as the present one since many will have been in work and therefore have some sort of pension. But at present, Glasgow's social deprivation is severe by British and European standards and is aggravated by the culture of Glaswegians; this includes aspects which affect health (diet, exercise and smoking), education (high drop-out rates, poor exam results and poor skills) as well as high teenage pregnancy rates and significant drug addiction.

Is social deprivation reversible?

The city pays a high price in terms of lost economic activity, high social and health costs and the side effects of a large population of drug addicts. Plus, there is the frightening fact that deprived Glaswegians, whose only error was to be born in one culture rather than another in the same city, lose as much as two decades of life.

Can the culture be changed? Glasgow's economic recovery appears to have improved the lot of 50,000 who found employment during the dozen years up to 2005. These tended to be people living in a household with two adults. Those living alone were less successful, particularly if they had no dependents. As the numbers of unemployed decreased, the number on invalidity benefit remained fairly constant; remarkably, fully one-third of the sick or disabled were aged less than 45. This also points to a hard core that is unlikely to take a job under any circumstances.

The government, in one form or another, must believe that it is possible to reclaim the others for it has spent about £120m per year and European funds provided a further £52.6m per year for seven years from 1999 to try and deal with deprivation. The methods used for the programme were not piloted and largely depended on persuasion through the dissemination of information and some support. As usual targets were set and an early assessment of progress was not very optimistic. Between 2002 and 2003, the number on Incapacity Benefit in Glasgow fell from 61,000 to 59,300, the number on Job Seekers' Allowance was down from 18,800 to 17,300 and the number of lone parents receiving support had fallen from 17,400 to 16,600. However, the main target was the number receiving income support and this remained unchanged at 40,300.

Thus it was a typical government undertaking with few pilot projects, lots of money spent and a whole forest of targets. It may be too early to judge its success but the Scottish Executive were at it again, announcing their proposals for reducing deprivation under the slogan 'Closing the Opportunity Gap' in July 2004. They were:

- To increase the chances of sustained employment for vulnerable and disadvantaged groups – in order to lift them permanently out of poverty
- To improve the confidence and skills of the most disadvantaged children and young people – in order to provide them with the greatest chance of avoiding poverty when they leave school
- To reduce the vulnerability of low income families to financial exclusion and multiple debts – in order to prevent them becoming over-indebted and/or to lift them out of poverty
- To regenerate the most disadvantaged neighbourhoods – in order that people living there can take advantage of job opportunities and improve their quality of life
- To increase the rate of improvement of the health status of people living in the most deprived communities – in order to improve their quality of life, including their employability prospects
- To improve access to high quality services for the most disadvantaged groups and individuals in rural communities – in order to improve their quality of life and enhance their access to opportunity

This was followed by the inevitable announcement of targets to hit. The main weapon used to try and hit these targets is to pay people to exhort the socially deprived to change their behaviour.

But is this approach sensible? Can people with little motivation and appalling personal problems be persuaded by lectures on healthier lifestyles and the need for qualifications? I suspect that the arguments do not seem that important to people who feel hopeless or to the young who believe in their own immortality or to drug addicts who cannot plan further ahead than their next fix.

The quality of housing and the appearances of the estates can be, and many have been, improved, more jobs can be and have been created, but can the culture be changed? The evidence to date shows that Glasgow's deprivation burden remains largely intact.

Other approaches have been tried elsewhere. Putman reviewed successful projects that had been operating in the US for some years, undertaken by a variety of agencies from churches to businesses. They all had common themes. All involved the people of the community concerned. Prescription from outsiders was counterproductive and the first task was to convince the locals that they would run the project even if those who had started the initiative thought that mistakes were being made. The organisers confined their role to implementing the decisions of the community. Self-help was the golden rule. This system built up networks in the communities where few had existed before. Networks were thought to be the key to success. In terms of health, people with more networks live longer than those without. Deprivation in Glasgow is associated with isolation, where many middle aged and elderly people live alone and often rely almost entirely on their families for support. Whether Putman's approach is viable in such a large community as the deprived areas of Glasgow is doubtful because the organisation required would be very complicated. It has been tried with some success in small areas such as parts of Easterhouse. However, this approach presents serious problems for councillors because it necessitates loss of control to the locals who make the plans which necessarily involves expense. This is against all their instincts and usual custom.

Mentoring young children, particularly boys of single mothers, may help especially if the mentors are volunteers and old enough to be perceived as surrogate grandparents. One scheme in the United States, Adopt a Grandchild, seeks men over 50 to see if their input can help boys develop more positively. No results have been published. This is unlikely to be acceptable in the UK at present when men are seen as predators with little to offer except danger.

The police also have a role which is very difficult. It is almost impossible to prevent the violence that arises when individuals or groups cross boundaries which separate one gang's territory from another's. Yet, unless this can be achieved, boys find it difficult to take advantage of facilities like sports centres or libraries that lie outside 'their' territory. This encourages youths to seek protection in their own gangs. The police also appear to many to support the rights of the disruptive against the rights of the constructive thus limiting the ability of communities to deal with their problem families. This prejudice is very difficult to prove but there are so many stories of men being indicted for assault when trying to protect their neighbourhood from young hooligans that it may be true.

The numerous governmental initiatives have done little to alter the culture of deprivation except that the number in work is steadily increasing. All the other initiatives have yielded disappointing results. The reasons why social deprivation has proved so difficult to eradicate are not clear but, at the end of the 20th century, monetary poverty was not the main cause. A culture had grown up which led to dysfunctional families, often housed in ghettoes of hopelessness, producing generation after generation of deprived offspring drifting to its fate rather like the reinforcements sent to France in the First World War.

PART 3
THE FUTURE

CHAPTER 10

INDEPENDENCE?

In 2007, Britons celebrated the 300th anniversary of the Union in a surprisingly half-hearted fashion considering its historic success and the benefits that it has brought to both sides. The Scots have performed well above expectations; after all, the English really only wanted to secure their northern border but they also got the Scottish Enlightenment which had such far reaching effects for the world; Scottish regiments became the shock troops of the army as an empire was won; Scottish contributions to the industrial revolution were considerable as were their discoveries in science and medicine. Even some Scottish cultural traditions have been adopted as the best of British. Who knows how much would have happened if Scotland had remained a poor independent neighbour of England? But Scotland has also reaped huge benefits; from the Navigation Acts in the 18th century which gave Glasgow a start in colonial trade; from the Empire which provided a major market for its industrial products in the 19th century as well as an outlet for the younger sons of many families; and from political evolution shared with one of the more innovative states in Europe. Even the economic performance of Scotland in the first decade of the 21st century is far better than most pundits allow, with the historic gap with England all but closed. Everyone cites the difference in the growth of GDP between England and Scotland, but, if Scotland is compared to the English regions outside the Southeast and with Wales, the record is quite respectable particularly if the loss of population is factored in.

So why change a winning formula? There are three main arguments for independence: sentiment, constitutional instability and economic potential.

Sentiment with some statistics

Some Scots have a gut feeling that the time has come to seize home rule on the grounds that a nation needs its sovereignty. This feeling is surprising given how inextricably mixed the nations have become. Each census since the Second World War has found more English living in Scotland than the one before (see Figure 10.1) rising from 222,000 in 1951 to 409,000 in 2001 when they made up about 8% of the population. This is dwarfed by the number of Scots living in England, which increased 565,000 in 1951 to 796,000 in 2001. Thus migrant Scots make up about 1.6% of the population living in England but, more importantly, about 16% of Scots have moved south.

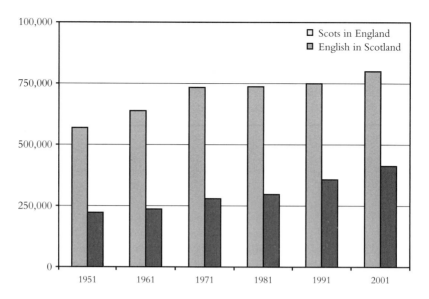

Figure 10.1   Number of Scots living in England and English in Scotland at the time of each census after WW2.

Source: The censuses of England and Scotland taken from *Being English in Scotland* by Murray Wilson

In 2000, the year before the last census, 47,823 people moved to Scotland and 47,766 left the country. The figures for the four major cities are shown in Table 10.1.

Table 10.1   Number of people who moved to the four major Scottish cities from the rest of the UK in 2000. Source General Registry Office for Scotland report on 2001 census

City	Glasgow	Edinburgh	Aberdeen	Dundee
In	4,739	9,639	2,088	1,474
Out	5,299	8,406	2,681	1,342

More people moved to Edinburgh from the rest of the UK than to the other three cities combined. This includes all immigrants; some may have come from Ulster or Wales but most will have been English. Indeed, for the last half of the 20th century, the English were by far the largest immigrant group, although the rate of migration was not as high as that of the Irish in the middle years of the 19th century, but there was no famine to spur it.

Exchanges between the two nations since Union have been so extensive that the genetic make-up of the two countries must be well nigh indistinguishable (even if it was different to start with, which Stephen Oppenheimer doubts). Yet the feeling of difference is still remarkably strong. It does not seem to help that millions of English people have Scottish blood flowing through their veins and many Scots are more English than they may like and both have numerous relatives on the other side of the border. Yet, however close the ties of blood and history, a distinct feeling of being different persists. The intensity of this feeling has waxed and waned with the fortunes of the British Empire which was a truly British undertaking. In the early days of the Union, enlightenment figures like Adam Smith tried very hard to Anglicise their accent, and many Scots talked about North Britain. While the going was good, Scots were fully paid up members and contributors to the Union and Glasgow was proud of its title 'the second city of the Empire'.

However, as British power diminished, the mood changed. The feeling of difference intensified after the Second World War. Many feel it without necessarily wanting independence; they just want to maintain a clearly different Scottish entity. I remember a report of one Scotsman living in Manchester who took his son to watch England playing Scotland in a European competition. He was not sure how his eight-year-old son would react – after all he had been bought up in England and spoke with a Mancunian accent. When England scored their second goal and it was clear that Scotland would lose, he looked down at his son and saw tears on his cheeks. 'Stewart, you've passed the test' was his reaction.

How have the Scots preserved their sense of identity through 300 years of history shared so intimately with the English? Commentators often cite the separate legal and educational systems as well as the difference in the churches. They rarely mention sport. I suspect the existence of separate football and rugby teams may be the most powerful of all reasons for the survival of the feeling of difference. For year after year Scotland played England and tribal loyalties were reinforced. After all, if two football teams can split a town in two, they can also help divide a nation. Sport also leads on to other complaints. Many feel that the BBC is English because it presents programmes for English ears. How many Scots have been tormented by repeated refer-ences to 1966? Some of my friends will not even watch World Cup matches until England has been knocked out because they find all the hype so excruciating – which of course is true to an unsympathetic ear. On the other hand, how many even notice how often the Lisbon Lions are introduced into TV conversations or press articles? The first song my son learnt in primary school was 'We're on the march with Ally's army, we're going to the Argentine' which of course the English were not. Every nation celebrates its successes and it is hard to criticise the BBC for focussing on the hopes relevant to 85% of its listeners.

Another less appealing method of preserving identity is to nurture a sense of grievance. Most English people arriving in Scotland have some story of petty aggravation to report although rarely offered except in a formulaic way as though the person was going through a little ritual. English people moving to the Highlands are denigrated as White Settlers even though they may have helped restore economic life to many villages. Until recently, this sort of petty persecu-tion was not censured because it was considered reasonable perhaps because of the fear that the English might swamp local culture, especially in remote areas where comparatively few English settle but where their numbers are disproportionately significant. Most of the English go to the Central Belt and particularly to Edinburgh where, in 2001, they made up 12% of the population compared to just 4% in Glasgow. But the feeling of animosity is stronger in Glasgow.

One might expect the incoming tide of English people to dilute the feeling of separateness but this has not happened partly because they, the English immigrants, go native. After a while, the English begin to share the Scots' view of their southern countrymen and by the time that their grandchildren grow up, an English family has been replaced by a Scottish one.

Many feel very strongly about being Scottish and quite weakly about being British. Surveys show that in 2005 about 40% of people living in England thought of themselves primarily as English compared to nearly 80% of those in Scotland who thought themselves primarily Scot-tish. The proportion who thought they were primarily British was 47% and 17% respectively. The feeling of being British has declined on both sides of the border because in 1992 about 62% living in England and 25% in Scotland felt British. If the question is asked more starkly, 'are you British or English/Scottish', only 16 per cent of English people said they were 'English, not Brit-ish', compared to 26 per cent of Scots who said they were 'Scottish, not British.'

In 2006, there appeared to be an even more important change of sentiment. Do the English want the Union to survive? That year, I visited friends in London and was struck by their change in attitude. The tendency of some Scots to say that they support any team playing England has been known for years but for some reason went down badly in 2006. Why should we, they said, support Andy Murray if he clearly has no reciprocal loyalty? Why is it that the First Minister expressed the same opinion while supporting the Union politically and in receipt of a generous block grant from the UK exchequer? If the English lose their sympathy for the Scots, independence for Scotland must be almost inevitable. Shortly after that visit, an opinion poll asked whether people favoured independence for Scotland. Whereas 52% of Scots said they favoured separation, an astonishing 56% of people in England agreed. Fully 60% of people living in England thought the higher level of public spending per head in Scotland was unjustified, a view supported by 36% of Scots. On the question of loyalty in sport, an ICM poll in 2007 found that 70% of English people said they would support a Scottish team playing football or rugby against a nation other than England and only 14% would support whoever was playing Scotland. This compared with 48 % of Scots who said they would back England with 34% supporting their opponents.

So sentiment on both sides of the border may be pushing towards separation. But there is a huge difference between opinion poll evidence and the way people would actually vote if the question were put in a referendum. The English, of course, will not be asked, but if they make it plain that they find the Union more trouble than it is worth, the Scots are more likely to vote for a divorce. But are these prejudices enough justification to break a partnership which has been so good for both countries?

Constitutional instability

There are two constitutional arguments for independence. The first is that the European Union is destined to be the major power representing Scots and English alike. Only it will be big enough to negotiate with the United States, China and Russia as an equal. It already negotiates for all constituent countries on climate change and agriculture and is an increasingly important voice in foreign affairs, for example in dealing with Russia. If the attention of the United States turns eastwards, defence may also become an EU undertaking. If it operates at that level, there is less and less need for Westminster. It would be far more efficient to have two levels of government: Brussels and Edinburgh. The former would be responsible for foreign affairs, defence and disputes between the European nations; the latter would be responsible for all local services and for taxation. The British seem very slow to recognise the importance of the EU perhaps because it is always presented so negatively by the press. If this were to happem, the administration of government would be much improved (see later).

The second reason is the celebrated West Lothian question, raised by Tam Dalyell back in 1977 when devolution was first debated in Westminster.

> For how long will English constituencies and English Honourable members tolerate … at least 119 Honourable Members from Scotland, Wales and Northern Ireland exercising an important, and probably often decisive, effect on British politics while they themselves have no say in the same matters in Scotland, Wales and Northern Ireland?

The referendum on Devolution in 1997 resulted in 74% of Scots and 84% of Glaswegians approving the project. The first elections for the Scottish Parliament were held in 1999 and, perhaps luckily, led to a coalition of which the senior party was the same as had won the UK election in 1997. This helped to disguise the constitutional mess that devolution brought about. It became possible for Scottish and Welsh MPs to vote on matters that pertained only to England but English MPs had no influence on similar legislation in Scotland and Wales. The West Lothian question can only remain unanswered if the English feel it does not matter. Increasingly, I think, they will resent the privileged position of Scottish MPs. Why should a Scot representing a Scottish constituency be in charge of a department which has no responsibilities in Scotland?

The powers taken over by the Scottish Parliament are:

- health
- education and training
- local government
- social work
- housing
- planning
- tourism, economic development and financial assistance to industry
- some aspects of transport, including the Scottish road network, bus policy and ports and harbours
- law and home affairs, including most aspects of criminal and civil law, the prosecution system and the courts
- the police and fire services
- environmental management
- natural and built heritage
- agriculture, forestry and fishing
- sport and the arts
- statistics, public registers and records.

If the English ever decided that no MP for a Scottish constituency could head a department which had devolved duties, career opportunities for an aspiring Scottish politician would be limited to departments dealing with powers reserved for Westminster which are:

- the constitution
- defence and national security
- fiscal, economic and monetary system
- trade and industry, including competition and customer protection
- transport (not particular to Scotland) including railways, transport safety and regulation
- social security
- medical ethics: abortion; human fertilisation and embryology; genetics; xenotransplantation and vivisection.
- broadcasting
- foreign affairs
- the civil service
- immigration and nationality
- energy: electricity, coal, oil, gas, nuclear energy
- employment
- equal opportunities.

This would restrict the careers of many Scots at Westminster. It is even possible that sentiment in England will turn against the idea of a Scottish Prime Minister, which is ironic given that several recent party leaders have been Scottish.

There have been some solutions proposed to solve the West Lothian Question:

A separate English Assembly dealing with the same matters as the Scottish Parliament does. This would be symmetrical but it would pose some problems. Where would it sit? What would be the role of the House of Lords? Would the Lords merely scrutinise Bills from the House of Commons, a much reduced workload? Who would scrutinise Bills passed by the parliaments of England, Scotland, Wales and Northern Ireland? What happens when a different party is in power in the English and the UK parliaments, particularly if English MPs sit in both parliaments and are in opposition in the UK Parliament but in power in the English Parliament? Would the English Parliament push for an extension of their powers in the same way as some want the Scottish Parliament to do? Since England makes up 85% of the population of the UK, the temptation for their Parliament to dominate the UK Parliament might prove irresistible.

Regional Parliaments Another possibility is that England be divided into regions perhaps those used by the Office of National Statistics but given more historic names such as Wessex, Mercia and Northumbria. Each region would have a population about the size of Scotland's and their own regional assembly given the same powers as the Scottish Parliament. This would be stable and workable because Scotland would be on a par with other units of its size. The main problem may be getting the English regions started. The Labour Government set up eight Regional Development Agencies for this purpose at the same time as Scotland's parliament was restored. The London Development Agency came a year later.

Under the Regional Development Agencies Act 1998, each Agency was given five statutory purposes, which are:

- To further economic development and regeneration
- To promote business efficiency, investment and competitiveness
- To promote employment
- To enhance development and application of skill relevant to employment
- To contribute to sustainable development.

The RDAs are run by personnel appointed by the Secretary of State at the Department of Trade and Industry. Each consists of 'not less than 8 nor more than 15 members'. That represents quite considerable patronage for the Secretary of State. They are, therefore, more like Scottish Enterprise than the Scottish Executive. The Labour Government hoped to develop them into local parliaments but an attempt to introduce such a system foundered when a plebiscite for an elected Regional Assembly with restricted powers was rejected by the people of the Northeast of England. Whether this was because the Assembly did not have enough powers or because the voters thought it an unnecessary extra layer of government is not clear, but the answer is important because Regional Assemblies are the most logical solution to the West Lothian Question but are unlikely to succeed unless supported by public opinion. Some encouragement may be taken from the Welsh experience. The majority for a Welsh assembly in the referendum in 1997 was wafer thin, but after a few years' experience of better government, enthusiasm increased.

Local Councils have the great advantage of already existing. In the 19th century, large cities like Manchester, Liverpool and Leeds benefited, as did Glasgow, from strong local government which had local priorities and ambitions. Diversity was much more marked than today. The experience of government in the Second World War and the setting up of the Welfare State afterwards led to extreme centralisation of power. Big plans and big government were popular both with politicians and with the people. Since then, the trend has not been reversed although, typically, politicians out of power say they want to devolve power but lose their enthusiasm once elected. Local councils, themselves, are probably too small to provide the unit for devolved power but with amalgamations could provide the continuity to achieve Regional Assemblies.

There can be little doubt that devolution would improve the quality of government. The administration of the Health and Education services, for example, has been wasteful and inefficient as each change in ministerial policy was rolled out across the country. Why is it that politicians are so reluctant to design experiments to study the practicality of their policies? Regional Assemblies would be ideal for this sort of trial so that disasters are only local and not national.

One reason that the record is so bad is the aggression of the press to ministers in general, and Prime Ministers in particular. Journalists seem to hold the prime minister responsible for:

> every sprained ankle in the land. 'The reason that British prime ministers look so exhausted when they leave office', says Tony Travers of the London School of Economics, 'is that they not only do the job that George Bush or Angela Merkel is doing; they also do most of what the states or Lander do too'.
>
> Source: *The Economist* Feb 2007

Politicians have been forced to accept responsibilities for matters of management rather than policy, and managers they are not. This has led to centralised systems micromanaging detailed administrative processes. Tony Blair's method was to set targets so that he could tell whether money spent by government was doing the job he had set. To monitor these targets, a huge administrative force was assembled. The Local Government Association, a pressure group, claims it costs about £2.5b a year. And you can see why: each major hospital may have 100 administrators, about the same number as consultants, whereas 30 years ago there may have been a dozen or so. But targets, like any measurement, distort the performance in two ways: functions with no targets get neglected; and targeted activities lead to changes in practice so that the targets appear to be met but may not be in reality. For example, some Health Trusts met their waiting list targets by the simple measure of having a waiting list to get onto the waiting list that was being assessed. But spare a thought for ministers who are probably capable, hard working and motivated individuals; what else can they do when the press holds them responsible for everything that goes wrong? I bet they feel that they would rather swing for their own faults than someone else's.

Devolution of power to the local level has huge advantages both in freeing up ministers to do more strategic planning and thus improve the quality of legislation centrally, and in transforming the quality of services delivered locally. If this model were followed, the UK parliament would end up dealing only with matters to do with finance, defence, foreign policy, the legal system and immigration. Locally elected politicians would take the rap for local problems.

Therefore, the West Lothian Question could be solved by devolution in England but for that to happen, some brave British cabinet (or Prime Minister) will have to shed power which is not easily done particularly when there is no popular enthusiasm for it.

Abstention Another proposal which has been canvassed is that Scottish MPs should simply abstain on questions which affect England only. This is unworkable since the government that introduces legislation may not have a majority among English MPs. Therefore, it would be almost powerless and England would have weak government in those matters devolved to Scotland. How would a bill of which the majority of English MPs approved but the cabinet disapproved be put before the House? Stalemate would result.

If no constitutional arrangement satisfying both English and Scottish voters can be found, both English and Scots may decide that independence for Scotland would be the best solution.

Economic potential

The third reason to consider independence is the potential boost it could give to the Scottish economy. The most vexed question is whether a Scottish Independent Government would have enough revenue to continue to fund public services at their present level. Most London based commentators accept that the rest of the UK subsidises Scotland and that the Scots are hooked on these subsidies. At first sight, this appears to be correct. The expenditure per head of the four parts of the UK is shown in Table 10.2.

Table 10.2   Comparative spending per capita in the four countries of the UK

Country	Amount per head per year		% of UK	
	2003/4	2004/5	2003/4	2004/5
England	£5,940	£6,361	96.4	96.9
Scotland	£7,346	£7,597	119.2	115.8
Wales	£6,901	£7,248	112.0	110.4
N Ireland	£7,945	£8,216	128.9	125.0
UK	**£6,164**	**£6,563**	**100.0**	**100.0**

Source: Government Review of Expenditure and Revenue in Scotland 2005 and 2006.

Scots have more spent on them than the English or Welsh but less than the Northern Irish. There are some good reasons, and some not-so-good, for this. The most convincing is the relative size of Scotland. With only 8.2% of the UK population, Scotland has about 32% of its land mass and therefore has more remote communities to support – and island communities are particularly expensive. There are about 100 inhabited islands around Scotland with a combined population of 100,000 (about 2% of Scots). The scattered communities have to be provided with education, health services and transport, all of which are expensive and account for a large part of the increased spend on these services in Scotland. The size of the country and its long coastline also lead to increased spending on fisheries, agriculture, forestry and transport. There is a net flow of university students from the rest of the UK to Scotland which, together with the four-year courses, leads to increased costs, however welcome the incomers are. For historical reasons, there is more public housing in Scotland which has proved very expensive. Exactly why central government should help councils who have run disastrous housing policies is not clear but they have done so, recently wiping off nearly a billion pound deficit for Glasgow City Council. Health problems are more severe in parts of Scotland and therefore admission rates to hospital are higher. However, once the healthcare and educational needs of isolated communities have been provided, the difference in spending on these services is much the same in England and Scotland (see Table 10.3).

Table 10.3.   Public spending in £/individual by different departments in Scotland and the UK

	Scotland £ per head	UK £ per head	Scotland (UK = 100)
Social protection	3,007	2,702	111.3
Health	1,513	1,369	110.5
Education and training	1,160	1,093	106.1
Public order and safety	376	400	94
Transport	329	262	125.6
Housing and community amenities	252	132	190.9
Recreation, culture and religion	183	111	164.9
General public services	166	96	172.9
Employment policies	158	61	259
Environment protection	154	106	145.3
Agriculture, fisheries and forestry	124	87	142.5
Enterprise and economic development	123	109	112.8
Science and technology	47	29	162.1
Total	7,597	6,563	115.8

The relative weight can be assessed by the ratio in Scotland to UK. Since total spending per head in Scotland is 116 % that of the UK, any ratio below that means that a lower proportion is spent in Scotland than in the UK. Source: Public Expenditure Statistical Analyses 2006

The proportion of the Scottish and UK budgets spent on health, education and social protection is less in Scotland than the UK average, even though the absolute amounts are a bit higher. Indeed, these three departments which account for three-quarters of the amount spent on each individual are only responsible for £416 (less than half) of the difference in expenditure. The rest comes from smaller departments with employment (an extra £97 per head) and housing (£120 more per head) showing the largest differences. Only an extra £67 per head was spent on transport which, considering the size of Scotland and the numerous isolated communities, is surprising.

The famous formula which led to this 'favouring' of the Scots was devised by Joel Barnett in 1978 as a short term stratagem for avoiding repetitive arguments in cabinet about who gets how much. It divided the funds allocated to a service so that England received 85%, Scotland 10% and Wales 5%, reflecting their relative populations at the time. However, the population of Scotland fell during the following years whereas England's rose so that Scotland received more per capita than England. The difference in spending between the different countries may be narrowing (see Table 10.2). But, whether independent or not, Scotland is a more expensive country to run at a given level because of the factors listed above.

Although more is spent on each Scot, it does not mean that Scotland is in fiscal debt to the rest of the UK. No one accuses Londoners of being hooked on subsidies although each Londoner has more spent on him or her than is spent on each Scot because they also contribute most in taxation. Those most 'hooked' are the ones who receive most and contribute least. The ONS has published the five NUTS 2 regions with the smallest and largest differences. In West Wales and the Valleys, social benefits are almost the same as tax receipts, whereas in Inner London they amount to only 35%.

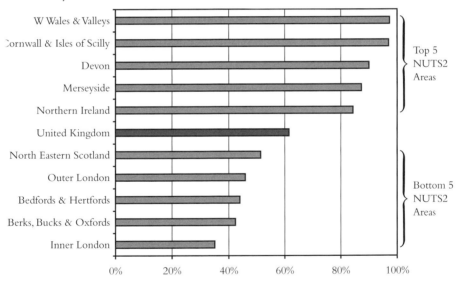

Fig 10.2   Impact of Redistribution 2005. This shows the amount paid out in social benefits by government to different regions as a percentage of tax income from the same regions.

Source: ONS 2007

No Scottish region appears in the graph except North Eastern Scotland which was the region with the fifth biggest gap, receiving about 50% of its tax contribution in social benefits. If the income from North Sea Oil is attributed to Scotland, then the balance is even more in Scotland's favour. Thus the Scots are not the biggest beneficiaries when tax contributions are taken into account.

To examine the viability of a budget in an independent Scotland, the Government Review of Expenditure and Revenue in Scotland (GERS) is an interesting starting point. Scotland received £47.7b in 2004/5 from the UK government but revenues from Scotland were only £36.4b. The deficit of £11.3b, 4.8% of the Scottish GDP or a formidable £1,176 for each Scot, is well above what would be acceptable to the European Central Bank if an independent Scotland were to apply to join the Euro. But it had decreased from 6.2% the year before when each Scot received £1,350 – so it is narrowing, according to Government statistics. These figures take no account of North Sea Oil.

The Scottish National Party vehemently disagrees. Its paper, 'Scotland in Surplus' produced in 2006 argues that, on the contrary, Scotland is in budgetary surplus and subsidises the rest of the UK by about £1b per annum. Their estimate is based on Treasury figures for the year 2006/7 and was a prospective estimate. If the Chancellor's figures were wrong, then the conclusions of the SNP would also be wrong. The SNP predicted that tax raised in the form of income tax, national insurance, corporation tax including from the North Sea, death duties, etc. would be £35.3b. But in addition receipts from customs, taxes on tobacco, alcohol and betting, landfill tax and others would add a further £16.3b. Therefore, total tax raised in Scotland was predicted to be £51.6b which, after some adjustments, increased to £54.1b. Expenditure, both identifiable and non-identifiable (i.e. defence and Foreign Office costs) came in at £53.4b. Therefore, Scotland's fiscal position in 2006/7 should yield a surplus of £700m, quite a healthy position and one which would be viewed favourably by the European Central Bank.

The difference between the two estimates is mainly due to the income generated by North Sea oil. GERS estimated it at £5.3b in 2004/5 and the SNP anticipated receipts of £11.6b in 2006/7. Part of the difference may be due to the different years in which the two studies made their estimates as government receipts from the North Sea are volatile. Two factors suggest a big jump in revenues: first, Chancellor Brown increased the Supplementary charge to Corporation Tax (SCT) on oil production from 10% to 20% so that companies essentially paid Corporation Tax at 50%. Second, the price of oil increased dramatically in 2006. The Chancellor assumed a price of $57 per barrel and the SNP thought $65 a barrel more realistic. The Red Book for the Budget in 2006 estimated that revenues from North Sea Oil would be £10.2b and the SNP added another £1.9b because of the expected higher price of oil.

Therefore, Scotland's predicted budgetary surplus in 2006/7 depended on the amount of oil recovered, its price, and the rate of the pound against the dollar. Two things seem certain: that the price of oil will increase dramatically as demand exceeds supply; and that the amount recovered from the North Sea will decrease equally dramatically. How this equation will play out is uncertain, but the North Sea while it lasts would be a great fiscal help to an independent Scotland.

The SNP seem to have extrapolated from the results of their survey to conclude that Scotland has been in surplus over the last 30 years. This is not justified by any figures in 'Scotland in Surplus' which is only a projected budget for a single year. Almost certainly, the GERS estimates, which are retrospective and produced annually, are much nearer the mark.

Even if Scotland's putative budgetary surplus is a figment of the SNP's imagination, it does not follow that independence would be unworkable or even bad for the Scottish economy. Let us assume that North Sea oil revenue is stable for the next ten years, because increasing prices are balanced by reduced production, and yields revenue of about £8b per annum; the Scottish budget would be in deficit of about £2b equivalent to 2.3% of GDP, which is manageable and within the guidelines of the European Central Bank for countries wishing to join the Euro. There would be no black hole in the new state's finances.

Independence could have some clear-cut economic benefits. In Chapter 6, I outlined some of the ways in which the dominance of London and the Southeast of England slowed growth in the economies of the northern English regions and Scotland. The most pernicious effect is the historically high interest rates imposed by the Bank of England. The Southeast has one of the most buoyant economies in Europe and the Bank always raises interest rates to restrain its over-exuberance. Never has it required to rein in the economies of the Northern regions of England, Scotland or Wales. High interest rates have a pernicious effect on regions with slower growth. As a rough rule of thumb, for each percentage point that interest rates are raised, growth is suppressed by about 0.3%. If, over the years, the Bank has set interest rates an average of two percentage points higher than is necessary for the Scottish economy, its growth will have been suppressed by about 0.6% each year which is a major reason why the Scottish trend growth rate is lower than that of England. If interest rates were 2% lower, the trend rate of growth would increase from about 1.9% to 2.5%, similar to that of the UK now. This is the single most persuasive economic argument for independence but does depend on Scotland having an independent currency or adopting the Euro. Interest rates set by the European Central Bank have, so far, been much more suitable to Scotland's needs. Alex Salmond's recent decision to stay with the pound sterling means that an independent Scotland would forgo this advantage until it adopted the euro.

Other economic advantages of independence include the ability to improve transport links with Europe and America. The present arrangement, dominated by London, disadvantages the northern English regions and Scotland. Creating an airport hub in the Central Belt would im-prove access for business and tourism. Ferry services to northern European ports may reduce the cost of using busy English motorways and contributing to the congestion around the M25. An independent government could pursue these policies more vigorously.

Immigration and energy policies are two more areas that have a direct bearing on the local economy and could undoubtedly be improved by an independent government.

However, there would inevitably be changes to the economy following independence. At present, it is over-reliant on the Public Sector. Scotland's GDP (excluding oil) in 2005 was £86.3b, and government's non-oil tax income was £36.4b or 42% of GDP and its expenditure was £47.7b, or 55% of non-oil GDP. Even with oil revenues of £8b, would it be wise to tax an economy at a rate of half its GDP? Sweden and Denmark apparently thrive on it but their model relies on social cohesion which is clearly lacking in Scotland. France also has a tax take of almost half its GDP and its public services and infrastructure are certainly better than in Britain but its economy has not been nearly so vigorous in recent years.

The SNP's plans for taxation are not yet firm. However, in January 2007 they made a couple of announcements that suggest that they hope to raise extra revenue from the English. First was an eye-catching proposal.

> The Scottish National Party's leaders say they will seek to impose a levy on Trident if the party leads the Scottish Executive after May's election.

> The SNP wants to impose a £1m toll on every nuclear weapon which is brought into Scotland. SNP leader Alex Salmond said the 'Trident toll' would use devolved powers over local taxation.
>
> Source BBC News, Jan 2007

Next, their spokesman said that a Scottish government would claim £2b for the Scottish share of the huge bonanza that fell into Chancellor Brown's pocket with the sale of licences for the third generation of mobile telephones. These proposals were good tub thumping stuff, however unrealistic. Any divorce settlement is likely to be more generous if both sides feel some sympathy for the other. Offending the English would almost certainly be counter-productive since there are countless ways in which they could poison the divorce. This approach is, in any case, curious since the SNP say that the Scottish fiscal position is secure, so why go in for this bear-baiting?

Table 10.4   GDP/head of 15 EU countries

Rank	Country	Index of GDP/head
1	Luxembourg	215
2	Ireland	133
3	Denmark	123
4	Austria	122
5	Netherlands	121
6=	Belgium	118
6=	UK	118
8	Sweden	115
9	Finland	113
10	France	111
11	Germany	108
12	Italy	107
13	Spain	98
14	Greece	81
15	Portugal	74

The indices are adjusted for purchasing power and are based on the average GDP/head of the 25 countries of the EU in 2003 of which the average is 100.
Source: Eurostat quoted in the *Herald*

The SNP regularly point out that small European countries have better economies than their bigger neighbours, a point which is largely true (see Table 10.4). Denmark and Holland have higher GDP per capita than Germany (though Germany is still feeling the effect of reunification), Belgium than France (is this because reform in France is almost impossible or because investment in the Paris region has disadvantaged the country at large?) and Austria than Italy (which is compromised by the incorrigible South) and Ireland than Britain (however, Ireland's Gross National Product, for definition see p.91, is not nearly as good as its GDP and if GNP per capita were used as the yardstick, Britain may be the better). The only clear-cut exception is Spain which does better than Portugal. Therefore, there are extenuating circumstances which the bigger countries could use to refute the claim. However, small countries certainly do well in the European Union.

The SNP proposes to follow the economic policies of some of these small countries.

Corporation Tax would be reduced in order to encourage inward investment and try to reproduce the extraordinary success of the Irish economy. An investment fund from the tax income from North Sea Oil would be set up for the benefit of future generations of Scots as the Norwegians have done. Given their rather rosy view of the Scottish fiscal state described above, this seems like spending and saving the same pot of money.

It also has plans to promote small businesses:

> Under the SNP proposals, business rates for firms with a rateable value of £8000 a year or less will be abolished. Businesses with a rateable value of £8000 to £10,000 a year will receive rates relief of 50 per cent, while those with a rateable value of between £10,000 and £15,000 would get 25 per cent off their bills. Other businesses will benefit from our commitment to parity with English business rates.

Any tax cuts would have to be balanced by a reduction in public spending or an increase in other taxes in order to prevent the PSBR rising above the 3% of GDP necessary to permit entry into the euro. The SNP has nothing to say about this. In short, the economic plans of the SNP for management of the budget of an independent Scotland are far from clear partly because it is difficult to sort out what is politics and what is policy. A period in office would be highly desirable.

Why has Alex Salmond opted to retain the pound Sterling, at least in the short term? There are three possible reasons. First, it would not be worth the trouble of setting up an independent currency to cover the gap before adopting the euro, assuming that is the immediate target. Second, by sticking with Sterling, the inevitable dose of uncertainty associated with independence would be reduced. It so happens that Scotland is going through a fairly comfortable phase at present and radical proposals for the economy may appear unattractive to an electorate voting on a referendum for independence. Third, the performance of an independent currency would be difficult to predict. What would the balance of trade be? England is Scotland's biggest trading partner and no one measures the balance of trade between the two countries. Therefore, it is impossible to predict whether Scotland would be able to export enough to pay for the imports from England. If the balance is in England's favour, the currency would depreciate and Scots would be poorer when buying foreign goods or travelling abroad, including to England. Interest rates might have to be raised in order to prevent devaluation thus mitigating one clear advantage of independence. On the other hand, a new Scottish government could chose to accept the depreciation, maintain low interest rates and wait for an export led recovery, something of a rarity in recent UK history. The intervening period would be one of belt tightening which the new Government may be unwilling to inflict because it would seem to confirm the Jeremiahs who warned that Scotland would be poorer outside the Union.

Another problem would be the health of the financial sector on which the Central Belt has become heavily dependent. It is unlikely that the London offices would switch investment away from Glasgow and Edinburgh unless the regulatory and tax burdens or economic volatility increased after independence. Therefore, if Scotland were to adopt lower interest rates and its currency depreciated, the financial sector might take fright which would be very damaging. Since the Public Sector would also be reduced in size after independence, two of the motors of the Scottish economy may misfire at the same time, leading to a reduction in retail sales and other parts of the urban economy. Tourism might benefit but there would be an uncomfortable period before growth in manufacturing picked up the slack left by downsizing of the financial and public sectors. Unemployment and social spending would increase making it more difficult for the new government to reduce taxes.

Therefore, it is not surprising that the SNP's policy is to join the euro as quickly as possible and to stick with Sterling until then. The possible growth in manufacturing is not worth the turmoil that an independent currency might cause, especially if it is to be changed for the euro as quickly as possible.

Even without a separate currency, there are areas in which an independent government could make a difference. Control of immigration policy would be a huge advantage. Although the majority of immigrants after the Second World War were English, in the last three years Poles, Latvians, Lithuanians, Estonians and other new members of the European Union have arrived in large numbers and given a non-inflationary boost to the economy. Since the Scottish population is in danger of falling below 5 million in the next few years, the importance of encouraging immigration can hardly be exaggerated. Recent decisions such as Public Finance Initiative (PFI) investments for public projects, changes to the pension system and the costs of climate change are all cheques written by this generation to be paid for by the next one. This will be bad enough, but if there are fewer workers paying for more pensioners, the burden may be extreme especially if the young also have to repay university loans and take out large mortgages. Therefore, the power to encourage immigration would be a huge bonus.

In 2004, Jack McConnell introduced such a policy, the Fresh Talent initiative, which included the following decisions:

- From summer 2005 any non-EEA student graduating from a Scottish higher or further education institute with an HND, degree, masters or PHD will be eligible to apply for leave to remain for up to two years without requiring a work permit.
- In October 2004 the government set up a relocation advisory service for people considering settling in Scotland. This one-stop service offers a wide range of advice on everything from employment, accommodation, visas and work permits to Scotland's health service, cultural life and leisure activities.
- Appointed a Scottish Enterprise secondee to join the relocation advisory service to offer employers advice on how to recruit staff from overseas.
- Funding for 22 scholarships for students from overseas who want to study for a Masters degree in Scotland. The Scottish International Scholarship Programme will start in 2005/06 and there will be nine scholarships for students from China, six for Indian scholarships and two each for students from South Africa, Australia, and Singapore as well as one for a student from New Zealand.
- We have granted Scottish Networks International £225,000 over the next three years to provide a total of 20 work placements. The funding will also be used to enhance the experience of a further 200 overseas postgraduates.
- The government has set up a challenge fund for universities and colleges to help them provide international students with opportunities to enjoy all their new home has to offer, and to make decisions about whether to stay here at the end of their studies.

These are remarkably modest but represent the best that could be achieved given that immigration policy was not devolved. An independent Scotland could be much bolder.

Independence could also lead to a greater nimbleness in government if the constitution were designed to promote it. The world is facing devastating challenges through climate change and globalisation. Speed of reaction in redesigning the economy to serve in the new conditions is vital. Democracy, particularly in a large diverse country, has many advantages but it does take overlong to react to new threats or opportunities. Even the mundane issue of planning control can put a severe break on progress. A good example is the present inquiry into the advisability of a new power line needed to bring renewable energy from the periphery of the country to the major cities. This is a vital development and may be delayed for five years while the project is examined to assess whether its value is worth the visual impact on a beautiful part of the country which is already crisscrossed with power lines. Meanwhile, it takes years to connect up new sources of clean energy to the grid and the companies that build the new plant have to bear the cost of delays. Government should be able to give different levels of urgency to projects, with the most urgent being fast-tracked through the planning system.

Another example of costly delays through government inertia is the lack of clear guidance of how future power supplies are to be generated. Is nuclear power on or off the agenda? The nuclear energy industry has waited years for a decision and now it is probably too late to build new installations to cut carbon dioxide emissions before global warming becomes critical. The government also stalled on a plan by BP to sequester carbon dioxide in one of its exhausted oilfields in the North Sea and so pioneer a new industry. This was potentially very important but the delay was so long that BP closed the oilfield and abandoned the project. A government of a small country may be able to make key decisions more quickly and be more responsive to key local projects than is possible in a country of which Scots make up less than 10%.

But it is only right to acknowledge that Scotland gets a fair crack of the whip when it comes to many aspects of national life. Take the lottery as an example. In Table 10.5, the total amount spent in selected regions in different categories is compared with the amount spent in Scotland between 1995 and 2006.

Table 10.5   Amount awarded to Scotland and selected English regions by the National Lottery for various purposes between 1995 and 2006 Source National Lottery website 2007.

Country/ region	Population	Arts	Charitable	Heritage	Millenium	Sports	Health, education and environment
Scotland	5,062,011	236,400,161	357,623,404	428,150,807	246,972,510	130,810,513	322,763,992
Yorkshire	5,037,000	148,415,748	272,684,246	270,217,229	98,261,418	194,151,834	254,042,481
Southwest	4,928,434	134,883,634	257,596,708	362,538,492	141,195,755	213,202,843	195,065,210
London	7,172.091	988,604,747	794,547,735	744,899,911	925,379,453	415,925,937	434,145,453

Yorkshire and the Southwest, with almost identical populations as Scotland, received less in all categories except sport. On the other hand, London did better in every category. Once again, Scotland does worse than London but better than the English regions.

Tourism tells a similar tale. London received about 13.9 million overseas tourists in 2005, just over 50% that came to England. But Edinburgh with 1 million foreign tourists came second and Glasgow with 700,000 comes fifth after Manchester and Birmingham. Scotland received 2.5 million of the 30 million who came to the UK, or just 8.3%, in line with its share of the UK population. Tourism accounted for 142,000 jobs in 2000 or 7.5% of all Scottish jobs (7.6% in Glasgow and Clyde Valley).

The UK earned £14.2b from overseas tourism in 2005, dwarfed by the £32.2b spent by Britons abroad. This deficit of £18b accounted for nearly half the UK's balance of payments deficit in that year.

Visits to Scotland between 1995 and 2003 ran at about 20m per year, so UK citizens account for about 90% of all visitors and 75–80% of earnings from tourism (Americans spent most per visit). Altogether, tourism contributed between £4b and £5b per year to the economy during this time – about 6% of GDP.

Would tourism be better served by independence? Probably not, since Scotland already has its own promotional organisation, VisitScotland, which is an independent body set up to:

* provide strategic direction to the industry, marketing Scotland and its tourism assets worldwide
* provide information – and inspiration – to visitors so they can experience the best of Scotland
* provide quality assurance to visitors and quality advice to industry partners to make sure the industry meets – or exceeds – visitors' expectations
* promote partnerships across the industry to make sure we all reap the economic benefits of collective effort.

Its budget was £42m in 2005–6. It is unlikely that independence would lead to any improvement. Furthermore, the English are the major customers of Scottish tourism. In 2003, around 16.5 million tourists from elsewhere in the UK took overnight trips to Scotland and they spent about £3.6 billion. Would independence affect this? In particular, would the English continue to come if they thought the Scots were anti-English? The tone of the discussion during the negotiations for independence could be a key factor.

The links between the Scottish economy and the rest of the UK are so strong that independence must be assessed in terms of its effect on those links. As has been seen, Glasgow's revival owes much to incoming investment, not least from England. Would this be put in jeopardy or even reversed if Scotland became independent? Glasgow competes with Manchester, Leeds and other English cities. Would investors choose to put their money in their home market with the same currency and the same regulations rather than in a city using the euro and with different taxes and regulations? The answer is that they would invest in Glasgow if the skills were available at a competitive rate and the tax burden were favourable, but all other things being equal, they would chose cities in their own country. And Scots would do the same.

One of the features of Glasgow's economy in recent years has been the loss of local companies to outsiders. Head offices have become rarer in Glasgow which makes the economy less robust in times of trouble. And the loss of head offices may continue. Of the ten biggest companies, Scottish Power has been taken over by a Spanish firm; British Energy is unlikely to survive as an independent company; Clydesdale Bank is owned by the Bank of Australia; and Abbey by a Spanish bank; Weir group has recently refused to deny rumours that it is in discussion with a Swiss company; and Hewden's is part of the Finning Group. Only four of the ten largest companies listed in Table 5.8 have their headquarters in the region. Surrendering major firms is likely to be to the long term detriment of the country since foreign owners seeking rationalisation of their business may well chose to make redundancies in the Scottish branch of their empire rather than in their own country. Would an independent Scottish government be more willing to protect our crown jewels?

Conclusions

The arguments for and against independence are finely balanced unless you are a true believer. As far as sentiment is concerned, there is a lot to be said for independence as a way of making Scots responsible for their own fate but this means that the possibility of failure is also on the cards. When Scotland was last independent, it organised the disaster of the Darien Adventure and Scottish incomes were well below those of England. Being part of the fourth largest economy in the world does provide a degree of insurance. Furthermore, independence would only increase sovereignty somewhat since the European Union determines the rules of much of the game. Indeed, the English attitude to Europe bears a striking resemblance to the Scottish attitude to the Union.

Constitutionally, independence might be the easiest way out of the West Lothian Question's impasse.

Economically, Scotland does well out of the union in terms of government spending but suffers in that interest rates are always too high. It is interesting that Glasgow's economic recovery followed Black Wednesday in 1992, after which interest rates fell substantially. Independence may be followed by a period of lower government spending and reduction in public services with increased unemployment before the benefits kick in.

What is likely to happen? The betting must be that Scotland will be independent within 20 years, pushed as much by growing antipathy amongst the English media which will harden the resolve of convinced nationalists and weaken the resistance of preferential unionists.

CHAPTER 11

GLASGOW 2050

The city in mid-century has had to reckon with two major developments. First, global warming proved to be more vicious than predicted in the Intergovernmental Panel of Climate Change's (IPPC) fourth report. The reasons were the leaking of methane into the atmosphere as the permafrost melted in Siberia and Canada and the melting of the Greenland and Antarctic Ice Caps were greater than anticipated. Second, independence for Scotland was not followed by the promised gains to the economy but evidence of renewed growth is beginning to emerge.

To start with global climate changes: the IPCC built up conclusive evidence that linked increasingly apparent changes in the world's climate with the increasing concentrations of greenhouse gases of which carbon dioxide (CO_2) was the most important. When people came to appreciate exactly how seriously they themselves would be affected and when they heeded the lesson of the Stern Report that it would be much more economical to reduce emissions than to deal with the consequences of global warming, they demanded a solution. It also helped that there was widespread panic that the shortage of oil would cause war between nations competing for the remaining supplies if other sources of energy were not developed. The definitive climate treaty was signed in 2012. It was radical, far reaching and received the approval of the scientists on the IPCC. Strangely, the main opposition to this course came from people who thought it was already too late to save the world and presumably thought that they should continue to enjoy their lives and let their children pay the price.

In the period leading up to the treaty, it was clear that there were four sorts of countries; developed and increasing their emissions of CO_2 such as the US and Australia; developed and modestly reducing their emissions exemplified by European countries; developing and rapidly increasing emissions such as India, China and Indonesia; and undeveloped countries with stable outputs such as most African countries, some Asian, Central American and South American countries. The differences between the four groups were startling at the end of the first decade of the new century. Australia and the US produced about 19 tons of CO_2 per person, each European just less than 10 tons per year, China had increased to 3 tons per person per year and India, Indonesia and Brazil to about half that; and the poor undeveloped countries hardly produced any – each Nigerian less than half a ton per year. The major iniquity of this imbalance was that it was the people who had contributed least to the catastrophe who were expected to suffer most. It is true that the people of the developed world felt their guilt with amazing lightness.

The standard adopted by the Climate Treaty of 2012 was that each individual was entitled to an output of 2 tons of CO_2 per year and that each country was responsible for adopting policies that would achieve that target by 2050 at a rate of reduction agreed for each country, usually 2.5% per year. Countries with outputs below this level were able to sell their carbon ration to countries with excess production. The rich and not so rich competed for the finite number of quotas, forcing up their price and this resulted in an unparalleled transfer of wealth from rich to poor in the first two decades of its operation. The old problem of corruption in many of the recipient countries was minimised by strict auditing of budgets with inspections to make sure that money was spent as intended. The treaty allowed confiscation of the carbon allowance from countries that failed one of these inspections and even the most venal of presidents was careful not to kill the goose that laid the golden eggs. Furthermore, the banking system was organised so that it was more difficult for the big men of these countries to salt away the odd billion pounds. No one pretends that the system has worked perfectly but the education and health services in most of the poorest countries have improved quite impressively and a new generation of healthier, educated graduates should be emerging from their universities soon. The money was also urgently needed to pay for measures to alleviate the worst effects of the changing climate – planting on hill slopes to reduce the threat of river flooding, building up sea defences, increasing water reserves and other measures that might help to mitigate the worst of the expected changes. It is still not clear whether the reforms have come in time as drought in many countries of Africa and Asia has reduced agricultural production and a significant proportion of the wealth transferred has had to be used to buy food from the developed world although programmes of genetic manipulation of various crops should mean that production will increase even in areas quite severely affected by drought.

As far as the developed countries are concerned, once the treaty was signed and clear goals defined, change happened at a remarkable pace, creating new industries and services while making others obsolete. Car manufacturers, for example, have proved to be fantastically innovative and cars are now more expensive but have reduced emissions to an average of about 25g of CO_2 per 100 Km, about 10% of the emissions at the beginning of the century. On the other hand, air traffic fell precipitately once people were given an individual carbon quota. Most chose local mobility in the shape of energy efficient cars rather than flights to exotic destinations which had become fashionable 50 years before. Transportation costs have become a major problem for several industries and activities. Businesses have reacted by franchising local production so that manufacturing, while still owned by a few large companies, is now spread more widely in smaller units supplying local populations. This has dramatically reduced the size of international freight transport, whether by sea or air and spread manufacturing output more evenly. It was somewhat surprising to realise how much CO_2 ships emitted as they had always been thought to be efficient users of diesel. Re-design has begun including the use of huge kites to power the ships downwind. Hulls have become narrower for any given length which improves efficiency but reduces carrying capacity so that only goods that cannot be produced locally are transported.

Conferences are now rare events and only called when a particular problem requires the attendance of critical individuals and their teams. Jamborees like the G8 summits, NATO gatherings and even meetings about climate change have been abandoned. Instead, negotiations are conducted by tele-conferencing. The professions, and particularly the medical profession which had been hooked on large international conferences, realised that information could be disseminated and discussed without anyone having to be away from their base. Teaching lectures, including state of the art lectures, were simply put on websites created by particular professions and specialties. Even sporting exchanges have been reduced. The Olympic Games takes place every six years. Football's World Cup and other competitions such as the European Cup still take place every four years but the qualifying rounds have been much reduced. No longer does Spain have to play the Faroe Islands home and away. Instead there are regional competitions played over a short period in selected countries with the winners qualifying for the finals. The net effect of these changes has been a dramatic reduction in the size and value of the conference and tourist industries.

Agriculture also had to adapt. The absurdity of a million litres of milk crossing the Channel in both directions ended when food miles were priced realistically. This led to the re-emergence of local suppliers who have adopted new techniques to grow the fruits and vegetables which had become popular with customers during the period of cheap transport. The traditional meat industry has, on the other hand contracted for two reasons: it is no longer feasible to export carcasses around the world, but even more important was the sheer inefficiency in the use of land. Therefore, agriculture has specialised in the most efficient ways of growing cereals and fruits. Genetic engineering has proved invaluable in maintaining output in areas of water shortages. In the West of Scotland, large greenhouses, heated by renewable energy, have been constructed in the Clyde valley and Ayrshire to supply fruits and vegetables never grown in Scotland before. Clever breeding programmes and genetic engineering coupled with artificial heating has enabled most of the fruits formerly imported from warmer countries to be grown locally although at a considerable increase in price. Many have had to give up nectarines and mangoes but make do with apples and pears. A distinct seasonal rhythm has returned to the menus of the world.

The climate of the West of Scotland has changed with more rain and more frequent and violent storms. Winters are not as cold but fine summers are a rarity. Despite this, the country has got off lightly compared to other parts of the world. The Mediterranean countries have suffered repeated droughts and even the North of France and the South of England have many more summers with below average rainfall. Further away, Northern and Southern Africa, Central and Southern Asia and Australia are in dire straits (see Figure 11.1). Much of the Southern United States has been severely affected and agricultural production has fallen catastrophically. Mercifully, Northern China has escaped with only a slight reduction in rainfall although even that has proved insufficient to maintain the population of the early part of the century. Mass migration is the most dangerous consequence of global warming to Northern Europe. If droughts get more serious, as many as a tenth of the human race could be propelled towards the remaining fertile regions of the world. Some extreme remedies have already been applied. Bangladesh, which has begun to disappear beneath the waves, has been sealed off from India by an electrified barrier running the length of their common border. Americans are migrating to Canada at an unsustainable rate even though desalination has been used to supply the coastal regions of the US.

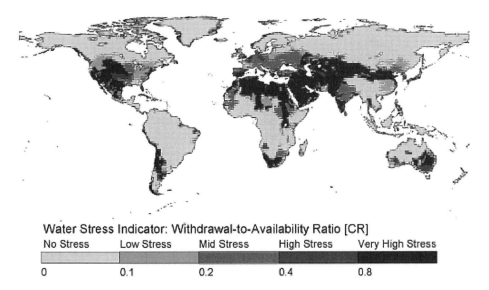

Water Stress Indicator: Withdrawal-to-Availability Ratio [CR]

| No Stress | Low Stress | Mid Stress | High Stress | Very High Stress |

| 0 | 0.1 | 0.2 | 0.4 | 0.8 |

Fig 11.1   Water availability in regions of the world in 2005. Stress is measured as the proportion of water withdrawal to total renewable resources. In this map, an overall value of 0.4 (40 %) indicates high water stress.

Source: World Water Council 2005

Lack of water has presented Scotland with a whole new industry. Pipelines flow from the Scottish freshwater lochs south to the East and Southeast of England. Figure 11.2 shows freshwater availability in England in summer 2001. Since then water supplies have become much more precarious in the years of drought which now occur almost every other year. Water imports from Scotland keep agriculture and industry going in England during these droughts.

Tankers dock at deep water terminals constructed off the west coast where they are filled with fresh water piped from the nearest loch and then taken to the Middle East and countries around the Mediterranean. This trade not only generates as much income as oil delivered during its heyday at the end of the 20th century but also helps to sustain life in those areas, reducing the threat of migration. Glaswegians don't like getting wet but every cloud now has a silver lining.

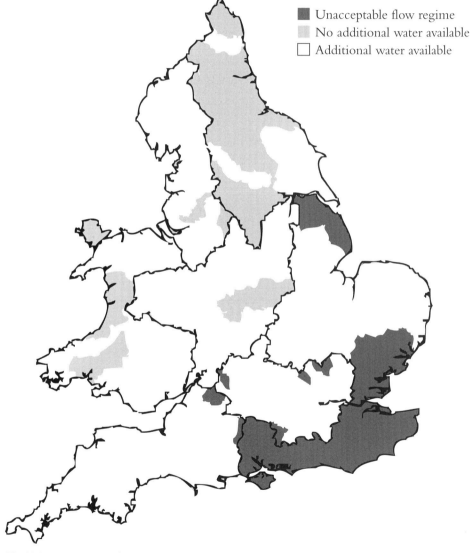

Fig 11.2   Assessments of water availability in 2001

Source: Sustainable-development.gov.uk

Scotland achieved its CO2 emissions target in three ways. First, electricity was generated from a mixture of nuclear, hydro, wind, wave and tidal sources with coal used only as a back-up. The results of wind power, which received the largest share of the early investment leading to the construction of large numbers of both onshore and offshore windmills, have been a little disappointing. Most were built in the first 20 years of the century and have worked a bit erratically and now deliver about 15% of the country's requirements. Hydro-electrical projects have been expanded and contribute 20%. The contribution of nuclear power is diminishing but still generates about 30%. Radioactive waste has been buried in deep underground bunkers for 20 years, so far without any problems; the initial protests died down quite quickly because the government's energy plan was a major issue in their successful election campaign of 2015. By that time, even doubters had accepted that the unwelcome consequences of unrestrained global warming were on a different scale to the dangers arising from the storage of radioactive waste.

Tidal lagoons have proved to be a good investment. They consist of walls built from ordinary aggregates and rubble, as used in marinas and breakwaters, enclosing an area of sea of between two and ten square miles about a mile offshore in shallow water. At low tide, they look like harbour walls but almost disappear at full tide. The walls of the lagoons are raked at about 30 degrees. Power is generated by water rushing into the lagoon through turbines as the tide comes in and flowing out through the same turbines as the tide ebbs. There are, therefore, predictable patterns of power production and periods of inactivity. The latter have been minimised by subdividing the lagoons with less substantial walls so that different levels can be created within each lagoon. Therefore, when extra power is required, the internal sluices are opened and water flows through another set of generators from one part of the lagoon to another. This not only reduces the down periods to a minimum but also provides reserves so that variations in demand can be accommodated. Since the size of tides on the coasts of Scotland is not as large as in, for example, the Bristol Channel, the power produced has been correspondingly less. The figures are, however, quite impressive. A total area of lagoons of about 100 square miles provides about 20% of Scotland's electricity. The initial investment was considerable, but the infrastructure has proved relatively cheap and simple to maintain with an expected life of 100 years. Over the lifetime of these structures, power from tidal lagoons is probably the cheapest.

Coal-fired power stations, using locally mined coal, produce the remaining electricity, but, more importantly, are used to fill gaps when the wind fails or the reserves held in the tidal lagoons are insufficient or the nuclear reactors are down for maintenance or repair. Carbon dioxide capture has been incorporated in the plants but it is still not clear how much leaks from the old oilfields into which it is being piped and stored.

Second, energy used for home and office heating has been drastically reduced. The government made insulation of buildings a top priority. Infra-red photography has been used for the last 25 years to monitor heat loss from buildings. Owners are held responsible for meeting the exacting standards set by laws introduced in 2020. This required all new housing to be securely insulated and also to have micro-generating plants – wind turbines, solar panels or geo-thermal units – whichever was appropriate for the site. Geothermal heating has also been widely adopted in the estates of Glasgow, the council having started this programme in 2010, taking the lead from Woking in Surrey which had pioneered its use successfully towards the end of the 20th century. As a result of these measures, household use of mains electricity or gas for heating has fallen by about 50% compared to 2000.

Third, transport was tamed to some extent. Improvement in the efficiency of cars meant that habits had to change less than expected. Even so, their use has been significantly reduced because of road pricing and because the centres of many towns, including Glasgow, have become car-free zones. Battery technology has improved considerably and all cars are now hybrid, direct descendants of the original Toyota Prius, which is now a collector's item. Most cars are run on a mixture of bio-diesel or ethanol. These changes were really inevitable, and not just because of the treaty obligations to cut CO2 emissions. The world production of oil peaked in 2015, and output fell dramatically thereafter stalling the emerging economies of India and China. The price of oil exploded which made other sources of power much more competitive and accelerated the conversion to green energy. Coal came back into fashion but power stations were built to capture emitted carbon which was stored in whatever sub-terrain depository was available – in Scotland's case these were the emptied North Sea oilfields. However, the cost of motoring has doubled in the last 50 years. Cars are more expensive to produce and their markets have contracted with the renewed impoverishment of large parts of the globe, particularly South and East Asia, the middle and west of USA and southern Europe.

Aeroplanes have not achieved sufficient gains in efficiency and so prices of air travel have risen hugely, reducing foreign travel and air freight to a fraction of its size at the turn of the century. Now, if someone wants to visit their family in Australia, it costs them the equivalent of seven years' carbon ration. Not many go more than once in a lifetime. Marine transport has also suffered from the scarcity and expense of diesel.

Of all the consequences of global warming, rising sea levels are likely to hold the greatest direct threat to Glasgow. In the last 50 years, sea levels have risen 50 cm compared with only 17 cm in the whole of the 20th century. Between 1993 and 2003, the sea rose by 3.1 mm each year, half of which was due to thermal expansion of the water, but since then the rate has accelerated; between 2040 and 2050, it had risen to nearly 2 cm a year as terrestrial icecaps melted and drained into the oceans. The process remains incomplete. The prevailing opinion is that there will be at least a 7-metre rise by the end of the century. Not surprisingly, there is an intense debate about what to do. A 7-metre rise would cut the motorway to Greenock, the Dumbarton Road in Clydebank, not to mention the Expressway in Glasgow itself. All the expensive Clydeside developments of the first two decades of the century would be under water: the Southern General Hospital, one of Glasgow's two main hospitals, the SECC, the BBC headquarters and all other developments at Pacific Quay – plus Glasgow Airport. The cost of replacing these functions would be enormous. A rise of 14 meters would flood the junction of Gallowgate and High Street in the east and the base of the hill up to the University in the west. Thus the Kelvingrove Museum would be under water. Since a complete melt of the Antarctic ice-cap would result in a rise of more than 50 meters, plans to protect the city have to be ambitious; there is little point in building an expensive barrage only to find that it is inadequate. The worst case scenario is becoming less and less likely because there is evidence that the amount of carbon dioxide in the atmosphere is stabilising, even though the temperature is still rising.

The favoured option for the defence of Glasgow is the construction of a barrage in the shallow waters of the Clyde below Dumbarton, but so far there has been little agreement on its specifications. Others have been more decisive, with Singapore building a rampart around the island designed to withstand a rise of 14 meters. The government will have to decide soon because it may take 10 years to construct. Most of the rest of the sea-level towns and villages of Scotland will simply be abandoned and replaced by new build on higher ground. There has been some thought of resettling villages on floating pontoons which could cope with any rise in sea level and leave more land free for agricultural use. Of the bigger cities, Edinburgh, Dundee and Aberdeen may lose their dock and harbour areas but Inverness would be hardest hit with about a third underwater should the expected 7-metre rise occur. New coastal railways and roads will be required in many areas.

All this required and still requires huge resources which have led to higher taxes and charges than during the era of cheap oil. This caused sustained anguish and hardship but was essential to meet treaty obligations and the population realised that doing nothing was not an option. The standard of living of most Scots fell precipitously in the early years of the century and has remained below those levels. Food and heating take up a larger proportion of expenditure but the population has become much more active as football, cycling, tennis and other sports have replaced foreign travel.

The other main threat to Scotland is the danger caused by huge migrations of populations on a scale never before seen. As China, India and Africa suffer shortages of water and agricultural land, significant numbers, measured in millions, may move north into Siberia and west into Northern Europe. This process began early in the century, was reduced by the transfer of funds from the carbon rich to the carbon poor countries, but drought and sea level changes have set it accelerating again. Such is the threat posed by these migrations that most borders have been closed and armed. Scotland's geographical position on the outskirts of the EU is, for once, a huge advantage. Its border is largely protected by the draconian laws introduced by England and its increasingly efficient border guards which enforce them. The main function of the English and Scottish armed forces is to prevent illegal immigration. This has already led to unpleasant incidents in which boats of illegal immigrants were sunk in the Channel with considerable loss of life. But the threat of waves of climate refugees pouring northwards from Africa and westwards from Asia may have horrific consequences in mainland Europe. Since most of the southern European countries also suffer badly from water shortages and the consequent decline in agricultural production, they are in no position to absorb the migrants. Therefore, the British Isles, Scandinavia and other northern European countries are seen as the most desirable destinations. The English Channel and the English defence forces should keep the flow to manageable levels. Some shiploads of migrants may aim for Greenland, Iceland and Scotland but the expanded navies of target countries are expected to be able to manage.

World population has stabilised at about 8 billion and is expected to fall to 6 billion over the next 50 years due to rapidly reducing birth rates and accelerating mortality in much of Africa and Asia. Europe's population is also falling but replacement by immigrants has maintained the overall numbers in northern Europe.

So Glasgow has survived relatively intact while many cities around the world are threatened by water shortage, rising sea levels and/or mass migration. The growth of the economy has begun to accelerate after a prolonged period of stagnation. The regional economy has become much more self sufficient and skill shortages are easy to solve by selective immigration. The future looks fair. That is not to say that Glasgow has not suffered from global warming. It has, with regular hurricanes and an increase in rainfall to about 1,500 mm per year. Houses and drains have had to be adapted to cope with the more extreme conditions. But it is so much better off than the vast majority of coastal cities and indeed all types of cities nearer the equator.

The price of both goods and food has increased so peoples' disposable incomes have fallen as have house prices. Second homes became impractical, increasing the supply of houses and this was a major contributor to the reduced cost of buying in many parts of Scotland thus breathing new life into many highland and island communities. Holidays abroad, once an essential part of life, are now prohibitively expensive and that part of the family budget has been reassigned to food and local leisure activities.

Glasgow is once again a manufacturing city, with a population of about 750,000, producing goods for the home market usually on franchise from foreign companies and some high-value lightweight products for export.

Independence for Scotland has, on the whole, been beneficial even if the first years have been very hard. It has enabled the government to make decisions much more quickly than before. Nuclear weapons were repatriated to England shortly after the divorce and the Clyde shipyards closed without the orders from the Royal Navy. Government spending first decreased as tax revenues were not nearly as encouraging as the SNP had promised in their election campaign. The numbers working in the public sector were reduced from 25% of the working population at the time of independence to fewer than 20% now. Then taxes had to be increased to build the new infrastructure needed to cut CO_2 emissions and to deal with the more powerful storms that regularly hit the west coast. Social deprivation actually got worse in Glasgow in the early years of independence. In short, the first ten years of independence were a time of misery, perhaps not on the same scale as the 1690s just before the Act of Union, but quite unpleasant enough for many to yearn to return to the Union.

The picture changed for a number of reasons. First, Scotland adopted the euro. Interest rates were about 2% lower than those set by the Bank of England and this encouraged businesses to borrow for investment and research. The fruits of the planning of previous Governments became apparent when clusters of small high tech companies developed in the major cities.

The second factor which led to the turnaround was that Scotland was seen as a relatively safe haven against the problems of global warming so that it became a leading location for inward investment. Many firms wanted to transfer their operations to the Central Belt because of the political and civil stability that Scotland offered. The Government was able to choose the businesses that they wished to encourage. London's pre-eminence as the business capital of Europe was eroded as it became an increasingly unpleasant place in which to live. Londoners have been leaving the city for most of the century, at first in small numbers, but then in droves. Many businesses transferred their headquarters northwards although not many to Scotland, if only because the rather messy divorce 25 years before had resulted in mutual hostility which took years to settle.

On the other hand, the relatively benign consequences of global warming in Scotland and its relatively de-regulated market have made Scotland an increasingly attractive place for inward investment by firms operating in southern European countries which have suffered most through climate change. The population of Scotland has increased by 10% during the last 20 years and immigration rules were designed so that Scotland could pick and choose the immigrants it wanted.

Social changes

So Glasgow was well placed geographically to ride out the storms created by mass migration. It had envious water reserves and the warming climate meant that its population could be fed from locally produced food. How had it progressed socially?

Social deprivation had been the outstanding problem of Glasgow at the beginning of the century affecting a large part of the population with high levels of addiction, crime and illness. Money had been poured into the city to try and end these evils with little result. An army of exhorters had been paid to persuade erring citizens to mend their ways but their message had gone unheeded. The following extract is a good example from a government paper of 50 years ago.

> The National Teenage Pregnancy Strategy is set out in the Social Exclusion Unit Report on Teenage Pregnancy launched by the Prime Minister in June 1999. Its action plan for reducing the rate of teenage conceptions and getting more teenage parents into education, training or employment covers four categories:
>
> - A national campaign – to improve understanding and change behaviour
> - Joined-up action – to co-ordinate action at both national and local levels
> - Better prevention – to include better education and access to contraception, to target at risk groups and reach young men
> - Better support – for pregnant teenagers and teenage parents.

The Government has established the Teenage Pregnancy Unit in the Department for Education and Skills (DfES) with an extensive programme for reducing teenage pregnancy rates, particularly for those under the age of 16.

The tone of this approach is that behaviour can be influenced by government making people aware of the consequences of their actions. Should the various arms of Government also act effectively, that is in a joined-up manner, the desired result would be achieved. It failed totally. Exhortation was discredited as a way of changing destructive behaviour.

Independence meant that less money was available. Since the failure of the exhortation projects had become obvious even to the politicians who had set them up, they were all scrapped. Unemployment benefits were also cut. These measures might have been expected to cause a surge in the crime rate and indeed there was for some years but not to epidemic proportions. This was because another programme aiming at cultural change was put in place at about the same time.

Ministers reckoned that the youth of the deprived areas should be offered attractive alternative activities, to the gang culture of the poorer communities and they chose sport and music as the likeliest to succeed. Government poured money into deprived areas to build facilities to cater for these activities. Parks laid out more football fields; basketball courts, indoor tennis courts, hockey pitches and swimming pools were all built so that almost any game could be taken up by anyone interested. Glasgow began to resemble an Australian city of 20 years earlier. Coaching was made available for most sports. Local teams were formed, some based in schools and some in clubs, to take part in the various sponsored leagues. Friday evenings became swimming galas for many schools with a race every five minutes starting with 6-year-olds and working up to 16-year-olds. Each swimmer was timed and given a certificate to show how he or she was progressing. Tennis courts, running tracks and even the velodrome, perhaps one of the best legacies of the 2014 Commonwealth Games, were all busy with teams practicing and competing in the sponsored leaugues. Members of cycle clubs swarmed in large numbers over the countryside. Each child was formally assessed early in primary school and advised which sport would be the most rewarding for him or her to pursue. This was really designed so that every child would know of the opportunities available. The police helped by ensuring that the gangs' territorial boundaries did not prevent children from accessing the parks, fields and sport centres and they also stopped vandalism of the facilities by rigorous monitoring.

You may ask why a previously apathetic population should have embraced sport with such enthusiasm. Well, apart from the ready availability of the facilities, there were numerous local competitions in many sports which were sponsored with substantial prizes available at local and district levels. Leagues were set up in all sorts of sports to foster the competitive spirit. Prizes included cups, promotion to a higher league and also quite liberal cash payments which were enough to encourage parents to keep their children motivated. Celebrities were asked to take an interest and part of the motivation for the youngsters was meeting and talking to people they admired. It also helped that parents could leave their children in supervised premises while they went out shopping. Families were enthusiastic because they now saw sport and music as a way out of deprivation. Sport became a bit of an obsession with Glaswegians so the level of fitness of the younger generation was far better than that of their parents. For example, the threatened epidemic of obesity did not hit Glasgow nearly as badly as Liverpool or Birmingham. But the main prize was that sport brought children into the orbit of adults, particularly men who had achieved some sporting fame. It was easier for the boys to see alternatives to the then prevailing counter culture and their school work improved accordingly. In short, sport broke the cycle of deprivation by changing the values of the deprived.

An equivalent programme was run for music; schools hired teams of musicians so that each pupil who showed an interest in learning an instrument could have individual lessons; school choirs were formed but it proved difficult to interest boys in singing. Altogether, music was not as successful as sport although it did lead to a number of successful bands which brought Glasgow some international fame. Of course, Glasgow still has problems but they are on the same scale as in other cities. Deprivation scores have improved as a result of improving health and educational achievments. The number claiming benefits began to fall satisfyingly after about ten years of this new programme.

Another policy has also shown some promise. The City Council was persuaded by a small and eccentric pressure group of the relevance of research showing that children of two-parent families did better than children of one-parent families. The evidence had been available for several years but it took quite a long time to be accepted probably as a result of the feminist movement which had led many to believe that fathers were a luxury, a good thing if they behaved properly but to be packed off if unsatisfactory. The other reason was that, self-evidently, many children brought up by a single parent do very well. But the studies showed that in comparisons between large numbers of children brought up by one parent and another group with two parents, the latter, on average, did considerably better.

Previous policies had been designed to ensure that the children of single parents did not suffer acute want. Mothers were given social housing and benefits which enabled them to become independent of their parents. This escape route was, of course, largely taken up by daughters of problem households, who themselves became poor parents, thus increasing the size of the problem. By contrast, parents who waited until they had saved sufficiently to bring up children without state assistance paid taxes that supported the unemployed single parents. In this way the prudent indirectly supported the imprudent. The percentage of children born to single parents had remained obstinately high in Britain, while falling in other European countries. At the turn of the century, it was double that of Germany, three times that of France and five times that of Holland. And nowhere was it higher than in Glasgow.

Early pregnancy is both a result of social deprivation and a cause, much like alcohol or drugs. Vicious cycles are notoriously difficult to break. Skinner showed years ago that reward is a far better way of influencing behaviour than punishment. The reward must be tangible, preferably immediate and significant. The City Fathers decided that they would see if rewards to parents could break the cycle of deprivation. They resolved that the rewards should be large and offered for easily verifiable and desirable events. The reward was also designed to encourage a belief that the recipients have a stake in society. Since in Britain owning your own home is a potent symbol of belonging, families were rewarded by being offered part ownership of their house. If a mother was over the age of 21 and married when her first child was born, she was rewarded with a fifth of the value of their house. If the father was still at home when the child went to school and had not been in prison during the crucial five years, he was awarded another fifth of the value of the house. If the child subsequently went onto to do well in school and sit highers, the family received £3,000 for every higher passed at grade A, B or C. Any parents who had two successful school children owned most of their house and many felt motivated to get a job in order to buy their house outright. They thus felt they had a major stake in their community. Now poorly qualified parents know there is a relatively simple recipe for gaining some control of their lives and this has bought results, albeit slowly over the last 20 years.

These bounties were only available to people living in defined areas of multiple deprivation such as Keppochhill, Royston, Calton, Bridgeton and Dalmarnock. One consequence was that outsiders moved into the areas to reap the benefits: this was encouraged because they had a beneficial impact on the prevailing culture through their ambition for their families. Schools' performance improved since the increase in the number of interested pupils created a critical mass which tipped the balance in favour of discipline and willingness to learn. Parents too had a selfish reason for supporting teachers' authority in matters of discipline. Advice on how to keep the family going in the desired direction was available but the example of neighbours succeeding was probably the most important aid.

The Council was persuaded to adopt this policy because the system then in operation was extremely expensive. The cost of the various schemes to end deprivation had been enormous. At the turn of the century, government was investing about £120m (plus £50m of European money) each year on projects designed to mitigate or reverse deprivation in Glasgow but all the expense and effort had little impact on their chosen target of reducing the number receiving benefit. There were other costs of deprivation: each heroin addict had to raise about £18,000 per year to sustain his or her habit which may have cost the city about £300m each year. Inevitably crime led to prison where each prisoner cost about £28,000 per year. Fewer lone parents went out to work in Glasgow than elsewhere and each one staying at home cost the nation about £10,000 per year.

The Council argued that the proposals may or may not help towards reversing deprivation. If they were successful, the overall cost may increase in the short term but would pay for itself many times over in the longer term as the problems caused by drugs, violence and health diminished. If they failed, the cost would be minimal because no one would claim the rewards.

With parents in more control of their lives, with the opportunities offered by sport and music, children now have a model that appears attainable and superior to the gang orientated culture of the earlier period. It took about a generation to show significant improvements. In the last 10 years or so, it has become clear that deprivation is indeed decreasing and that Glasgow's problem is now not much worse than in other cities such as Edinburgh or Leeds. Some argue that the policies adopted by the Council were not that effective and that the immigrants that have come into the deprived areas of the city were more important in changing the culture of despair. Whatever the reason, all are impressed by the turnaround and are optimistic that deprivation will not be the shame of Glasgow as it has been since the Industrial Revolution.

So Glasgow and its region are thriving in 2050, benefiting from the new jobs in agriculture and manufacturing. Its population has increased, as has that of most northern cities in Europe and America. It remains Scotland's largest city although not as prosperous as Edinburgh or Aberdeen. It has achieved regular economic growth after the unpleasant recessions of the 2020s. Employment has picked up again and is back to the levels of the early part of the century. And, perhaps best of all, there are signs that deprivation is on the wane. The way of life is less orientated to consumerism, if only because disposable incomes are still less than they were 50 years ago, and more towards sport which has reduced some of the excess mortality suffered by the grandparents of this generation. Cultural activities have increased as the size of the middle class has increased. Glasgow is now less a working class city than since the dawn of the industrial revolution 250 years before.

POSTSCRIPT

I wrote this book between my retirement in 2003 and summer 2007 which explains why there are different dates for different data. The promotion of Gordon Brown to Prime Minister and the success of the Scottish Nationalists in the 2007 elections occurred after I had finished but do not really affect the conclusions that I reached.

The Credit Crisis of 2008, on the other hand, changes everything. It is likely to have huge consequences for the country and for Glasgow. It accentuates and validates the problems with the economy that I raised in Chapter 6. The key question is whether it represents a temporary problem or a hinge point in history. If the former, then we just have to tough it out, but if the latter, as I think, then the strategy should certainly be changed. Glasgow's recovery relied on a vigorous retail trade and a thriving service sector spearheaded by the financial services. Both are likely to suffer long-term damage. Local entrepreneurial flair contributed little although the seeds may have been sown for this to emerge over the next few years.

At a Scottish level, the Credit Crunch has changed the perception of Independence. The failure and rescue of the two major Scottish Banks has led to a radical reassessment. Both required large sums of capital to rescue them and are now partly owned by the UK Government. The huge sums necessary extended the finances of a nation of 60 million and would have been quite beyond the capacity of a nation of five million. The SNP has been unable to explain how an Independent Scotland would have coped. This may colour the debate on Independence for decades to come – always provided that the outcome within the UK is seen as satisfactory.

The world itself may be very different when recover eventually comes. Everyone in the developed world will be poorer, spending a greater proportion of their income on food, heating and taxes for several years to come. Many families will cut back on luxuries and holidays. The spending power of teenagers will be severely reduced as parents struggle to meet their bills and employment becomes more difficult to find: this may have important social consequences and could reverse what advances have been made in the reduction of social deprivation over the last decade.

With luck, the systems to encourage entrepreneurial activity that the Scottish Executive (now Government) has put in place will bear fruit and increase our share of manufacturing. However, it is unlikely to lead to much employment, at least directly.

What should the City Council do? Up until now, it has been determined to increase the prosperity of the city as judged by the GDP per head and it has been remarkably successful even though its target of promotion to the top quartile of European cities was never achieved and is never likely to be achieved. A more appropriate target may be to aim to increase the citizens' contentment. This is, of course, a very fuzzy concept but it has recently received some attention. The wonderfully named Index of Happiness has been established. There is a correlation between it and GDP up to a certain level after which happiness is unaffected by further increases in GDP. This is common sense; it is hard to be content when you cannot fill your stomach. Once that point has been reached, a choice becomes available: would you rather be richer or happier? The Council's choice up to now has been to try to be richer. That is a much easier target to understand and it has had considerable success in the process. But the going will get much tougher from now on.

Two main enjoyments of recent years have been recreational shopping and travelling. In an era when opportunities to continue to pursue these activities are much reduced, citizens may feel deprived. If this is inevitable, Local Government should try to reshape the city so that it is a place where the young and not so young can entertain themselves for minimal expense. The principle should be to encourage networking of any sort at any age: the more networks, the better for the health of individuals and for societies. This may mean building more facilities in strategic areas of the city so that they are easily and safely accessible. The facilities may be sporting or cultural, whatever local people want. Schools should ensure that all children join some extra-curricular activities and teachers and others should be paid extra for developing them. Transport around the city could be made easier by developing cycle routes and installing facilities for the safe parking of bicycles. The aim would be to reduce isolation and provide an alternative culture to that destructive tradition that has ruined too many generations.

In an age of increasing fuel costs and insecurity of its supply, the Council can make the city less vulnerable. The UK Government has been indescribably slow in coming to any decision about how electricity should be generated and the First Minister has ruled nuclear power out of the mix for Scotland. The City Council of the 19th century would undoubtedly have acted. Now, it could do worse than copy the initiatives of Woking Council which have halved its use of energy and cut its carbon dioxide emissions by three-quarters since 1990. To achieve this, it has developed a network of over 60 local generators of various types to power, heat and cool municipal buildings and social housing. Many town centre businesses are also connected to this local energy supply. In and around Glasgow there has been considerable investment in wind turbines but they are unlikely to provide more than a fraction of the needs of the city. Rivers powered the start of the Industrial Revolution, so why not use them by building numerous small hydro-electric schemes which could be added to the mix?

If the Council can somehow create a more neighbourly city with a wealth of interconnections achieving a Scandinavian level of trust between its citizens, then Glasgow may become world class again.

INDEX